NYPD

CONFIDENTIAL

Also by Leonard Levitt

Conviction: Solving the Moxley Murder

An African Season

The Long Way Round

The Healer

"Mbeya Dreaming" in *Going Up Country* (edited by John Coyne)

As Editor

The Brothers of Attica by Richard X. Clark

Power and Corruption in the Country's

GREATEST POLICE FORCE

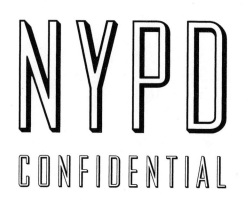

NYPD

CONFIDENTIAL

LEONARD LEVITT

Thomas Dunne Books

St. Martin's Press / New York

HV
8148
.N5
L395
2009

THOMAS DUNNE BOOKS.
An imprint of St. Martin's Press.

NYPD CONFIDENTIAL. Copyright © 2009 by Leonard Levitt. All rights reserved. Printed in the United States of America. For information, address St. Martin's Press, 175 Fifth Avenue, New York, N.Y. 10010.

www.thomasdunnebooks.com
www.stmartins.com

Library of Congress Cataloging-in-Publication Data

Levitt, Leonard, 1941–
    NYPD confidential : power and corruption in the country's greatest police force / Leonard Levitt. — 1st ed.
        p. cm.
    Includes bibliographical references and index.
    ISBN-13:   978-0-312-38032-8
    ISBN-10:   0-312-38032-1
    1. Police corruption—New York (State)—New York—History.   2. Police administration—New York (State)—New York—History.   3. Police—New York (State)—New York—History.   I. Title.
    HV8148.N5L395 2009
    364.1'3230883632097471—dc22

                                                            2009007602

First Edition: July 2009

10 9 8 7 6 5 4 3 2 1

To S, J, and M—as always.

CONTENTS

ACKNOWLEDGMENTS

Writing a book is never easy. Writing a book about the New York City Police Department—where lack of cooperation is the norm and retaliation is an accepted part of police culture—can be especially challenging.

Nonetheless, there are plenty of men and women in the NYPD who have important things to say, although most of them are reluctant to attach their names to them. To the few who have, I am especially appreciative.

To those outside the police department who have allowed me to interview them, facilitated interviews with others, read parts of the manuscript, or verified the accuracy of their quotes, I am further appreciative. They run a wide gamut and include George Arzt, Ron Bellistri, Wayne Barrett, John Clifford, Mike Doyle, Chris Dunn, Ed Gavin, Michael Horowitz, Robert Johnson, Tom Kelly, Ed Koch, Marvyn Kornberg, Debbie Krenek, Walter Mack, John Marzulli, Randy Mastro, Judge Milton Mollen, Brigid O'Connor, Al O'Leary, Judith Regan, Thomas Reppetto, Marvin Smilon, Joe Valiquette, Murray Weiss, Mary Jo White, and Denny Young (who couldn't remember anything he ever said to me).

I'd also like to thank Bill Bratton for answering the one question I asked him; Iris Quigley for locating my old *Newsday* articles; and John Miller, who spoke to me until he stopped speaking to me.

Finally, there are the dozens and dozens of people, both inside and outside the NYPD, whom I cannot publicly acknowledge but without whose help this book could not have been written. You guys know who you are and I love you for it.

I'd also like to thank my agent, Julia Lord, whose support for this project, even during my darkest moments, never wavered. Ditto, my editor, Peter Joseph, who made this book at least 20 percent better.

Once more, I marvel at Susan Levitt, who, yet again, put up with the author for another two years. (She says it wasn't so bad.)

TIMELINE

November 1965	Mayor John Lindsay elected and appoints Howard Leary police commissioner.
October 1970	Lindsay appoints Patrick V. Murphy to succeed Leary.
Fall 1971	Knapp Commission corruption hearings
April 1972	Fatal shooting of police officer Philip Cardillo inside a Harlem mosque
May 1973	Lindsay appoints Donald Cawley to succeed Murphy.
Fall 1973	Police headquarters is moved from Centre Street to One Police Plaza, across the street from City Hall.
November 1973	Mayor Abe Beame elected and appoints Michael Codd police commissioner.
July 1976–August 1977	Son of Sam killings
November 1977	Mayor Edward Koch elected and appoints Robert McGuire police commissioner.
January 1984	Koch swears in Benjamin Ward as the city's first black police commissioner.
April 1984	Palm Sunday massacre
November 1989	Mayor David Dinkins elected
1990	Dinkins appoints Lee Brown police commissioner.
1990	Homicides reach record high of 2,245.
August 1991	Crown Heights riots
July 1992	Dinkins appoints Mollen Commission on police corruption.
October 1992	Ray Kelly appointed police commissioner.
February 1993	World Trade Center bombing
1993	Homicides fall below 2,000 for first time in three years.

November 1993	Mayor Rudolph Giuliani is elected and dismisses Kelly.
January 1994	Giuliani appoints William Bratton police commissioner.
May 1994	Bratton; his deputy commissioner, Jack Maple; and Chief of Patrol; Louis Anemone, institute Compstat.
July 1994	Mollen Commission issues final report. Giuliani rejects it.
1994	Homicides fall 18 percent and Bratton calls it the largest decrease in history.
February 1995	Giuliani appoints Mayoral Commission to Combat Police Corruption.
February 1995	*New Yorker* magazine article credits Bratton with the city's drastic crime reductions. Giuliani forces resignation of Bratton's spokesman, John Miller.
January 1996	*Time* magazine issue of January 15 places Bratton on its cover.
February 1996	Bratton signs six-figure book deal with Random House to write his autobiography, *Turnaround*.
March 1996	Giuliani dismisses Bratton.
April 1996	Giuliani appoints Howard Safir police commissioner.
1996	Homicides fall below 1,000.
August 1997	Haitian immigrant Abner Louima is sodomized in the bathroom of a Brooklyn precinct.
1998	Homicides fall to 633.
February 1999	Four white cops in the Bronx fire 41 shots, killing an unarmed African immigrant, Amadou Diallo. They are acquitted.
August 2000	Giuliani appoints Bernard Kerik as Safir's successor.
May 2001	Kerik signs six-figure deal with publisher Judith Regan to write his autobiography, *The Lost Son*.
September 11, 2001	Second attack on the World Trade Center.
November 2001	*The Lost Son* is published.
2001	Giuliani leaves office.
November 2001	Mayor Michael Bloomberg elected.
January 2002	Bloomberg swears in Ray Kelly as police commissioner.

May 2003	Ousmane Zongo, an unarmed African immigrant, is shot and killed in a botched police raid. Officer is convicted of negligent homicide.
May 2003	Alberta Spruill, 57, dies of a heart attack after police, acting on incorrect information, throw a flash grenade into her Harlem apartment.
May 2003	The White House sends Kerik on a six-month assignment to Iraq to rebuild the Iraqi police force. He stays only three months.
October 2003	Intelligence Division detectives sent to New Jersey and Pennsylvania to investigate terrorism without informing local state authorities or FBI.
2003–2004	Intelligence detectives sent across the country to spy on protest groups planning to demonstrate at 2004 Republican National Convention.
January 2004	Richard Neri, a white police officer, shoots and kills Timothy Stansbury, a 19-year-old black youth. A grand jury determines that Neri fired his gun accidentally.
November 2004	President Bush nominates Kerik to head Department of Homeland Security.
December 2004	Kerik withdraws nomination, citing problem with an undocumented "nanny."
April 2005	Mark Pomerantz, chairman of the Mayor's Commission to Combat Police Corruption, resigns after Kelly refuses to provide information and Bloomberg refuses to intercede.
June 2005	Bloomberg appoints former Knapp Commission counsel Michael Armstrong to succeed Pomerantz. Armstrong says there is no need to investigate the police department under Ray Kelly.
June 2006	Kerik pleads guilty to two misdemeanors in the Bronx for failing to report $165,000 in free renovations to his Bronx apartment by a company with alleged mob ties.
September 2006	Detectives fire 50 shots, killing Sean Bell, an unarmed black man, and wounding his two friends. The officers are acquitted.

November 2007   Kerik indicted in federal court on 16 counts of fraud, tax evasion, and lying during his nomination to become Homeland Security director.

October 2008   Kelly writes to Attorney General Michael Mukasey, accusing the Justice Department of refusing to approve electronic surveillance of terrorism suspects. Mukasey says Kelly's actions would be "contrary to law."

October 2008   Bloomberg succeeds in convincing the city council to vote to amend the two-term mayoral limit law, and he decides to run for a third term.

NYPD

CONFIDENTIAL

Introduction

"There are many cultures in the New York City Police Department, but corruption is the strongest one," Chief John Guido used to say.

Friday afternoons, as the week wound down, Guido would hold forth to me in his corner office on the twelfth floor of Police Plaza, with its skyline view of Lower Manhattan that looked north past the old federal courthouse and down over the tenements of Chinatown. "And they're often the sharpest guys," he said. "Guys who are always hustling, thinking of ways to make a buck."

Better than any member of the department, Guido knew about police corruption. After the Knapp Commission scandal of the early 1970s—the result of the revelations of Detective Frank Serpico—exposed the NYPD's organized and systemic corruption, Guido headed the department's Internal Affairs Division for fifteen years, longer than anyone in its history. Balding and barrel-chested, his every other utterance an expletive, he personified the department's macho image. Yet despite his forty-year police career, he was never part of the NYPD culture. The son of immigrants who never learned to speak English, he was a voracious reader. He had a master's degree in political science, and was one of the few Italian-American chiefs in an Irish-dominated department that resented both his heritage and his aggressive pursuit of corruption.

"The Irish thought the job was a calling," Guido liked to say. "To me, it was just a job." I took that to mean that many in the police department viewed it— or rather the image of it—as sacred, and exposure of its flaws as sinful. Such protectiveness had allowed cops over the years to shake down citizens, whether merchants, construction site foremen, tow-truck operators, or bookmakers. Because those arrangements were supposedly private, they would not tarnish the department.

Guido disdained this hypocrisy. The consummate outsider, he did not mingle with colleagues. He refused to attend formal police functions like retirement dinners or testimonials staged by wealthy police buffs. He maintained he did not want to compromise himself by fraternizing with people he might some day have to investigate. He liked to say he never owned a tuxedo and that he wouldn't hire anyone at Internal Affairs who did. "I never socialized with other chiefs," he would tell me, "and I was never afraid to alienate people."

At the height of his power, he underwent life-threatening cancer surgery, but hid his condition by using vacation days to secretly schedule the operation. "So many people wished I had cancer," he said, "I didn't want to give them the satisfaction."

Guido kept the police department's darkest secrets, and it was my good fortune as a police reporter that he allowed me to stumble upon some of them. One was the truth behind the 1984 murder of twenty-five-year-old transit cop Irma Lozada, the first female officer killed on the job in New York City. Pursuing a chain snatcher who ran out of the subway, she and her partner split up. In a weed-filled lot, she confronted the thief, who overpowered her and shot her in the head with her own gun. Her body lay undiscovered for three hours because the partner waited ninety minutes before reporting her missing.

Guido was skeptical of the partner's account: He hadn't heard the gunshot, apparently because of noise from a passing Long Island Rail Road train. To test the noise level, Guido placed fifty officers at intervals along the train tracks. When a train passed, one of them fired a shot. The others all heard it.

And there was more that Guido knew. Earlier, Lozada had slipped away for a few hours to go shopping. While Guido suspected cowardice on the partner's part, I wondered if his motives were less sinister. I wondered whether in not reporting her missing, he thought he was covering for her. Never imagining she was in danger, he assumed she had slipped away to do more shopping.

The police department never made public Guido's findings. Instead, the

Transit Police—which operated separately then from the NYPD though theoretically under its jurisdiction—covered up Lozada's lapses and portrayed her as a heroine. It also obscured her partner's mistakes by awarding him a commendation at a ceremony at Police Plaza. To maintain their image, they publicly praised a cop who had unwittingly left his partner to die.

That is how the New York City Police Department often operates—sacrificing truth for image while acting in secrecy and in silence. More ominously, such silence is countenanced, even encouraged, by City Hall. This can be especially pernicious because the NYPD—the nation's largest and arguably most powerful law enforcement agency, with 36,000 officers—is a world to itself, and its mores and values sometimes clash with the society it is bound to protect. Loyalty to fellow officers and to the image of the department is paramount. Bravery, such as capturing a violent felon or protecting the life of one's partner, is not only respected but expected.

Indeed, the NYPD has performed great acts of heroism. The NYPD landed helicopters on the roof of the World Trade Center to rescue people after the 1993 bombing and helped evacuate thousands from the Twin Towers after the second Trade Center attack in 2001. Twenty-three police officers lost their lives there. The NYPD has also solved some of the most complex homicides. In 1977 detectives found the Son of Sam serial killer through a ticket found on a parked car near the scene of his final murder.

Then there is the silence. Unlike the mafia, another secret society to which the department is sometimes compared, the police culture does not, at least officially, countenance violence. But like the mafia, it recognizes the code of *omertà*. Break the NYPD's Blue Wall of Silence and acts of retaliation and ostracism follow—from tossing a cop's locker to slashing his tires, or as may have been the case with Serpico, allowing him to get shot.

"That's why," said Guido, "it will never change."

The NYPD's culture of silence has led to horrendous acts of corruption and brutality. Both these forces run through the department's history. Over the past hundred years, the department has struggled to overcome them. Over the past hundred years, it has failed.

Since the late nineteenth century, as chronicled by the muckrakers Lincoln Steffens and Jacob Riis, both of whom worked as police reporters in New York City, citizens have been aware of the department's widespread corruption. The city's first major police scandal, in 1894, exposed by the crusading Rev. Dr. Charles Parkhurst, involved prostitution, extortion, counterfeiting, voter fraud, and brutality, and led to the formation of an anticorruption body known as the Lexow Commission. Similar scandals with similar commissions have followed every twenty years or so with depressing regularity.

The most far-reaching scandal of the past two generations occurred in 1970. From Serpico's revelations, the Knapp Commission the following year exposed organized and systemic corruption at virtually every level of the NYPD. Despite reform, yet another scandal surfaced twenty years later. The department-wide corruption of the past had mutated into pockets of violent cops in league with equally violent drug dealers.

The culture of silence has also hindered efforts to combat police brutality. Over the past decade, the most notorious abuses have all had racial overtones. Amadou Diallo, Ousmane Zongo, Timothy Stansbury, and Sean Bell—each of whom was fatally shot by police—were all unarmed men of color. Moreover, the silence that infected an entire Brooklyn precinct permitted the most horrendous act of police brutality imaginable. Inside the precinct's bathroom, an officer used a broom handle to sodomize a Haitian immigrant, Abner Louima.

At the highest levels of the NYPD, the culture of silence reflects the arrogance not merely of power but of ego. Each administration I have covered has had a backstory, a largely unreported, behind-the-scenes dynamic with invariably far-reaching consequences. The backstory of the modern NYPD is how its leaders have allowed their personal agendas to undermine their stated goals to frame foolhardy, if not disastrous, policies.

Former mayor Rudolph W. Giuliani's signature claim is his reform of the NYPD, which led to unprecedented crime reductions. Yet he forced out William J. Bratton, the police commissioner who instituted those reforms, and gave no credible explanation. As Bratton's successor, he appointed Howard Safir, a longtime friend, whose policies led to one of the most heinous acts in the department's history—a forty-one-shot barrage by four officers that killed the unarmed Diallo. Next, Giuliani defied logic and common sense to appoint as commissioner his former driver and bodyguard, Bernard B. Kerik, who was subsequently indicted on corruption charges.

Similarly, the signature claim of current NYPD commissioner Raymond W. Kelly has been his revolutionary policies in fighting terrorism. Yet bitter over personal grievances and past resentments, he has nonetheless refused to cooperate with other law enforcement agencies engaged in the same fight, turning potential allies into rivals, to the detriment of both the NYPD and all New Yorkers.

Perhaps it is inevitable that men like these brook no questioning of their authority. Both Kelly and Giuliani—who served as de facto police commissioner during most of his eight years as mayor—have closed the NYPD to public scrutiny. Under Giuliani, such routine disclosures as overtime earnings or the race of victims shot by police were removed from public purview. Is it coincidence that the two most egregious acts of police brutality—the sodomizing of Louima and the fatal police shooting of Diallo—occurred during his tenure?

Despite Mayor Michael Bloomberg's campaign promise in 2001 of "more transparency," the police department under Kelly is now more closed than it was under Giuliani. While Giuliani's belligerence intimidated reporters into silence, Kelly threatens them with "consequences" for negative stories. In addition, for the past two decades, there has been no effective departmental oversight. The NYPD, with City Hall's acquiescence, has undercut the agencies entrusted with that role.

Hovering over the department today is 9/11. Fear of another terrorist attack serves as a cloak, hiding much of what the police department is doing, or not doing, in matters not related only to terrorism. The department refuses to acknowledge that an increasing number of cops are accused of corruption. Through a series of federal lawsuits, we have learned that the Intelligence Division—which Kelly enlarged to fight terrorism—has sent detectives across the country and abroad to spy, apparently illegally, on political protest groups that planned to demonstrate in New York City.

Meanwhile the city's media, which began serving as cheerleaders as crime fell in the 1990s under Giuliani, has gone into a post-9/11 swoon, all but relinquishing their critical faculties. The *Daily News*, which once called itself "the honest voice of New York," has unquestioningly supported the Intelligence Division's clandestine activities. The once-pliant *New York Post* has recently reversed course and become a department critic after its reporters became victims of Kelly's retribution.

Through my columns—first in *Newsday* and later online—and in this book, I have attempted to report some of these truths about the police department. In so doing, I found myself becoming an outsider like Chief Guido. Although I have covered the NYPD for twenty-five years and had a long-standing relation-ship with Kelly, he revoked my press credentials and banned me from Police Plaza because of my reporting. Neither he nor two of the book's other major subjects—Giuliani and Bloomberg—responded to my requests for interviews, although scores of other police officials, both past and present, some on the record, more anonymously, did speak with me.

Not long ago, I drove out to visit Guido. He is eighty-two years old now, a grandfather many times over, and he lives with his wife in a large, wooden-frame home in Queens that he purchased and renovated after his retirement from the NYPD two decades ago. Since then, he has had nothing to do with the department. "When I retired, I was finished with the job," he says. Yet his in-sights are no less valuable than they were twenty years before. As we do when I visit him, we drove through an industrial area across the Van Wyck Expressway to lunch at a Portuguese restaurant, where he always insists on paying. Yet if I expected a sympathetic ear, I was disappointed. When I told him of my report-ing difficulties with Kelly and the department, he merely shrugged. "Hey, Lenny," he said, "that only means you're doing your job."

ONE

Evidence of Things Not Seen

i.

I met Frank Serpico at the Knapp Commission corruption hearings in the fall of 1971. What I remember is how unlike a cop he seemed, how he kept apart from his so-called fellow officers. He had a bushy black beard, and when I spoke to him, he cocked his head like an ancient. Eight months earlier, he'd been shot below his left eye. A .22-caliber fragment had lodged in his brain and rendered him deaf in his left ear.

When Serpico was shot, many feared the worst—that someone in the police department had tried to kill him. Ever since he'd alleged his Bronx plainclothes unit was taking payoffs, he'd been a marked man. By coming forward he had betrayed the police department's code, its "blue wall of silence," which held that cops didn't turn in, or "rat out," fellow officers. Serpico received so many death threats that the department provided him with twenty-four-hour bodyguards, though in its bumbling fashion, one happened to be the former partner of his unit's bagman— the person who collected the money—whom Serpico had accused.

Mercifully for the department, a drug dealer, not a cop, had shot him, although some, Serpico included, believed the department had deliberately chosen not to provide adequate backup after his partner called in sick that night. After he was rushed to the hospital, Mayor John V. Lindsay, the police commissioner, and the top brass trooped to Serpico's bedside to pay homage to the man whose claims of corruption they'd ignored. The mayor couldn't ignore him now, and pronounced Serpico "a very brave man."

By then it was obvious to all New Yorkers that Frank Serpico was indeed a very brave man. He had risked his life to expose the NYPD's pervasive and systemic corruption. Misunderstood by the department, which had never known a cop to come forward unless seeking personal gain, and disparaged by City Hall, which feared antagonizing the police department, Serpico in the end had gone to *The New York Times,* which splashed his story across page one. Public pressure led Lindsay to appoint the Knapp Commission on Police Corruption. Its revelations became a watershed in the department's history.

Serpico was thirty-five years old then and I was five years younger. Perhaps because we were close in age, perhaps because Serpico felt more comfortable with a reporter than with his own kind—the police—we began a friendship that continued, intermittently, over the next four decades. I was then a reporter for *Time* magazine with the lofty title of "correspondent," and this was my first brush with the NYPD. I was a middle-class boy from Long Island who had never seen the inside of a station house. Like most middle-class folk, I regarded the police as society's protectors, the good guys.

The Knapp Commission painted a darker picture. It would hold three weeks of public hearings, baring the innards of the police department for the world to see. The NYPD would never be the same.

Sitting every day in the dour, high-ceilinged chamber of the City Bar Association, I became versed in a new language. A "pad" was a systemized payoff. A "KG" was a known gambler. Cops engaged in minor corruption were "grass-eaters"; those on the take in a major way, "meat-eaters." I heard how cops shook down store owners, hotel managers, construction foremen, and tow-truck operators; how gamblers, loan sharks, and drug dealers paid cops off. In Harlem, gamblers paid off in heroin, which cops provided to informants.

The corruption was not confined to the lower ranks. The hearings revealed how the top brass ignored and even abetted it. The chief inspector, the department's highest uniformed officer, acknowledged accepting gifts from businessmen. The chief of detectives refused to turn over his files of suspect detectives to the chief of internal affairs. A confrontation in the chief of detectives' office ended in a fistfight. The chief of internal affairs left, bruised and empty-handed.

The first deputy commissioner, John Walsh, refused to help federal authorities investigate cops suspected of dealing drugs. A note from his subordinate to another department official stated that the first deputy "doesn't want to help lock up local police." "Let them arrest federal people," Walsh told him.

In its final report, the Knapp Commission put it this way. "The department was given reason to suspect that some of its members were extortionists, murderers and heroin entrepreneurs and made no attempt to verify these suspicions or refute them." When the commission questioned the top brass about this, they suffered what the final report described as "memory lapses." Even a novice like me understood what that meant: like corruption, the blue wall of silence extended to the highest levels of the police department.

Attempting to explain the police mentality, an Internal Affairs Division captain told the commission that cops viewed themselves as surrounded by hostile forces that wanted to destroy the department. In response, they developed loyalties to each other and would not inform on fellow officers. Superior officers were also reluctant to act because they did not want to reveal their weaknesses by acknowledging they had been unable to control their subordinates.

Sitting through every day of those hearings, I realized how little the public or even the city's public officials knew about what went on inside the New York City Police Department. I also realized that when it came to the police, things are not all that they seem. The Knapp Commission's story line didn't convey the full picture. As appalling as the testimony was, there remained pockets of honesty and decency within the NYPD that went unheralded and, I suspected, were probably more prevalent than the corruption. At one hearing, a witness described a Queens command as rife with dishonesty. The next day, its commander appeared before the commission to deny the allegations, pointing out flaws in the witness's testimony. The commission publicly apologized to him.

At another hearing, twenty-three-year-old George Burkert, a tow-truck operator from Astoria, Queens, told how two cops on Manhattan's Lower East Side had ticketed him and a friend twenty-six times in thirteen minutes because he refused to pay them bribes. Burkert related his story to cheers and laughter from the hundreds of spectators. He seemed to personify all honest New Yorkers whom the police had mistreated, as well as their Walter Mitty fantasies of rising up in anger at official injustice. "I just had enough of it," Burkert testified. "I got tired of getting tickets for nothing." When he completed his testimony, the audience applauded him.

The following year, the two cops who had ticketed him were indicted. As their trial began, the charges were suddenly dropped. Burkert and his friend were charged with perjury. They had apparently concocted their entire story. Four civilians testified Burkert and his friend had run a series of red lights. The two cops had chased them in their patrol car and on foot before arresting them. The jury, however, voted 10–2 for acquittal and the judge declared a mistrial.

Serpico and the Knapp Commission also provided me with a story I was too inexperienced to appreciate. After his superiors had ignored his accusations, Serpico met with Jay Kriegel, a top aide to Mayor Lindsay, who told him of City Hall's reluctance to become involved. Soon to declare for the presidency, Lindsay needed a friendly police department, should race riots erupt the following summer as they had in other American cities.

Before the hearings began, I interviewed Kriegel at City Hall and asked what seemed an obvious question: Had he passed Serpico's allegations of police corruption on to Lindsay? Instead of answering, Kriegel led me from his office and walked me around City Hall Park. There he told me he had informed the mayor. At the time, I didn't understand why Kriegel took me to City Hall Park to tell me this. Watergate—and the exposure of President Richard M. Nixon's secret tape-recording system—was in the future. Years later, I would surmise Kriegel had taken me outside his office, thinking that as we walked I might not take notes, or that in such an informal outdoor setting a young reporter like me might not appreciate the import of what he was saying. If those were his reasons, he was at least partially successful. I did not take notes, and although I did file a story, it was unfocused enough that my editors at *Time* reduced his remarks to a sentence. Referring to the Knapp Commission, the story said only that Lindsay "was slow to react."

Testifying before the Knapp Commission some months later, however, Kriegel gave a different version. Protecting Lindsay, he denied what he had said to me in City Hall Park. Under oath, he stated he had not passed on Serpico's information to the mayor. His testimony completed, he walked directly to me and asked what I thought. I was too stunned to say I thought he had lied to the commission—and too embarrassed to say he'd played me for a fool.

Later there was talk Kriegel would be indicted for perjury because his public testimony contradicted what he had told the commission in closed session. Nothing came of it. Lindsay's presidential bid fizzled. The police department revelations were so shocking that he lost any chance he had for reelection to a third term.

Serpico retired from the department. A book was written about him. A movie was made of his life. He became a household name, representing honesty and goodness. He went off to Europe and lived there for ten years. Though he did not know it then, he had altered the department for generations.

The top brass, from the police commissioner on down, also retired. With their departure, the New York City Police Department saw the end of an era. For me, my career as a police reporter was just beginning.

ii.

Four months after the Knapp Commission hearings ended, the riot Mayor Lindsay had feared erupted. For the past couple of years, killers known as the Black Liberation Army had randomly assassinated police officers across the country. On May 19, 1971, patrolmen Nicholas Binetti and Thomas Curry flagged a car at Riverside Drive and 106th Street for a minor traffic violation. BLA gunmen inside the car riddled the officers' patrol car with machine-gun fire, seriously wounding them. Two days later, patrolmen Waverly Jones and Joseph Piagentini, walking out of a housing project in Upper Manhattan, were ambushed. Jones was shot in the head and died on the street. Piagentini was shot thirteen times and died in the back of a radio patrol car en route to the hospital. On January 27, 1972, the BLA executed two rookie officers, Rocco Laurie and his partner Gregory Foster, in the East Village. Three or four men had passed them on the corner of 11th Street and Avenue B, then shot them in the back. As the officers went down, the men stood over them and continued firing. Foster was hit eight times and died instantly. Laurie took six shots and died on the operating table.

Poor in the best of times, race relations in New York City in the early 1970s were at another low. Those random police shootings, as well as Lindsay's desperate efforts to identify with black New Yorkers, had fueled the anger of many whites, including the largely white police department. Tensions culminated on the morning of April 14, 1972, at a Harlem mosque after a civilian 911 dispatcher received a pseudonymous telephone call. "This is Detective Thomas, 28th Precinct. I have a 10-13 [officer needs assistance] at 102 West 116th Street."

"What floor?" asked the dispatcher. "Second floor," the caller replied, then hung up. He did not mention that the building, near Lenox Avenue, was Nation of Islam Mosque Number 7, headed by the notoriously antiwhite minister Louis Farrakhan.

Police officer Philip Cardillo and his partner Vito Navarra rushed to the mosque. In the reception area, Navarra asked a man talking on the telephone whether police officers were inside the building. The man ignored him. Navarra bounded past him and up the stairs to the second floor. A dozen Muslim men appeared and forced him back down.

Two other cops, Ivan Negron and Victor Padilla, said they saw Cardillo trying to push past the Muslims to reach Navarra. "Bring the cop down or let us go up and get him," Padilla shouted to the Muslims. They refused.

Five other officers arrived, including a sergeant. A dozen Muslims forced them outside, leaving Navarra, Negron, Padilla, and Cardillo inside alone. All but Cardillo fought their way out. There were shots. Negron said later he saw Muslims on top of Cardillo, who'd been hit in the side. His service revolver had been taken. Police later recovered it in the reception room with a spent bullet. He died six days later. He was thirty-two years old, the father of three children.

Meanwhile an angry crowd of a thousand had gathered outside the mosque and the police called for reinforcements. The crowd threw rocks, burned a city bus, overturned an anticrime team's gypsy cab, and roughed up a white female reporter. For the next three hours, a full-blown riot raged. To end it, the police allowed a dozen suspects they were holding in the mosque's basement to leave without identifying them. Police later claimed Farrakhan had promised they would appear at the 24th Precinct, on Manhattan's West Side, where the investigation was moved. None showed up.

No one was convicted of Cardillo's murder. The repercussions of a police officer's unsolved killing reverberated through the department for the next decade. The day of Cardillo's funeral, his commander, Deputy Inspector John Haugh, resigned in disgust, blaming the NYPD's failure to publicly affirm that Cardillo had acted properly on entering the mosque. Within days, the department issued written rules for sixteen "sensitive locations," including Nation of Islam Mosque Number 7, forbidding officers to enter such places without a supervisor. It turned out there had been an unwritten agreement to that effect with Mosque Number 7. So strictly did the department follow their new rules that for the next two years, the police department prevented ballistics technicians from entering the mosque to gather evidence from Cardillo's shooting.

In 1974, the dean of the mosque's school, Louis 17X Dupree, was indicted for Cardillo's murder. At trial, he claimed that either another cop had shot Cardillo or Cardillo had shot himself. The first trial resulted in a hung jury, the second in acquittal.

In 1980, a Manhattan grand jury under District Attorney Robert Morgenthau investigated the Cardillo shooting. It did not indict anyone but issued a report that excoriated the department. The police investigation, the grand jury said, had been "curtailed in deference to fears of civil unrest in the black community. . . . The long-term interests of justice in apprehending criminals were overridden by the short-term concern of preventing civil disorder."

The grand jury also criticized the department for "inexcusable detective procedures." It specifically cited the release of the Muslim suspects before they were identified. Echoing the Knapp Commission of a decade before, the grand jury accused the department's top brass of "persistent lapses of memory." It found a "concerted and orchestrated effort by members and former members of the police department to impede" the Cardillo investigation and the grand jury's inquiry. The Knapp Commission may have rid the police department of its systemic corruption, but it had apparently failed to breach the blue wall of silence.

Within the department, blame for the suspects' release fell upon Benjamin Ward, a black lieutenant whom Lindsay had appointed deputy commissioner for community affairs. Ward, who had rushed to the mosque after the shooting, denied releasing the suspects. As a civilian deputy commissioner, he argued, he lacked authority to give such an order. No one believed him. So furious was the police union, the powerful Patrolmen's Benevolent Association, that its president, Robert McKiernan, declared in its official publication *Front and Center* that Ward "should either resign or be fired."

Not until eleven years after the shooting did the truth about what happened at the mosque emerge. A long-hidden document cleared Ward, who would become the city's first black police commissioner. I would play a role in uncovering it.

iii.

In 1983, I opened *New York Newsday*'s police bureau. During Lindsay's second term, police headquarters had moved south from Centre Street, where it had been for a hundred years, to a fourteen-story, red-brick, fortresslike building known as One Police Plaza. The building was completed in 1973, the year before Lindsay left office. It was his final legacy to the police department.

In the eleven years since that shooting, racial tensions in New York City had only worsened. The Black Liberation Army had been subdued, but black New Yorkers were now accusing the police department of systemic brutality. In the summer of 1983, Michigan congressman John Conyers came to New York and held three days of public hearings on the subject. A few months later, Mayor Edward I. Koch—who invariably sided with the police, angering virtually all black New Yorkers—announced Ward's appointment as police commissioner.

In the years since the mosque shooting, the department's anger toward Ward had only intensified. The PBA's president Phil Caruso publicly mocked him, calling him "Bubba." It seemed the union's opposition might sink his appointment.

Then *New York Newsday*'s court reporter Gerald McKelvey made a discovery that changed everything. McKelvey, who shared my office at One Police Plaza, knew the court system as few did. He was close to the then–state's chief judge Lawrence Cooke, and would later become a special assistant to Morgenthau. McKelvey had read the 1980 grand jury report, which mentioned a document known as the "blue book," so-called for its blue cover. The blue book was the police department's internal investigation of the Cardillo shooting. According to the grand jury report, it had been "circulated only among the upper ranks of the department."

Because the grand jury did not indict anyone, all testimony and evidence had been sealed, and only its final report made public. Figuring the Cardillo family had filed a wrongful death suit against the city, McKelvey sought out the family's lawyer, who brought in six boxes of discovery material. In the first box McKelvey found the blue book.

We opened it in our office at Police Plaza and began reading. Officially entitled "Report and Analysis of Muslim Mosque Incident of April 14, 1972," it had been prepared a year after the shooting, between March and June 1973, under

James Hannon, the chief of operations, then the department's highest-ranking uniformed officer. It began with the phony 911 call, went through Cardillo's rushing into the mosque, and cited the riot raging outside and the call for police reinforcements. It described the appearance at the mosque of three black heavyweights—Ward, Farrakhan, and Harlem congressman Charles Rangel. According to the blue book, Farrakhan and Ward "took the position that the street would return to normal if the police were removed from the area, including the mosque."

At that point, the tough-talking, cigar-chomping chief of detectives Albert Seedman arrived. A Jew, described as "more Irish than the Irish," Seedman, according to the blue book, "assumed the responsibility of the investigation." Then came the key sentence. As Gerry and I read it, we looked up and stared at each other without speaking.

"These facts, plus uncertainty that all persons involved were in the basement, led to the reluctant decision by Chief Seedman to move the investigation to the 24th Precinct on the promise of Mosque officials to produce the detainees thereat." There it was. Seedman, not Ward, had ordered the suspects' release. Ward may have urged that police officers be removed from the area, but it was Seedman who had allowed the suspects in a police officer's murder to leave the premises without being identified.

"Seedman," the blue book added, "continued his investigation in the Mosque but after about 15 minutes either Rangel or Farrakhan approached him and told him that they had better get out of the Mosque or there would be trouble; that they could not control the crowd outside. Seedman now felt that with the reduced uniform presence protecting the scene outside, he was in an untenable position."

According to the blue book, Seedman said that the decision to transfer the investigation to the 24th Precinct was his. He explained that "no police officers at the scene could identify any person remaining in the basement as being involved in the incident." He added that either Farrakhan or Rangel had promised he would produce the suspects at the 24th Precinct.

I couldn't reach Farrakhan, but Rangel denied making that promise. "I couldn't promise anyone to the precinct," he told me as we prepared the *Newsday* article. "For me to negotiate over a bunch of hoodlums with an officer I didn't know is . . . ridiculous."

For eleven years Ward had been blamed for something he apparently hadn't done. The code of silence that prevented police officers from coming forward about corruption also prevented top department officials from revealing the truth about the mosque. How much easier to blame a black man and department outsider whose "position" to remove officers from the mosque implied a cowardly retreat from the murder scene of a fallen comrade than the flamboyant, tough-guy chief who personified the department's macho image. The code that protected the guilty had, in this instance, condemned the innocent.

Seedman, I subsequently learned, had retired just two weeks after Cardillo's shooting. Had he done so, like Cardillo's superior, the embittered Inspector Haugh, because of what he had regarded as the department's pusillanimous response to the mosque incident? I doubted it. More likely, Seedman felt his decision to release the suspects spelled the end of his career. Surely he never suspected the department would cover up that decision for a decade.

By the time I caught up with him in November 1983, he held the more prosaic position of chief of security for Alexander's Department Stores in Queens. "What is this document?" he said when I confronted him with the blue book. "I never heard of it." But when I told him what the blue book said about his releasing the suspects, he acknowledged his role. When I asked why he hadn't owned up to it and had allowed Ward to twist in the wind all these years, he meekly replied, "What good would it have done?" What good, indeed!

New York Newsday's front-page story on November 17, 1983, assured Ward's appointment as police commissioner. Mayor Koch, who said he had never heard of the blue book, waved the paper on the steps of City Hall and crowed, "Thank God for Newsday's uncovering the report." Ward tacked a copy of the story to his office door.

Our discovery had exposed another police cover-up, this one buried so deep that literally no one could find it. The day the story appeared, Koch asked the Manhattan district attorney and the police department for copies of the blue book. Not one could be found. The New York City Police Department's Public Information Office, on the thirteenth floor of Police Plaza, had some two dozen officers, a number of whom with long-standing ties to reporters and editors. Yet not one person acknowledged knowing anything about the blue book. The department's prim and savvy deputy commissioner for public information, Alice T. McGillion, who knew as much about the department's intricacies as any civilian, said she, too, had never heard of it. Neither she nor anyone else at Police Plaza or City Hall could explain why the report, completed ten years before, had never surfaced. Had the situation been reversed—had the blue book exonerated Seedman and blamed Ward—I suspect *that* information would surely have seen the light of day.

This led me to another discovery about the police department: Official silence can be tantamount to a cover-up. One might naïvely think that Ward, buried by official silence for over a decade, might as commissioner have sought more openness or transparency for himself and the police department. But less than six months after *Newsday*'s discovery of the blue book, these same forces were marshaled to protect him. Once again, there was a cover-up. This time, the abettors were not merely in the police department but at City Hall. That was where the decisions were made.

On the rainy Palm Sunday night of April 15, 1984, just a few months after ward's inauguration as commissioner, I was one of a half-dozen reporters keeping vigil outside a house in the Brownsville–East New York section of Brooklyn. The house was located in the 75th Precinct, which had the city's highest murder rate. Earlier that day, ten women and children inside that house had been shot to death. Some had been struck at close range. One was a baby in her mother's arms. The killings, drug-related, became known as the Palm Sunday Massacre— the largest mass murder in city history.

Because I was the only reporter there who covered the police department, I noticed something the others didn't. Standing outside in the rain, I watched every top police and mayoral official, Koch included, arrive—everyone except Ward. I also noted that Ward was absent from that evening's news conference, held at the 75th Precinct, and from the second, the following day at Police Plaza. When I asked McGillion about Ward's absence, she told me he had been at his vacation house upstate—unreachable.

Not until six months later did I uncover the truth. By then I had learned Ward was a drinker. At the PBA's convention that summer, he had drunk so much that before he stepped inside the police helicopter returning him to headquarters, he urinated on the helicopter door in front of scores of union delegates. The incident was never reported in the newspapers. Perhaps to seek leverage over him, a PBA official told me the union would officially deny it had occurred.

Nonetheless, it became the talk of Police Plaza. It occurred to me then that had Ward been at his upstate vacation house during the Palm Sunday Massacre, as McGillion claimed, the department could have reached him by telephone—unless he had been in no condition to respond. When I confronted her with this, she blurted out the truth, or at least a sanitized version. The night of the massacre Ward had been, as she put it, "on a holiday on a car trip in his own car visiting various places between Baltimore and Washington. It was social," she added.

"He didn't leave a number," she continued when I asked why the department couldn't reach him. "He says he didn't leave a number. He realized when he came back that there was a problem he hadn't left a number."

I later discovered what McGillion had selectively omitted. The married Ward had been on a three-day bender, traveling with a girlfriend to motels between Baltimore and Washington, D.C. During those three days the department had been unable to locate him. A further embarrassment arose when he returned to New York the following Wednesday for a meeting at City Hall. His car broke down on the New Jersey Turnpike. Fearing he would be late, he telephoned the department's highway patrol, which sent a car to meet him and his girlfriend at the New York State line.

But when I asked City Hall about Ward's absence, it was Mayor Koch who stonewalled. He denied Ward had been unreachable. "*You* say he was unreachable. We don't," said his spokesman, Tom Kelly, who had been one of the city officials to appear at the murder scene that Sunday night. "The mayor didn't try to reach him. He doesn't believe he [Ward] was unreachable."

Stanley Brezenoff, the deputy mayor responsible for supervising the police department, took a similar position. He said the department had never notified *him* that Ward was missing. Nor was he concerned, he said, because Ward regularly sent him memos telling him where he would be or where he could be contacted. Brezenoff even showed me the memo Ward had sent him on Thursday, April 12, three days before the massacre. It stated that Ward would be on vacation from Friday April 13 through Tuesday April 17. "During normal business hours," his memo read, "I can be contacted through my commanding officer, David Scott. . . . After business hours I can be contacted through the Operations Unit and First Deputy Commissioner Patrick Murphy will act as commissioner in my absence."

Koch, Kelly, and Brezenoff were so convincing that my editors at *Newsday* wavered for a week. "If Koch doesn't have a problem, why do we," asked *New York Newsday*'s top editor at the time. "Ten people are dead," I argued. "The head of the police department is missing. No one can find him and the mayor doesn't want to know where he is?"

The editor couldn't hold to his position for long. The story ran under the understated headline "For 3 Days, Police Brass Sought Ward." It began: "Police Commissioner Benjamin Ward was unreachable for three days last spring while his department tried to notify him of the largest mass murder in the city's history."

As soon as the story ran, the cover-up dissolved. Brezenoff acknowledged Ward "was not as reachable as he should have been," and added he had already spoken with him three times that day. "I wanted to know if in fact that he was reachable, if not, why not," Brezenoff said. "I wanted reassurance that it would not happen again."

Koch also offered an explanation. "It was something that should not have happened," he said. "You should always be in touch if you're a commissioner—certainly the police commissioner."

iv.

As the police department's spokeswoman, Alice T. McGillion was both clever and skillful. She—and the cops she brought into the Public Information Office—knew how to manage reporters. The best of them, like her freckled Lieutenant Thomas Fahey, could schmooze, joke, and swap stories. Fahey was so good at schmoozing he sounded as though he were providing confidential information when in fact he never offered more than McGillion wanted him to. Friendly as he might appear, there was never a question where his first loyalty lay. It was, as it should be, not to his reporter friends but to the NYPD.

Even though she was a civilian, the same could be said of McGillion. She, too, projected an intimacy with the in-house reporters at Police Plaza. She even threw a party at her apartment on Central Park West for reporters and her police staff. Such socializing fostered camaraderie, even trust, which, as I discovered, also made her treacherous.

I witnessed this at the end of 1983 just before Ward's appointment. It concerned the son of a deputy commissioner, then a probationary cop at the Police Academy. Celebrating the end of classes, he had attended a party at Kate

Cassidy's Pub on Woodhaven Boulevard in Queens. At 4:30 the next morning he was arrested in his car on the West Side of Manhattan, charged with being drunk and having sex with a prostitute.

His explanation was amusing. He claimed he had intended to drive from the party to his home on Staten Island but missed the turnoff on the Long Island Expressway and mistakenly took the Midtown Tunnel into the east side of Manhattan. Somehow he ended up on the West Side, on 38th Street and Eleventh Avenue, an area known for prostitutes. There, he said, he parked and fell asleep. He was awakened, he said, by two prostitutes whom he threw out of his car, then he went back to sleep. The next thing he knew, a sergeant was standing over him, placing him under arrest. According to the prostitutes—it turned out there *were* two—the young cop paid them fifty dollars for sex. But after being rousted by a passing Port Authority patrol car, he demanded his money back and held one of them hostage. The second prostitute fled and hailed a patrol car.

I was on vacation when the incident occurred. When I returned, I learned McGillion had alerted the in-house reporters and persuaded them not to write a story. She convinced them that had the incident involved any other probationary cop, it wouldn't be important enough for a story. That may well have been true. But any other probationary cop would have been summarily dismissed. "Probies," as they are called, have no union protection—not even a departmental trial—to defend themselves. The police department's position was that it was better to dismiss a bad probie before he obtained such protection. In fact, a few months later, a half-dozen probationary cops were dismissed for fighting at a tailgate party at Yankee Stadium. Unfortunately for them, the victim that time was the son of the PBA's private investigator, who came to me with the story.

With no story written about the deputy commissioner's son, he was able to remain a cop. The department allowed him to plead guilty to drunkenness, the least serious of his charges and an all too common failing in the NYPD. That was the story I wrote when I returned from my vacation. It ran under the headline: "Deputy Police Boss' Son Gets 2nd Chance at Job." But by then the department had embraced him. The only effect my story had was to embarrass his father, the deputy commissioner, who never spoke to me again. Although McGillion and I have remained friendly over the years, she says she has never forgiven me for having written that story. I have never forgotten how skillful she was in manipulating the media.

v.

I would report on a final cover-up in those years. This one was so bizarre that twenty-five years later I remain bewildered by it.

In March 1983, five men attended a midweek luncheon at the Altadonna Restaurant in the 106th Precinct in Queens. The five were: Queens district attorney John Santucci; the newly appointed head of the police department's Intelligence Division, Inspector Peter J. Prezioso; Queens district leader and Board of Elections commissioner Anthony Sadowski; the 106th Precinct's detective squad commander, Lieutenant Michael Doyle; and a mysterious figure named Salvatore Reale, rumored to be, in law enforcement lingo, a Gambino crime family "associate."

That term, however, belied Reale's true value to the Gambino crime family. He was its liaison to the city's political establishment—judges, politicians, and police. Such closeness between mobsters and the NYPD was not confined to the Gambinos or to the 106th Precinct. In 2006, two Brooklyn detectives, Louis Eppolito and Steven Caracappa, would be convicted of having murdered eight people for the Luchese crime family, dating back to the 1980s. Nonetheless, the relationship between the Gambinos—many of whom, like John Gotti, lived within the precinct's confines—and the cops in the One-Oh-Six, as it was known, appeared unique. The station house was considered a clubhouse, an annex to Gotti's Bergen Hunt and Fish Club. Mobsters held meetings in the precinct squad room.

The Altadonna restaurant, a favorite of Gotti's, was a point of contact between the Gambinos and the Queens political establishment. Its owner, Joseph Altadonna, had closed it for the day so that this unlikely group could meet in secret. He had pulled the blinds so that passersby could not see inside. To further ensure secrecy, each person entered through the kitchen, the same entrance favored by Gotti, then a ranking Gambino capo. Arriving around noon, the men spent the next fourteen hours eating and drinking at two long tables Altadonna had set up in the empty restaurant. Sadowski began by toasting Prezioso, the guest of honor. Reale ordered a bottle of Dom Perignon. Altadonna popped the cork. He then brought out hot antipasto, baked clams, mussels marinara, veal scaloppini, lobster oreganata, and linguine with white clam sauce, together with bottles of Pinot Grigio and Santa Margherita. Later that night, other visitors arrived. One was Reale's Israeli girlfriend, Roberta Mizrahi. Santucci spent much of the time with his arm around her. When the party broke up at 2:00 A.M., Reale paid the bill. It came to $1,825.

This luncheon meeting remained secret for three and a half years, until *New York Newsday*'s Ellis Henican reported it in the fall of 1986. Because Ellis was new to the city, I was asked to help figure out why Santucci and Prezioso, two law enforcement heavyweights, would spend fourteen hours in a locked-down restaurant with a reputed mobster.

Santucci and Prezioso offered different explanations. Santucci said the luncheon was "a belated celebration" for Prezioso's promotion to head the NYPD's Intelligence Division, known as Intel, then the NYPD division that investigated organized crime. This made Reale's presence all the more sensitive. Prezioso, however, said that at the time of the luncheon he had not yet been named to the Intelligence Division. He added that he had spent most of those fourteen hours speaking to Santucci about "family matters."

Doyle, who headed the 106th's detective squad and was said to be close to Reale, offered another explanation. He told Charles "Joe" Hynes, the special state prosecutor for police corruption—a position established in the wake of the Knapp Commission—that Reale and Sadowski had arranged the luncheon to discuss making Prezioso the NYPD's first Italian-American police commissioner. This arrangement, Reale told Doyle, had been sought by the Gambinos and sanctioned at its highest level so that they could control the city's other four organized crime families. The Gambinos would enact a toll from the other families for every illegal operation they opened—whether gambling, bookmaking, numbers, or after-hours clubs—in the five boroughs of New York. "Remember everything you see and hear at this meeting," Doyle said Reale had told him. "It will be important later on."

Doyle, who had become friendly with Ellis, told us that Sadowski—who was also a city elections commissioner—had even invited Mayor Koch. Asked about that in 2007, Koch said he didn't know Sadowski and could recall no such invitation. So was Doyle's story credible? Had a Gambino crime family mobster arranged a luncheon, attended by the Queens district attorney, to discuss making Prezioso police commissioner? Or was Koch's stated ignorance an indication that Doyle and Reale had exaggerated the luncheon's purpose?

What I did know was this: The New York City Police Department, like most major law enforcement agencies, has never had an Italian-American police commissioner. In a department long dominated by the Irish, Italians had become its largest ethnic group, with inevitable tensions and rivalries. Even today, more than twenty years later, these tensions and rivalries exist, though in a more benign and even humorous form. As Patrick Lynch put it after his election as PBA president in 1999 after two decades of Italian leadership, "Out with the tomatoes, in with the potatoes."

At the time of the Altadonna luncheon, the Irish still dominated the department's upper ranks. They were especially resentful of Internal Affairs Chief John Guido, who, as Doyle said, "hated Irish people and never went after Italian cops." Supposedly, Guido had warned Prezioso of the Irish as he rose through the ranks, saying, "Stay away from the donkeys and stick to your own kind." Whether or not Guido ever made such a remark, Doyle was forced to retire in October 1983, seven months after the Altadonna luncheon, while Prezioso was cleared of wrongdoing.

So how did Sal Reale figure into all this? Tall and muscular, with thick, gray-black hair, he was articulate, sophisticated, and impeccably dressed. He was said to have connections to the FBI and the NYPD and was seen with such politicians as Massachusetts Congressman Thomas P. "Tip" O'Neil and Queens Congresswoman Geraldine Ferraro. He boasted he had served as Ferraro's Queens County campaign manager and raised money for her 1984 vice presidential bid. Because politicians were reluctant to be associated with him [Ferraro denied to me that she knew him] Reale had a code name: "the Ambassador"—so called, as he put it, for "bringing people together."

That was the name he had left with O'Neil when he called him on O'Neil's private line in his congressional office from the Altadonna the afternoon of the luncheon. O'Neil wasn't in when Reale called, but the FBI was. Because the Altadonna was a favorite of Gotti's, they monitored the Altadonna's long-distance calls. When prosecutors subpoenaed Reale before a federal grand jury in Brooklyn's Eastern District to question him about the luncheon, he took the Fifth Amendment 121 times.

In the NYPD, Reale's connections were such that he possessed five press cards, which enabled him to pass through police lines at homicides and speak to the investigating detectives at crime scenes. He professed to have prior knowledge a decade before that Serpico was about to go public with his allegations of departmental corruption before the story broke in the *Times* and had warned his own contacts to avoid Serpico because he was wired.

Reale was also rumored to be the Gambino's man at LaGuardia and Kennedy Airports. In August 1983, five months after the Altadonna luncheon, he was indicted for labor racketeering at Kennedy. He was charged with extorting money from an air freight company in return for labor peace.

Santucci's spokesman denied the district attorney knew Reale. "He knew Reale was active in the community. He didn't think of Reale as anything other than a local businessman," the spokesman said. Prezioso acknowledged knowing Reale but said he knew nothing of his mob ties. It turned out the department had conducted a secret investigation of the luncheon before Henican's story ran, apparently because of Reale's indictment. In 1986, after the story, they conducted a second investigation. Both investigations cleared Prezioso of wrongdoing.

Then, in 1986, Guido retired. His successor, Chief Daniel F. Sullivan, who conducted the second investigation, said Prezioso had acknowledged meeting with Reale before joining the Intelligence Division. But Sullivan said there was no indication Prezioso had disclosed organized crime information to Reale or anyone else. Referring to the Altadonna luncheon, Sullivan said, "Our investigation found nothing to contradict what Prezioso said [had] occurred, that it was an amiable social meeting." But Sullivan conceded Prezioso had lied to police investigators about the number of times he'd met with Reale prior to the luncheon. In the first investigation, Prezioso said he had met with Reale twice. In the second, he acknowledged meeting with him at least five times. Sullivan said he accepted Prezioso's explanation—that he had originally "held back" about the number of meetings "out of embarrassment."

Was Sullivan serious? Either he was naïve or he was protecting Prezioso in yet another NYPD cover-up. And Sullivan certainly wasn't Italian. Nonetheless, in January 1987, after *Newsday*'s story ran, Ward transferred Prezioso to the police department's Criminal Justice Bureau, which served as a burial ground at Police Plaza for chiefs on their way out. Ten days later, Prezioso announced his retirement.

Meanwhile, I got to know Reale. He lived in Queens and invited Ellis and me to his home in Howard Beach, which was not far from Gotti's. He introduced us to his wife and cooked us a pasta dinner. Why was Reale so friendly while Ellis and I were reporting on him? I wondered. Perhaps "the Ambassador" thought he could charm us into writing favorably about him — especially with his sentencing on the labor racketeering charges coming up.

In 1987, he pleaded guilty before federal judge Jack B. Weinstein, who sentenced him to fifteen years in prison. But Weinstein, the chief judge of the Eastern District, which covers Brooklyn and Queens, then did something bizarre. Without explanation, he declared that imprisoning Reale would "likely result in his death, either by his own hand or the hands of someone else. He knows too much." He suspended Reale's sentence, placed him on probation, and banished him from New York for five years.

Reale, who had been living in Doyle's Vermont farmhouse, relocated to Scottsdale, Arizona. Then something extraordinary occurred. On February 6, 1990, federal agents in the southwestern Texas border town of Sierra Blanca (pop. 600) stopped a Lincoln Continental, leased to Doyle, that Reale was driving. According to newspaper reports, in the trunk they found $3.8 million in cash and an additional $96,000 in Swiss francs. Reale told the U.S. Border Patrol he had been "relocating" to Florida and that it was his "nest egg." Weinstein resentenced him to ten years for violating his parole.

A year later, in May 1991, Santucci resigned in the middle of his term. In a bitter parting news conference before six hundred people at the Queens County Courthouse, he blamed the media. "Hate is their business. There's no reputation they honor or respect," he railed. "Anyone in public office of Italian heritage is subject to association with organized crime." He accused *New York Newsday*, and me in particular, of anti-Italian bias and hounding him from office over the Altadonna luncheon. "If you want to do me a favor," he told the audience, "don't buy *Newsday*. And if you're in public office, exclude them from your news conferences."

Reale, meanwhile, served seven years in prison, then moved to Las Vegas. He and I kept in touch. He sent me cards each Christmas and Easter. When some years later a murder I had investigated led to the case's being reopened, he called to congratulate me. In 2007, as I prepared this book, he called me. He was in New York, visiting his sister-in-law. On the Saturday before Christmas, we met for breakfast in a diner in Whitestone, Queens. It had been nearly a decade since I had seen him. He was now sixty-seven years old, thinner, his hair all gray. Twenty-four years had passed since the Altadonna luncheon, but he spoke of it as though it were yesterday.

Yes, he said, he had arranged it. It had been just as Ellis had written it, to help Prezioso become police commissioner. It had been sanctioned at the highest levels of the Gambino crime family, by its then boss Paul Castellano, the same man Gotti would have assassinated two years later outside Sparks Steak House in Manhattan. Referring to the Altadonna, Reale said, "Do you think a meeting like that could have happened without Paul's approval? At that level, I had to get his okay."

I asked Reale about Santucci and Prezioso. Contrary to Santucci's claim that he didn't know Reale and was aware of him only as a local businessman, Reale said he had first met Santucci when the district attorney asked his help in finding Santucci's teenage daughter, who had disappeared and whom Santucci feared had been kidnapped. [It turned out she had run away with her boyfriend.] He said that he, Doyle, Prezioso, and their wives often went out to dinner together Saturday nights. "Pete and I had dinner at least fifteen times," he said. He added that it was Prezioso who had secured his five press cards at a cost of $5,000.

Then I asked Reale about his arrest at the Texas border. He said he had driven eight hundred miles east from Las Vegas. When federal agents stopped him, they confiscated the money. "They never arrested me," he said. "When they asked me where I'd gotten the money. I said I won it gambling, that I was very lucky. They didn't believe me. They wanted to know the names of the casinos." They then obtained a warrant and searched his house in Scottsdale from which they confiscated more money.

He maintained that when the agents at the border returned the money to him they shorted him $700,000. A similar scenario occurs in the movie *Casino*. Maybe the screenwriter got the idea from Reale. Maybe Reale got the idea from the movie.

"So where did you get the money?" I asked him. "And where were you taking it?"

"Let's just say the money was leaving Las Vegas, going to the right people," he said.

So was Reale telling the truth, about the money and about the Altadonna luncheon? If so, what did it mean? Merely the fact that the luncheon had occurred lent credence to the story's outline—that the Gambino crime family, with the help of the Queens district attorney, had sought to influence the selection of the police commissioner of New York City.

And what had been the response of the police department to the involvement of one of its top chiefs? Initially, they had accepted Prezioso's explanation that he had "held back" on his number of meetings with Reale "out of embarrassment." Only after *Newsday* reported the luncheon three years later did the department act, forcing Prezioso to retire. Once again, the NYPD had covered up for one of its own.

TWO

The Secret Meeting

i.

Like everyone else in New York City in the fall of 1993, I felt Ray Kelly deserved reappointment as police commissioner. During his fifteen months in office, he had taken control of a foundering city. Earlier that year he had served as the face of New York during the first attack on the World Trade Center. He had eased racial tensions by visiting black churches in a well-publicized attempt to recruit black officers. He had steered the department through another corruption scandal, the first since the Knapp Commission of two decades before. He had even begun to reduce the city's sky-high murder rate of the past two decades.

Yet here in the late fall of 1993, Kelly was forced to plead for his job. Despite his achievements, he had to arrange an eleventh-hour meeting with a resistant mayor-elect, Rudy Giuliani. The meeting was secret—so secret only a few people on either's staff knew of it. The media didn't report it. I wouldn't learn of it until ten years later. Kelly wouldn't acknowledge it until three years after that. Even its exact date is uncertain, though it appears to have occurred in the last days of November, just before Giuliani announced his selection.

Although lasting but a few minutes, that meeting would alter the lives of both men. It would serve as the foundation of the new mayor's political career, whose centerpiece would be his dramatic reduction of crime and his claim to "turning around" New York City. It would cause Kelly to leave New York for Washington, whence he would reemerge a decade later as a global leader against terrorism. It would also usher in a third man, William Bratton, who would orchestrate a revolution within the NYPD that was no less profound than the Knapp Commission's of two decades before. For the next fifteen years, these three men would become rivals and antagonists. During that time, they would barely speak to one another. They would denigrate each other's accomplishments while exaggerating their own. Yet between them, they would transform the New York City Police Department and personify the modern era of the NYPD.

I barely knew Kelly then. I would never get to know him, although I would delude myself into believing that I did. John Clifford, a sergeant on his staff, had flagged me about him early on. Clifford had been a detective in the Public Information Office, the department's public relations arm, known as DCPI, under Alice McGillion. He was, to say the least, unusual. The Public Information Office was expert in managing the media and presenting the department in a favorable light. Yet here was Clifford, who disdained reporters, who was brusque, if not rude. Sometimes he'd pause before answering a question, stare, sigh, then shake his head, implying in this world-weary gesture that he'd never heard anything so stupid. Other times, he'd simply hang up the phone because he felt a reporter's question was plain dumb. God only knows why they kept him there. It was one of the NYPD's mysteries that made covering it so frustrating yet so intriguing.

Unlike much of the NYPD, where rules were twisted and motives were serpentine, there was a purity to Clifford. He was loyal not only to the NYPD but to the concept of telling the truth, if not the full truth then at least to not telling a lie. When the department screwed up, as it often did, Clifford never equivocated. He simply refused to answer. So on those occasions when he spoke, I listened. Years later, after he had joined Kelly's staff, he said to me, "Kelly's the best commissioner the department ever had. He knows it better than anyone and he's smarter than all of them."

I had left Police Plaza by then. In the mid-1980s I had opened *New York Newsday*'s bureau in the Bronx, although I continued to report on the department. Because of Clifford, I took notice of Kelly. He had grown up on the West Side of Manhattan, where his father was a milkman, his mother a "dresser" for Macy's. He had joined the department as a police cadet, answering telephones while attending Manhattan College, where he also joined ROTC. Graduating in 1963, he was sworn onto the police force, then spent his next four years on active duty in the Marine Corps, including a tour as a first lieutenant in Vietnam. Returning to the NYPD, he was said to have graduated from the Police Academy first in his class and to have begun immediately studying for the sergeant's exam.

Because Kelly was short, perhaps five feet eight inches, just above the department's height requirement, his stature was the subject of jokes. Muscular, balding, his hair short in a military-style crew cut and with a canny half smile, he was called, in the trenchant humor of the NYPD, "Popeye." There was, however, nothing comic about Kelly. He stood ramrod straight and carried himself with a regal bearing. No officer dared call him "Popeye" to his face. Few addressed him by anything other than his official rank.

As he rose, he was spotted by Commissioner Ben Ward. In 1985, after a notorious "stun gun" incident—in which three officers in the 106th Precinct in Queens were found guilty of using a stun gun on black marijuana dealers—Ward fired the entire borough command. That included the precinct commander, executive officer, deputy borough chief, and the assistant chief in charge of Queens. Ward topped that off by removing the chief of patrol, the officer in charge of the day-to-day running of the city's seventy-six precincts. It was the NYPD's most widespread purge since the Knapp Commission. Ward then assigned Kelly to be the 106th Precinct's commanding officer.

Like Ward, Kelly had graduated from law school. He also obtained a master's degree from Harvard. When David Dinkins succeeded Koch as mayor in 1989, he brought in an outsider, Dr. Lee Brown, to head the police department. On Ward's recommendation, Brown appointed Kelly first deputy commissioner—the department's nominal second in command, whose duties, like those of the vice president of the United States, are as broad or as narrow as the commander-in-chief decrees.

About the only person Kelly had failed to impress was Ward's hard-charging chief of department, the snow white–haired Robert Johnston, whose nom de guerre was "Patton," after the World War II general. In 1986, while Kelly commanded the 106, Johnston was leading a seventeen-day manhunt for twenty-year-old Larry Davis, a Bronx drug dealer who had shot six cops when they came to arrest him. My recollection of Johnston was his arrival at an East Bronx command post on a winter night in full dress uniform and wearing a pith helmet, while directing his police army to close off street after Bronx street, building after building, trapping Davis like a rat. When Brown appointed Kelly first deputy, Johnston insisted he bypass Kelly in the chain of command and report directly to Brown. Apparently on Ward's recommendation, Brown agreed. That left Kelly with a title but with no defined responsibilities.

Dr. Lee Brown's three years as police commissioner would prove disastrous for the NYPD, just as many felt Dinkins's four years as mayor proved disastrous for New York City. A native of California, Brown had headed police departments in Houston and Atlanta, but he was never comfortable in New York. Often absent from Police Plaza, he was nicknamed "Out of Town Brown." Dinkins, however, referred to him, with his doctorate in criminology, as "Dr. Brown," as though his title of "Doctor" were more important than that of "Commissioner."

The two shared a philosophy called "community policing," a term then in vogue, in which cops walked beats under the theory that better police-community relations translated into less crime. A corollary of this was that crime's origins were societal, which the police could not solve. Under Dinkins, this became a self-fulfilling prophecy. During his four years as mayor, crime skyrocketed. In 1990, the number of murders—the bellwether crime that police cannot cover up or knock down to one of a lesser category—reached a staggering 2,245. The number hovered around 2,000 for the next three years while New York City's image came to resemble a Hogarth tableau, with panhandlers frightening passersby, squeegee men intimidating drivers at bridge and tunnel entrances, hordes of homeless sleeping in the subways, urinating and defecating in the streets, and marauding drug gangs terrorizing housing projects with random shootings.

There was a racial component to this. Most of the violence was committed by black and Hispanic New Yorkers. A decade before, Ben Ward, referring to blacks, had called this "our dirty little secret." Of course, most of the victims were also black and Hispanic. But it was the white victims who received the headlines. Brian Watkins, a twenty-two-year-old tourist from Utah, was stabbed to death on a midtown Manhattan subway platform as he tried to protect his mother from a gang of Hispanic teenagers. The Watkinses had been attending Dinkins's favorite event, the U.S. Tennis Open. In the Bronx, a white assistant district attorney was shot and killed by a passing gunman as he ate his lunch across the street from the courthouse. A *New York Post* front-page headline captured the city's fear and pain: "Dave, Do Something."

The reasons for the city's crime explosion, of course, went beyond Dinkins and community policing. The city's financial crisis of the mid-1970s had resulted in massive layoffs in the police department, reducing its force by a third. Then in the 1980s, a crack epidemic rippled through the city's minority neighborhoods. While the city's media reported both those causes, there was another that it ignored. Since the Knapp Commission corruption scandal twenty years before, the NYPD had undergone a revolution. For the next two decades, preventing corruption, rather than fighting crime, became its first priority. A cynical aphorism was born: No precinct commander ever lost his job because of a crime increase. But a corruption scandal could bring down an administration. So sensitive was the top brass to scandal that they discouraged precinct cops and squad detectives from making drug arrests. Instead, drug arrests were made only by specialized units. The result was that the police department all but abandoned narcotics enforcement. An explosion of well-financed drug gangs followed. The noble ideal of fighting police corruption had led to crime of a different kind.

No one inside the department discussed this policy change publicly. I learned of it only anecdotally from detectives, who shook their heads in bewilderment and resignation. They asked rhetorically whether the trade-off in increased crime was worth the supposed anticorruption gains. Nor did I ever hear a top police official publicly question the change in priorities for fear he would be considered "soft on corruption." After the Knapp corruption scandal, that was the last thing anybody in the police department wanted to be called.

To the cops, Dinkins appeared to side with the criminals. When the black racial rabble-rouser Sonny Carson, who had spent four years in prison for kidnapping and attempted murder, led a boycott of two Korean groceries, Dinkins ordered the police not to enforce a court order that banned protestors from picketing near the stores. When Michael O'Keefe, a white police officer, fatally shot Kiko Garcia, a Dominican drug dealer, and riots broke out after an eyewitness falsely claimed that Garcia had been shot in cold blood, Dinkins invited Garcia's family to Gracie Mansion, then paid for his funeral and the costs of flying the body to the Dominican Republic. Meanwhile, the police department remained silent. Not until three months later, only after a Manhattan grand jury determined Garcia had been carrying a loaded gun and had attempted to grab O'Keefe's, did the top brass have the courage to publicly defend him. The upshot was a politically charged PBA-led demonstration that September, where, with Giuliani in attendance, appearing to encourage them, out-of-control officers blocked traffic on the Brooklyn Bridge and swarmed the steps of City Hall, calling Dinkins "yellow-bellied" and a "washroom attendant."

At the same time, another corruption scandal was brewing. In New York's twenty-year cycle of such scandals, this one was right on schedule. The first signs had appeared in early 1992 with the arrest of police officer Michael Dowd, who had been running a ring of drug-dealing cronies out of a Brooklyn precinct. But the department's Internal Affairs Division had failed to apprehend him. Instead, police on Long Island, where he lived, arrested him. In June, Dinkins announced the formation of a corruption commission with citywide jurisdiction, headed by his criminal justice coordinator, former state appellate justice Milton Mollen.

But corruption was the least of Dr. Brown's problems. His bifurcated command structure, with Chief Johnston bypassing First Deputy Kelly, resulted in a disconnect at the department's highest levels—with tragic consequences. In the summer of 1991, a Hasidic Jew in the Crown Heights section of Brooklyn, driving in a city-sanctioned motorcade that was escorting grand rebbe Menachem Schneerson, ran a red light and fatally struck an eight-year-old black child, Gavin Cato. In retaliation, a black mob fatally stabbed a Jewish rabbinical student, Yankel Rosenbaum. Other mobs terrorized Jews in their homes, whose cries for help were captured in anguished 911 calls, which the police failed to answer.

Governor Mario Cuomo's 371-page report on the riot, written by his Director of Criminal Justice Richard Girgenti and issued in July 1993, captured this terror in chilling detail.

A caller from Utica Avenue to a 911 operator on Tuesday at 9:02 P.M.:

Caller: *Yes, police? . . . I've got big trouble!*
911 Operator: *. . . What do you mean by, big trouble?*
Caller: *Big trouble! Plenty of people around the house trying to open my door . . . plenty of people around the house. No police coming. Please help me. I got trouble! I've got my daughter!*

Another caller at 9:06 P.M. on President Street:

Caller: *They have just come in the door and are attacking my wife! . . .*
911 Operator: *Is this an apartment or a private house?*

Caller: *Private house. They're storming in through the windows—they're breaking the windows. . . .*

911 Operator: *Do you need an ambulance there? . . .*

Caller: *I need an ambulance right away.*

Another caller from President Street at 8:29 P.M:

Caller: *They're throwing more and more rocks. More and more windows are breaking. Now it's my house. . . . I called before. There's not a single cop in sight. How many times do we have to call before we get the cops over here?*

Cuomo's report attempted to explain the reasons for the police inaction. When the riots began, Chief of Department Johnston had just retired. His successor was on vacation and made no attempt to return. With a broken chain of command at the top and Kelly's undefined role as first deputy amorphous, the riots continued for three days—until Kelly finally inserted himself and took charge. Cuomo's report blamed both Brown and Kelly for not taking charge immediately.

"The Police Commissioner did not effectively fulfill his ultimate responsibility for managing the Department's activities to suppress rioting and preserve the peace," the report said of Brown. "Given the seriousness of the disturbances, it is unfortunate that the First Deputy did not assume a role in coordinating the development and implementation of a different strategy sooner," it said of Kelly.

These two police officials were hardly alone in being slow to react. The Anti-Defamation League, whose stated goals are to fight anti-Semitism and bigotry, made no public statement about the Crown Heights riots for three weeks.

Brown never explained his failings. With the establishment of the Mollen Commission, his departure—his wife was terminally ill, forcing their return to Houston, where he was subsequently elected mayor—became inevitable. Kelly, who became acting commissioner before formally succeeding him in October, also never explained why he waited for three days before taking charge. At a breakfast after his appointment, I questioned him about it. Most of the city's law enforcement establishment was there, and for a minute or two, he and I went toe to toe.

"Did Commissioner Brown contact you during the riot's first days?" I asked. Kelly refused to answer. "Did you attempt to contact Brown?" He refused to answer that as well. He said only that he had been kept "out of the loop."

At the time, I felt that Kelly's silence was due to his loyalty to Brown and the department. Later, as I came to know something of him, I was not at all sure. Clifford was right. Kelly knew the department better than anyone, and he was smarter than all of them. I wondered whether he had purposely refused to intercede in the first few days without specifically being asked to by Brown, allowing the commissioner to suffer the consequences of having kept him out of the loop.

ii.

Disengaged, perhaps, as first deputy, Kelly proved aggressively hands-on as police commissioner. Four months after his appointment, on February 26, 1993, a terrorist bomb exploded at the World Trade Center, killing six and injuring 1,042. Dinkins was in Japan and it was Kelly to whom New Yorkers turned. Like everyone in the city, I watched, transfixed, as he appeared on national television, standing shoulder to shoulder with Governor Mario Cuomo and Assistant FBI Director James Fox of the New York office. Kelly's mere presence—his muscular build, crew cut, and ramrod-straight bearing—help calm a shocked and frightened metropolis.

Unfortunately, neither the NYPD nor the FBI had connected the dots that might have prevented the attacks. Chief of Detectives Joseph Borrelli, who as a captain had played a key roll in capturing the Son of Sam serial killer, likely missed the first dot in 1990 when he attributed the fatal shooting of Rabbi Meir Kahane to "a lone gunman," El Sayyid Nosair. After the World Trade Center bombing, authorities realized that Nosair had been friends with two of the Trade Center bombers, one of whom had been a vocal supporter at his trial in 1991 and visited him in prison. Nor did either agency connect the dots after the Trade Center bombing. It turned out that Ramzi Yousef, who had masterminded the plot, was the nephew of Khalid Shaik Mohammed, the mastermind of 9/11.

Administratively, Kelly undertook an unprecedented effort to recruit black officers—something neither Ward nor Brown, his two African American predecessors, had attempted. Each Sunday morning, he appeared at black churches throughout the city. Although the number of recruits did not rise appreciably, his efforts filled a reservoir of goodwill among New Yorkers that would benefit him a decade later. One indication of Kelly's popularity among blacks fell under the law of unintended consequences. On December 7, 1993—a month after Giuliani's election but still a month before his inauguration—a black man named Colin Ferguson boarded a Long Island Rail Road train. In a gesture of dubious charity to New Yorkers, he waited until the train crossed into Nassau County, then shot and killed four white passengers and wounded nine others. When arrested, he carried papers stating that "New York City was spared because of my respect for Mayor David Dinkins and Commissioner Raymond Kelly."

As the 1993 election approached, Kelly could even take credit for a declining murder rate. Although the annual number remained around two thousand, they had leveled off from the 1990 high. By the end of 1993, Kelly's only full year as commissioner, they had dropped under two thousand.

Only one cloud appeared on Kelly's horizon, but it was a dark one. The arrests of officer Michael Dowd and his drug-dealing crew had again exposed the department's Achilles' heel, police corruption. Like the Knapp Commission two decades before, the Mollen Commission would unearth deep pockets of corruption that the department had failed to uncover. The heart of it lay in West Harlem's 30th Precinct. By the time the scandal ran its course, thirty-three officers had been convicted of drug-related crimes and the precinct would come to be known as the Dirty Thirty.

Echoing the Knapp Commission of two decades before, the Mollen Commission described a police culture that valued loyalty over integrity. "Honest officers fear the consequences of 'ratting' on another cop no matter how grave the consequences," the commission wrote in its final report. From the top brass down, it added, "there was an often debilitating fear about police corruption disclosures because it was perceived as an embarrassment to the department." The commission concluded that it had "allowed its systems for fighting corruption virtually to collapse. It had become more concerned about the bad publicity that corruption disclosures generate than the devastating consequences of corruption itself." The noble ideal of preventing corruption had turned into preventing disclosures about corruption.

Initially, Kelly resisted making changes. As knowledgeable as he was about the department, I was struck by another quality—his sensitivity to criticism.

When Chief Daniel Sullivan retired as head of Internal Affairs, Kelly promoted its number-two man, Robert Beatty, who was said to be Kelly's friend and whose brief tenure was marred by botched cases and alleged cover-ups. Only when the Mollen Commission proposed an outside monitor for the department did Kelly act. Before the commission issued its final report and recommendations, Kelly ran from the rear of the anticorruption line to the vanguard of the reform parade, taking the unprecedented step of appointing a civilian, a former federal prosecutor, Walter Mack, to oversee Internal Affairs. Still, Kelly refused to remove Beatty.

In the fall of 1993, the Mollen Commission held public hearings, and Beatty's failings came to light. Sullivan testified that Beatty had failed to inform prosecutors of 250 cases of serious corruption and that 40 serious corruption cases in the past five years had not been entered in IAD's files. Instead, said Sullivan, cases involving high-ranking officers were hidden in what was known as a "tickler" file. The commission produced a note Sullivan had written to Beatty about one such case. "Bob," it read. "Don't enter this one in any records until later. Assign to whoever you think is best fit to handle it."

Three weeks later, Kelly transferred Beatty to a newly created job as head of something called Information Systems, with no defined responsibilities. Kelly then attempted to cleanse his own reputation, down to the smallest detail. "Kelly phoned me last Friday to protest that I had maligned him in my column on police corruption," wrote Sydney Schanberg, then a columnist for *New York Newsday*. "He insisted he was not a 'close friend' of Beatty as I had written, and knew him 'only in a professional way.'"

iii.

None of what Kelly had achieved in his brief tenure—his serving as the city's public face during its first terrorism attack; his easing racial tensions; his lowering the murder rate; even his navigating the department through the Mollen Commission corruption hearings—appeared to interest Rudy Giuliani. Self-centered and self-righteous, unwilling or unable to accept the dissenting views of others, the newly elected mayor had made his reputation as the United States attorney for the Southern District of New York by convicting a string of mafiosi and corrupt New York City officials. His election in 1993 had been his second run for mayor against Dinkins, and he viewed his victory as revenge for his defeat four years before. That loss, in 1989, had seemed painfully unfair. First, his Republican enemy, U.S. Senator Alfonse D'Amato, had sabotaged him in the primary, supporting a wealthy dilettante, Ronald Lauder. The city's media had treated Giuliani as a law enforcement lunk, a bull in a China shop, in his first elective run. His campaign could gain no traction as the media piled on, lining up behind Dinkins, the city's first black mayoral candidate.

I had covered that earlier election. A story I wrote helped to alter its flow. Scrolling through the Dinkins campaign's filings, I had discovered an organization called the Committee to Honor Black Heroes. The Dinkins campaign had paid this committee $9,500 the week before the Democratic primary. But the group had no office, no listed telephone, and no known members. The Committee to Honor Black Heroes was a front for Sonny Carson. The Dinkins organization had apparently paid him off to shut him up.

Before my story, polls showed Dinkins leading Giuliani by double-digit figures. After it, reporters began examining Dinkins critically, discovering, among other things, that he had failed to file state income tax returns for four years. Though Giuliani lost the election, it was by only two percentage points.

Through my story, I became acquainted with him—or rather, with his staffers, Peter Powers and Denny Young. Powers was Giuliani's oldest friend and had run his campaign. Although said to be Rudy's hatchet man, he was approachable. Young had worked under Giuliani in the U.S. attorney's office. Short and bookish, he was open to listening and nothing like his boss. Giuliani was impenetrable. He was a born general. A relationship with him demanded not merely obedience but obeisance.

Four years later, after Giuliani defeated Dinkins, Young became Giuliani's counsel and asked if I might be interested in working in Giuliani's administration. No position was discussed, but I assumed it would be in his press office. I declined. Considering the relationship that developed between Giuliani and his thirty-year-old press secretary Cristyne Lategano, I probably wasn't the right person for the job.

Responding to the seeming anarchy of the Dinkins years, Giuliani's campaign theme had centered on preventing "street crime," as fifteen years later his presidential campaign theme would center on preventing terrorism. He went through the motions of including Kelly on his so-called short list for police commissioner, saying Kelly had "given great service" to the city. But Kelly's chances appeared doomed. To Giuliani, Kelly represented Dinkins's mayoralty. As Herman Badillo, perhaps the city's most prominent Hispanic politician and a key Giuliani backer, explained years later, "I told the mayor-elect, 'How can you promise change to people if you keep the same police commissioner?'"

Badillo favored William Bratton, Boston native and former chief of New York City's Transit Police, whose officers patrolled the city's hot, dank subway tunnels, a job even NYPD cops considered beneath them. Boastful and flamboyant, Bratton seemed a polar opposite of Kelly. If Kelly was a traditionalist, having served thirty-one years in the NYPD, Bratton was a maverick. He hadn't remained in any job long enough to qualify for the staple of law enforcement officials, his twenty-year pension. "I like to keep my options open. I never close any doors," he would say as he tangled with each of his bosses and quit one police position after another.

At Transit, he lasted only twenty-one months. But in that short time, he rejuvenated a demoralized force and sharply reduced subway crime. "He made a lot of big statements," said a law enforcement official, "but he backed them up."

Nobody had wanted him at Transit. "He was from Boston, didn't know the cops, and didn't know the subways," said the Transit Police's veteran spokesman Albert O'Leary. "He proved us wrong in spades. What I learned from him is that a person at the top of an agency can make a difference."

Like Dr. Brown's community policing, Bratton had a policing philosophy. His was called Broken Windows. First articulated by two academics, James Q. Wilson and George Kelling, the phrase refers to a building's broken windows, which if broken by vandals and left unrepaired, lead to more vandalism, then more serious crimes. Translated to subway policing, this meant, conversely, that preventing the most common subway crime—fare beating—would prevent more serious crime—robberies. So Bratton went after fare beaters. The result was a 13 percent drop in fare beating and a 40 percent drop in robberies. It was the first drop in subway crime in a decade.

While at Transit, Bratton had also brushed up against Dr. Brown. Bratton was not impressed. In meetings with Brown and his staff, Bratton noted in his autobiography, *Turnaround*, Bratton and his staff "always came with a prepared agenda. The NYPD didn't. Their senior staff sat in stone-faced silence, waiting to take their cue from Commissioner Brown."

He also had a dustup with Kelly. It involved a seemingly minor issue—the establishment of a warrant squad, then under the NYPD's jurisdiction, to arrest criminals who failed to show up in court. Bratton wanted to start his own squad, to target fare beaters with outstanding warrants. "Kelly wasn't happy with that," Bratton recalled in *Turnaround*. "'Take them away but we're not going to have anything to do with your warrants,'" Kelly told him. "That was fine with me," Bratton concluded. "[The NYPD] weren't serving my warrants anyway."

A more public spat involved Bratton's battle to upgrade the transit cops' weaponry—from the .38-caliber, six-round revolver to the 9mm, fifteen-round semiautomatic. As the city had become more violent, the criminals were becoming better armed than the police. The day of the Saturday night special was long past. Drug gangs and ordinary thugs were now armed with semiautomatic weapons. But Dinkins and the city's political establishment, including Brown and Kelly, opposed the upgrade. Their bottom line was they didn't trust the cops, whether in transit or the NYPD, with the guns.

As head of the Transit Police, Bratton didn't report to the mayor but to a board appointed by the governor, and he pushed for the weapons upgrade on his own. The Transit Police had hired a media consultant to put Bratton forward as a rival to Dr. Brown. His Boston accent began to be heard so often on radio and television that Don Imus mimicked him on his morning radio show. "Don Imus doesn't make fun of just anybody," Bratton boasted. His media presence pressured the Transit Authority board into voting for the upgrade.

Bratton's tenure at Transit proved so successful that when Brown resigned as police commissioner, Dinkins considered him as a successor, meeting secretly with him during the summer of 1992, before selecting Kelly. "I remember how disappointed Bill was that he didn't get the job," O'Leary recalled. "He called me on the phone as he was driving back to Boston. I said to him, 'Bill, don't you realize they did you a favor? Under Dinkins you'd only have been there a year. Now you'll be considered the number-one candidate of the next mayor.'"

Kelly, meanwhile, reversed his position on the nine-millimeter. The day after Giuliani's election, Kelly upgraded the NYPD's weaponry from the six-shot revolver to the nine-millimeter semiautomatic.

By then Bratton had become the number-two man in the Boston Police Department. Within a year, he became number one and was tangling again with his boss, the recently elected mayor, Thomas Menino. When the newly elected Giuliani asked him to consider returning to New York City, the two met secretly. Bratton then said the only thing that could have cost him both jobs, not one. He publicly announced that if he failed to win the New York position, his job as Boston's police commissioner would make "a good consolation prize." As New Yorkers would learn, such braggadocio was no aberration.

iv.

It was against the impending appointment of Bratton that Kelly sought an audience with Giuliani. To do this, he turned to the Staten Island borough president and former Republican congressman Guy Molinari. Molinari was considered, as the phrase goes, "a friend of law enforcement." This meant he was willing to support lost causes, sometimes with surprising results. The year before, he had managed to secure a pardon from President George H. W. Bush for an immigration officer who had been convicted of robbing bodegas in Upper Manhattan. More relevant to Kelly, Molinari had delivered Giuliani's key Staten Island vote.

Kelly apparently felt indebted enough to Molinari that, the following year, he endorsed him in an unsuccessful bid to become the county's district attorney. When I questioned Kelly he said he did it purely as a favor. "He's a good man. Nothing more than that." A decade later, though, when Kelly returned as police commissioner, he provided Molinari, then out of office, with a detective to serve as his driver and bodyguard. But Kelly remained as sensitive to criticism then as he had in his first term. The day after I wrote the story of Molinari's police detective, Kelly ended the practice.

The meeting between Kelly and Giuliani occurred at the Tudor Hotel on 42nd Street near the United Nations, in a suite of rooms rented for the day. Molinari did not attend. It was only Kelly and Giuliani and their aides. Kelly arrived first. A detective from his detail drove him. Carrying a leather portfolio, he took the elevator to the suite, where another aide from his office was waiting. Not one to display emotion, his nervousness was reflected only in his fingers drumming against his portfolio.

A few minutes later, Giuliani arrived with his aides. To avoid being spotted, they had entered through the hotel's rear door on 41st Street.

There were few formalities. After shaking hands, Giuliani sat down on a bed and began to question Kelly. Years later, Kelly would tell Wayne Barrett, the author of *Grand Illusion*, that Giuliani had sought his views on only two subjects. The first was what was known as "the Merge"—Giuliani's plan to merge the transit and housing police forces with the NYPD. The second was "street crime."

Another person present at the meeting offered an expanded account. When Giuliani asked Kelly how he would reduce street crime, Kelly began discussing community policing. Hearing those two words, Giuliani looked up at the ceiling, then turned toward an aide and in midsentence cut Kelly off. He rose, shook Kelly's hand, thanked him, and walked out the door. The meeting was over. Kelly's thirty-one-year career with the NYPD, including his praiseworthy fifteen months as police commissioner, had ended in fifteen minutes.

A day or two later, saying he was fulfilling New Yorkers' mandate for change, Giuliani announced Bratton's appointment as New York City's thirty-eighth police commissioner. Kelly was already a figure of the past. A *Daily News* editorial the next day said condescendingly of him: "Kelly was a good commissioner but not quite good enough to overcome the natural desire of a mayor-elect to pick him over his own person."

A *News* profile noted: "He seemed angry about the selection process, believes Giuliani wanted a new police commissioner from the start, and questioned the point of being subjected to interviews."

Kelly never forgave Giuliani for dismissing him. He never forgave Bratton for replacing him. Before the year was out, he dismantled his detective detail and personal staff, leaving Bratton to navigate his entry into the largest police department in the world literally alone. Kelly's curt congratulatory note—left on the carved mahogany desk used a century ago by their best-known predecessor, Theodore Roosevelt—bespoke his bitterness. Although Bratton denied seeing a note—"If there was one, I don't recall it," he said—two of his aides remembered it. Written on plain white paper, it consisted of four words: "Bill, Good Luck. Ray."

THREE

The Rise of Bill Bratton

i.

"Lenny, you and I are a lot alike," Jack Maple used to say to me. "We're orca whales. We swim apart from the pack."

A killer whale with attitude—that was just the sort of creature that appealed to Maple. He was both an iconoclast and an outsider to the New York Police Department, but he was, at least officially, one of them—and a big shot to boot. He'd been brought in with a mandate that was nothing less than to change the way the NYPD did business. Comparing me to an orca whale was apparently his idea of a compliment. An even greater compliment, I suspected, was comparing me to himself.

He and I had been circling each other since I'd begun writing a weekly column for *New York Newsday* about the department. The column had begun in the winter of 1994, about the same time Maple was appointed the NYPD's deputy commissioner of operations. In department parlance, we had been launched together.

Newsday had formally christened the column "One Police Plaza Confidential." Inside the NYPD, it was called "The Confidential." Like all the top brass, Maple was a reader. Unlike them, he was unafraid to admit it. Because of its insider insights and tales the department didn't want the public to learn, "The

Confidential" infuriated the bosses when it appeared Monday mornings. Worse, "The Confidential" resonated through the week as Xeroxed copies were passed around Police Plaza like samizdat.

I had attracted a small but devoted following. Maple, who could be both charming and frisky, loved to rag on me with the line, "Hey, Lenny, how are your four readers?" Fortunately for me, they included the top honchos both at Police Plaza and City Hall. One was Maple's boss, the new police commissioner, Bill Bratton. Another was *his* boss, Mayor Rudy Giuliani.

I think Maple was amused that the police department seemed unable to retaliate against me, as it did to others who reported critically, by withholding details of the city's menu of daily crimes. I, however, was immune from such pressures. My editors at *New York Newsday* had reassigned me to NYPD headquarters to chronicle Giuliani's so-called police revolution, and had in fact discouraged me from writing about daily crime. Rather, they had instructed me to focus on the policies and politics behind Bratton's and Giuliani's remolding of the police force, to seek out the hidden intrigues and dramas that form the daily life of One Police Plaza. Mine was a higher calling, I told Maple. I wrote about the bosses. That meant him.

Maple was not unlike all other police officials who talked to me to serve their interests. His was seeing himself portrayed not in dull department gray but in Technicolor. At the same time, I think "The Confidential" appealed to his untamed spirit. Although he had risen, or more accurately been appointed, to the top echelon of the NYPD, he never conformed. The location of his office reflected this. In a department of tradition and exactitude, he worked out of Police Plaza's ninth floor; all other top brass occupied the upper three, twelve to fourteen. Bratton himself hung his hat on fourteen.

Then, there were Maple's office furnishings. The centerpiece was not a desk with the requisite American flag and pictures of the commissioner on the wall. Rather, it was an espresso machine. Maple liked to welcome visitors by pouring the dark brew he cooked up into dainty porcelain cups. Next to the espresso machine stood a sink and above it, a mirror. Before it, Maple liked to preen, holding a scissors and trimming the hairs in his nose and the few remaining strands across the top of his head.

There was also a punching bag and gloves from the department gymnasium that hung on the back of his office door. Supposedly, these were for exercise, although I saw little evidence that Maple, at five feet eight inches and 220 pounds, ever threw a punch. Attempting to stop what he thought was a robbery outside Elaine's, the Upper East Side bar and literary salon that he and Bratton had taken to frequenting, he walked into a lover's quarrel. "The Jackster," as he liked to call himself, ended up with a black eye.

In fact the only person I saw him hit was me. Once, as he shadowedboxed about his office, he caught me, not quite by accident, in the solar plexus. "No gun, Jack," I said, raising my hands in mock surrender.

But the most obvious sign of his renegade spirit was his clothing. The stout, balding Maple dressed like a fop. Each day he appeared at Police Plaza in a brightly colored shirt, wide-lapel suit, bow tie, three-peaked white handkerchief in his jacket pocket, two-tone black and white Allen Edmunds spectator shoes, and a homburg. So who was he? I asked myself. A man who hid his physical shortcomings behind outlandish dress? Or someone so full, yet certain, of himself he didn't care what others thought? Maple never answered the question, but I tended toward the latter. As flamboyant as he was, he knew his limits. As he put it, "I am a bon vivant and get the prettiest girls, but I know that the day after I leave this job, I'll be just another stalker."

His father had been a postal clerk. In a revealing moment, Maple said to me he regretted his father had died before seeing what he, his son, had become. "He thought I was a bum," Maple said, shaking his head, a gesture that I sensed hid some personal pain. Well dressed or not, it was as a bum that Maple liked to present himself. He boasted of never graduating from high school and of having obtained a GED diploma, creating the illusion that he was a raw, semi-illiterate street tough. In fact, he was an inveterate reader who had passed a highly competitive exam to enter one of the city's elite high schools, Brooklyn Tech, and lasted there into his senior year. Instead of graduating, at age nineteen, he signed on as a trainee with the Transit Police.

Somewhere around 1980, he neglected to tell his wife that he had mortgaged their home, maxed out a pension loan, and borrowed $28,000 from the Money Store, then blew it all on clothes, a sports car, and the Oak Bar of the Plaza Hotel. Not that Maple was a serious drinker. He selected the Oak Bar not for its liquor but for the opportunity to mingle with its high rollers—to size up whether he was as smart as they were. It took him five years to figure it out. His money was gone, but he had determined that he was.

Bratton discovered him at the Transit Police, where Maple headed the Central Robbery Division. By then he had lost his house to the Oak Bar, to say nothing of his marriage. He slept in his office in the CRD's squad room, located on the first floor of the Board of Parole on 40th Street between Eighth and Ninth Avenues near the Port Authority Bus Terminal, a couple of blocks from Times Square. The floor was shaped like an L, the long side, the length of the building, with desks along the corridor and offices on either side. Maple slept on a cot in his office, wandered to the bathroom at the other end of the room in the early morning hours in boxer shorts and a Burberry raincoat that doubled as a bathrobe.

Before turning in, he would hit the Stage Deli, returning with huge sandwiches for anyone else who happened to be spending the night. One person was Detective Jimmy Nuciforo, who slept in the squad room once a week. He and Maple went back a long way. When Nuciforo made detective in 1987, he requested Maple's detective shield number and Maple gave him his detective ring. In 2005, when Nuciforo's son was born, he named him Jack.

But Maple was more than an eccentric. He was said to have scored a first on the Transit Police's lieutenant's exam. On the squad room wall, he kept his personal set of crime charts and pushpins. He kept so many charts and could recite all sorts of statistics on subway crime that he was known, after Dustin Hoffman's portrayal of an autistic idiot savant, as "Rain Man."

An outsider himself, Bratton realized he had a visionary in Maple, who saw these statistics not as mere numbers but as road maps to solving crimes. One of his charts showed an increase in teenage gangs who preyed on subway riders. Bratton allowed Maple to form a wolf-pack squad. Instead of arresting only one of the pack, closing the case, Maple's squad hung around to arrest them all, then tied them up in Family Court, which kept them out of the subways.

Maple's statistics also showed a 210 percent increase in robberies of Asians. He figured robbers targeted them because many were illegals who feared the police and were afraid to make complaints. Bratton allowed him to start an Asian decoy squad with Asian officers. They dressed in ties and jackets, wore "slum jewelry"—fake Rolex watches and gold chains—and pretended to be asleep or drunk at subway stops in Asian neighborhoods. As crimes against Asians fell, Maple's colleagues suggested a tribute: a statue of him in Chinatown's Confucius Square.

It was Maple who had urged Bratton to form the Transit Police's own warrant squad, which targeted violent robbery offenders, who, Maple knew, were also fare-beaters. The problem was that when transit police arrested a fare-beater and served him with a summons to appear in court, the fare-beater often didn't show. A judge then issued a warrant for his arrest. The warrant went to the NYPD, whose warrant squad worked only Monday through Friday, 8:00 A.M. to 4:00 P.M., when most people are out and about. Maple's warrant squad worked seven days a week, turning out each morning at 3:30 A.M. when most people are snug in their beds. Result: decreases not only in fare-beating but in robberies.

Then, in what Maple modestly described as "the greatest leap in law enforcement history," Bratton lifted him from the bowels of the Transit Police and installed him at One Police Plaza as the deputy commissioner of operations. That innocuous-sounding title belied Maple's importance. It was he — "the Jackster" — who would revolutionize the New York City Police Department. His creation was known as Compstat, the Computer Statistical Analysis System, which collected statistics on crime patterns and held all commanders accountable for crimes in their precincts. Maple had jotted down his four Compstat precepts — accurate and timely intelligence, rapid deployment of forces, effective tactics, and relentless follow-through — on a napkin at Elaine's. He modestly likened his approach to that of the Battle of Britain or Hannibal's crossing of the Alps.

Applied to New York, Compstat allowed the department to become proactive in stopping crime, rather than reacting to it, as it had for the past twenty years. Bratton would call Compstat the symbol of the department's newfound accountability. He, and subsequently Giuliani, would credit Maple with remaking New York into a safe place to live — although by the time Giuliani publicly acknowledged him, Maple was dead.

ii.

I got my first glimpse of Bratton when he appeared with Giuliani at a news conference to announce his appointment as police commissioner. Forty-six years old, with a moon-round face and skin pockmarked from childhood acne, he stood mellow and at ease at Giuliani's side, never raising his voice. Some police officers can fearlessly confront a gunman yet tremble before a microphone. Not Bratton, who had once talked a gunman into surrendering. He reveled in the media's glow. He was a natural before the television cameras—therefore, a natural in New York City.

"I admit it. I don't mind seeing my name in the papers," he would say in what was by any measure an understatement. Seeing a reporter or a television crew approaching, he would slow his step, place his hand inside his trouser pocket, and look disinterestedly away, which drew more attention than if he'd waved his arms or shouted to the heavens. With jaunty confidence, he had promised a 40 percent cut in crime over three years. "I brought to New York a lifetime of law enforcement and had led the turnaround in four major police departments, including the New York City Transit Police and the Boston Police Department," he stated with typical hyperbole. He may have turned around the Transit Police but he had accomplished no such thing at the BPD, having headed it for less than a year.

Standing beside Giuliani, he promised a new beginning for New York. He had returned, he said, "to restore order, to bring back to the streets of the city of New York a sense of well-being, to begin to improve the quality of life." Appropriating Winston Churchill's wartime cadence, he issued his own war cry, while never raising his voice: "We will fight for every house in this city. We will fight for every street. We will fight for every borough. We will win. We will take back the streets as we began to take back the subways. I did not come here to lose."

Strong words, I thought, but hardly original. After Mayor Koch's election fifteen years before, the department's new first deputy, Joseph C. Hoffman, had promised a similar assault on crime. Within a year, he retired, having concluded it was impossible to change the NYPD. "All the men we promoted have really got the same general mind-set as their immediate predecessors," Hoffman said. "It's a mind-set that tends to strongly resist any real change."

Was Bratton different? Did he truly believe he could change the New York City Police Department? Short of a cataclysm like the Knapp corruption scandal, did he believe he could alter a department whose recurrent lapses had continued over a hundred years? One of the more skeptical was Kelly, who said of Bratton's claims of cutting crime: "A lot of people aren't comfortable with this style. It goes to the question of what kind of policing we want in America. You can probably shut down just about all crime if you're willing to burn down the village to save it. Eventually, I think there will be a backlash and crime will be back up." Bratton, he added, "will be gone by then."

I got my first crack at Bratton a month after his inauguration when he paid a get-acquainted visit to *New York Newsday*. I asked him about the abuse of lucrative police pension benefits, one of which was the so-called heart bill. Under pressure from the PBA, the state legislature had mandated that any heart problem, even if congenital, was job-related. Reporter Kevin McCoy and I had conducted a yearlong investigation of these abuses. We had discovered that the top brass and top PBA officials exploited the system, which awarded officers supposedly injured in the line-of-duty a lifelong, tax-free pension equal to three-quarters of their last year's salary. Fearless, perhaps, when it came to catching criminals, these same officers metamorphosed when applying for their pensions into cripples, with bad backs, dislocated knees, and defective heart valves.

The most blatant example was Chief of Department Johnston's hearing disability. Five years after capturing Larry Davis, the commander known as "Patton," citing a line-of-duty injury, claimed permanent hearing loss. The cause, he maintained, was a firecracker that had exploded near him years before while policing a Rolling Stones concert. Johnston's hearing loss could well have been due to the natural aging process as he was sixty-three years old when he retired. Yet no baseline testing had been performed to determine that. Instead, the city awarded him a tax-free, three-quarters pension.

During the election campaign, Giuliani's team had promised to crack down on such practices. When I questioned Bratton about this at *Newsday*, we had a brief go-round. Then he shrugged and said, "Happy hunting." I took that to mean, "Okay, go ahead, investigate. You won't find anything under me."

I shrugged back.

So began "The Confidential."

iii.

My column may have been unique, but I was hardly the first reporter to probe beneath the surface of the NYPD. Police reporting in New York City has a long and fabled history, dating to the late nineteenth century when Theodore Roosevelt was a police commissioner and Lincoln Steffens and Jacob Riis were police reporters. Then police reporters worked across from the old headquarters on Mulberry Street from apartments, known as shacks. After headquarters was moved a few blocks to Centre Street, those apartments were combined into a building across the street from headquarters, called "the Shack." More than a hundred years later, the name endures. Today, inside One Police Plaza, reporters are confined to a second-floor warren of tiny, dirt-encrusted rooms. Insiders refer to it as the Shack.

In my imaginings, I viewed the circumstances of my reassignment to One Police Plaza as not so different from Steffens's to the old police headquarters on Mulberry Street a century before. For me the catalyst had been Bratton and Giuliani, who promised to reduce the city's staggering crime rate. For Steffens it had been the turn-of-the-century reformer, Charles Parkhurst, whose revelations led to the city's first body to investigate police corruption. That body, known as the Lexow Commission, after State Senator Clarence Lexow, was the progenitor of the more recent Knapp Commission, headed by a former prosecutor and later federal judge, Whitman Knapp.

I viewed Steffens's newspaper, the straitlaced *Evening Post,* as in some ways not unlike *New York Newsday.* Concentrating on financial news, it avoided sensationalism and had a small but influential readership. Until Steffens, it had no reporter on Mulberry Street. As Steffens explained in his autobiography, Parkhurst's revelations of police corruption offered "a good excuse for assigning a reporter to police headquarters: to report the police side of an opening controversy; and since the clergyman and I seemed to get along well together, I was the man to go."

Steffens's editors had instructed him to avoid the city's daily crimes, which seemed as plentiful as today's, although they were confined largely to the immigrant quarters, south of Fourteenth Street. His city editor, Henry J. Wright, told him that he was "not to report crimes and that sort of thing." Rather, said Wright, "You will keep in touch with Dr. Parkhurst, know what he is doing, and work with him for the purpose of reporting his findings with the police department."

To Steffens, then in his twenties, the police represented "a dark, mysterious layer of the life of a great city into which I had not yet penetrated." From that experience, he would become perhaps the country's foremost muckraker, poking into the mysteries of government not only in New York but in other large

American cities, and, forty years later, in the Soviet Union. My ambitions, to say nothing of my abilities, were more modest. To me the police department held all the layers of mystery I cared to unearth. Like an archaeologist, I would uncover one, only to discover another beneath it.

Despite the similarities I saw between Steffens and me, there were vast differences in our circumstances. At the turn of the century, a dozen daily newspapers thrived in New York City and their best reporters held no fear of the police. Consider Steffens's introduction to the notorious inspector Alexander "Clubber" Williams, so-called for beating both prisoners and reporters. Introduced to Steffens, Williams airily announced, "The *Post* has always despised . . . true police news but now when we are under fire, they are to have a man up here to expose, to clean us all out, us rascals." Pointing at Steffens, he added, sotto voce, "We'll see how long he stays here." To which Steffens responded, "I shall stay here till you are driven out."

Jacob Riis, who became Steffens's mentor, also held no fear. "That's the way to handle them," he told Steffens of his encounter with the Clubber. "They are afraid of me, not I of them, and so with you. You have started off on top. Stay there."

A hundred years later, the dynamic between the police and the media had altered. Approaching the twenty-first century, only three city newspapers remained. Not only police reporters but editors seemed reluctant to tangle with the police. Rupert Murdoch's *New York Post* veered slavishly to the side of authority. Virtually every mention of the word "cop" was preceded by "hero." The *Daily News's* Mortimer Zuckerman was a real estate man with business interests in the city. In 1993, the *News* had endorsed Giuliani for mayor over Dinkins. At the time, Zuckerman owed the city a $33.8 million forfeiture fee for failing to close a deal on the New York Coliseum site at Columbus Circle that he had purchased a decade before. After his election, Giuliani allowed Zuckerman to walk away from the property for $17 million.

Even the *New York Times* seemed susceptible to the police commissioner's blandishments. Twenty years before, its police bureau chief, David Burnham, had debriefed Serpico, then broken the corruption scandal that led to the Knapp Commission. Bratton, however, declared he wanted to "marry the *Times*."

At some point, the department had established the civilian position of deputy commissioner of public information, known as DCPI. By the end of the twentieth century, DCPI had three dozen officers. The NYPD, meanwhile, had become the largest and most powerful police department in the world. It may or may not have been the world's finest police department, but it had the largest staff of officers to tell the world it was.

Alice McGillion, who headed DCPI when I opened *New York Newsday*'s police bureau, was the most knowledgeable of them all. She would serve two commissioners over ten years and become first deputy, in 1989, under a third. From a reporting standpoint, her knowledge of the department made her dangerous, as evidenced by her role in the embarassing communications regarding Ward's Palm Sunday disappearance and the deputy's son's transgressions with prostitutes. Yet as *Newsday*'s discovery of the blue book had revealed, there were secrets within the department that even she didn't know.

I had a further handicap in my reporting. *New York Newsday* was the smallest of the city's daily newspapers. Aggressive as it may have been, it was never considered a New York City paper. It had begun in 1983 and it would close in 1995. For the next ten years, it would remain in New York as a scaled-back edition of a Long Island entity. And when that ended, when scandal and corporate forces closed down all but the last remnants of its New York operation, I was left to deal with the NYPD on my own.

iv.

Physically, nothing had changed at One Police Plaza when I returned from the Bronx, where I'd spent nearly a decade covering the district attorney's office, to begin "The Confidential" for *New York Newsday*. The Shack was the same as when I'd opened *Newsday*'s police bureau ten years before, and even more crowded. It was now jammed with four full-time crime reporters. But there was a difference. You could sense it. You could feel it. It was as though a fresh wind were blowing through the corridors of the building's fourteen floors. There was a sense of excitement, of fast motion, of new ideas, of big plans. There was a new vocabulary of "study groups," "focus groups," new phrases like "flattening the hierarchy" and "strategic intent." There was even a new word, "reengineering." Later there would be others — "stars," "superstars," and "Camelot."

But before he dealt with the future, Bratton faced an old-fashioned New

York City racial crisis. It began late Sunday afternoon, January 9, with an anonymous call to 911: "two men with guns" were on the third floor of a Harlem building on Fifth Avenue and 125th Street. The caller didn't say the building's third floor housed Nation of Islam Mosque Number 7, which had moved nine blocks from 116th Street, or that it was a "sensitive location." The mosque hardly fit the mental image of a mosque. There was no white marble, no minarets—in short, no external features that the police officers arriving on the third floor could recognize as pertaining to a religious institution. Instead, given only the address by the dispatcher, the cops—a male and a female officer—rushed inside. Muslim security guards tossed them down the stairs and into the street, stealing a gun and a police radio.

To Bratton and Giuliani, it was April 1972 redux. Outside, the temperature was dropping. A light snow was falling, the streets rock-hard under ice from a previous storm and an ugly crowd was gathering. Both the Muslims and the police called for reinforcements. A standoff ensued, the police controlling the outer perimeter, the Muslims the inner one.

Kelly had already resigned and left the city. His first deputy, John Pritchard, had resigned as well. Reluctant to appear at the scene before his formal swearing-in, Bratton dispatched the department's two highest-ranking black officers, Chief of Department Dave Scott and the courtly Manhattan borough commander Joseph Leake. Bratton stayed in touch with them by phone, as he did with City Hall.

He and Giuliani understood that their response to the crisis at Nation of Islam Mosque Number 7 would send a signal to the city—to blacks and to whites. Both men viewed the confrontation as an opportunity to demonstrate that the department's hand-wringing of the Dinkins era was over. But they disagreed over tactics. Giuliani demanded the police lock all the Muslims inside the building until they surrendered the men who'd attacked the two officers. Bratton sided with Leake, who was trying to broker a deal: The cops could search the mosque to recover the police gun and radio. The Muslims could leave after being identified.

"Giuliani kept calling me and Scott and Leake," Bratton recalled in his autobiography. " 'You have police officers injured. You have stolen police property. Why aren't you going in?' "

Reluctantly, Giuliani agreed to Bratton's compromise. Events then broke in their favor. Police recovered the gun and the radio and later arrested two suspects. Unlike the confrontation twenty-two years before, this one ended with no deaths or riots. And the city's media supported the police. The following week, in a gesture of reconciliation, Bratton agreed to meet with two Nation of Islam imams at Police Plaza. But apparently at Giuliani's direction, he canceled the meeting when the race-baiting Rev. Al Sharpton showed up with them.

A few days later, Bratton met with the imams at a Wall Street brokerage house, without Sharpton. That week, he was all over the newspapers and television. Black politicians praised him. Even Sharpton said Bratton's "actions show he wants to reach out." Congressman Rangel called him "a professional," adding, "It's the mayor who's not a politician." The following Sunday, the *Daily News* splashed Bratton's picture across its front page under the banner headline: "Top Cop Bratton: I'll End the Fear." The same day, an article he wrote about the mosque standoff appeared on the *News's* op-ed page under the headline: "No Choice. Cops Had to Go In."

Bratton justified the coverage by saying he needed high-profile media exposure to get across his message. As he put it, "Change was here and we were serious." The media, he said, "was the best and quickest way to express that."

What he was unprepared for was Giuliani. As Bratton described it in his autobiography, published four years later, the Sunday that his front-page picture appeared in the *Daily News*, Giuliani's newly appointed, thirty-year-old press secretary, Cristyne Lategano, telephoned Bratton's spokesman to complain. That evening, Bratton was summoned to City Hall. He says he wasn't told why—only to show up in Peter Powers's office. Powers, Giuliani's oldest friend, who had run his mayoral campaign, was now deputy mayor for operations. Most commissioners reported to him while Bratton reported directly to the mayor. That had been another of Giuliani's gripes about Dinkins. *His* police commissioner, Dr. Brown, had reported to a subordinate. As for Koch, Giuliani would complain that he hadn't been able to control Ward.

"*We* will control how these stories get out," Powers warned Bratton. "This business with the press and the TV shows and the interviews and the front-page profiles, these are going to cause problems." If it continued, he warned, Giuliani would find another police commissioner.

One week into what he'd described as "the number-one police job in America," Bratton had survived the crisis at Harlem mosque but faced another—this one personal and potentially job ending. If you fire me, how are you going to explain it to the city, he recalled in his autobiography. Yet he desperately wanted this job. As he put it, "I was finally in a position to have a significant impact on American policing, and I didn't want to give it up in one week. I bit my tongue."

Yet why was Bratton surprised by Giuliani's reaction? Even I, in my brief dealings with him during his first mayoral campaign, had understood that he demanded not just fealty but submission. Furthermore, a decade before, a similar incident had cost Bratton a top job in the Boston Police Department. In 1982, he had been profiled in a local magazine and baldly laid out his ambitions. "My personal goal is to become commissioner," he stated. "Be it one year or four years, that's what I want." That quote had so upset Boston's police commissioner Joe Jordan that he had Bratton transferred from headquarters to the city's outer reaches. So ended his first tour at the BPD. Shortly afterward, he resigned.

Had Bratton learned nothing from that? Neither in his autobiography nor in his subsequent actions is there a recognition he bore any responsibility for his failed relationship with Giuliani. As I prepared this book, I asked him that: Did he feel he bore any responsibility for that failure. He dismissed my question, saying only, "This is how I operate." Referring to Giuliani, he said, "We see things differently." Differently perhaps in one sense, but in another, they saw things exactly the same. As with Giuliani, the issue with Bratton was simple: who would get the credit. And with Giuliani, credit was a zero-sum game.

"Any time that week that a positive story had appeared that was focused on me, or on both the mayor and me, the Hall's position was that it should have focused solely on the mayor," he would write. "As far as City Hall was concerned, the *Daily News* had a photo of the wrong man on its front page. We didn't know the game was rigged. As smart as we all were, it took a while for that fact to register." But it never did register. Or if it did, Bratton no longer cared. The public never knew of this first-week confrontation. Not until a year later would the truth be revealed, and in a manner that New Yorkers had not seen before.

v.

The Bratton revolution began at Police Plaza his first week in office. He ordered all fifteen deputy commissioners and three-star "superchiefs," who ran the

Detective, Patrol, Organized Crime, and Personnel Bureaus, to submit resignation letters. While Kelly had maintained the top brass when he succeeded Brown two years before, Bratton fired a generation of them. To him, those old bulls, some with thirty-five or forty years' experience, were wedded to the status quo—and to Kelly. Kelly's former Internal Affairs chief Beatty "was a goner," the *News* reported. Walter Mack, the civilian Kelly had brought in to run Internal Affairs, would be out within a year.

From the sidelines, Kelly protested, saying Bratton was depriving the department of "hundreds of years of experience." No one was listening to him, either in the police department or in the media. Bratton, however, was mistaken in thinking Kelly loyalists might not be loyal to him. He discovered this when he appointed his three top people, all of whom had worked for the former commissioner. Rather, it was Kelly who considered them disloyal for accepting Bratton's appointments.

Bratton also brought to One Police Plaza a band of boulevardiers from different walks of life. Some like Maple came from outside the NYPD. Others came from outside of law enforcement. Peter LaPorte, Bratton's thirty-year-old assistant from Boston, became his chief of staff. LaPorte resembled a younger, cocky Bratton. He had worked for Bratton for a decade, first as an intern while at Northeastern University. Bratton trusted him enough that he used him to negotiate with enemies twenty years his senior.

Bratton's Transit Police media consultant, John Linder, became what Bratton described as his "change agent." Taking a survey of NYPD officers, Linder discovered that most viewed their jobs as staying out of trouble rather than policing the city. They viewed the department's first priority as writing summonses. Holding down overtime was second. Fighting crime was seventh.

Linder created the department's "cultural diagnostic," which he defined as "an analytic tool that determines the cultural factors impeding performance and the corrective values that must be employed as principles for organizational change." Flying in from his home in Corales, New Mexico, he would hole up in Bratton's fourteenth-floor office, writing Bratton's crime-fighting strategies at Roosevelt's desk late into the night, then sleep on Bratton's office couch. As for the cultural diagnostic, Bratton wheedled $137,000 from the Police Foundation—a nonprofit group of wealthy New Yorkers, founded after the Knapp Commission as an anticorruption measure—to pay Linder for such gibberish.

Bratton's spokesman, John Miller, was a wisecracking television reporter who carried a gun and shed his half-million-a-year salary to join the department. A tall, curly-haired bachelor, whom Bratton described as "aggressively single," Miller had made his reputation by chasing mobster John Gotti. He became so mob-struck he took to wearing the same $2,000 Brioni suits that he boasted Gotti wore. A cop buff since his teens, Miller had lied about his age to get his first job at a radio station, calling in crime tips by hanging around station houses, and listening to the police scanner. I once came upon him in the Public Information Office seated at an officer's desk, feet up, puffing a cigar.

Bratton hadn't known Miller before becoming police commissioner. He had preferred his Transit Police spokesman Al O'Leary. But the deputy commissioner for public information was Bratton's only appointment vetted by City Hall, an indication of Giuliani's media wariness. In fact, Giuliani, to say nothing of Bratton, might have been better served by the low-key O'Leary. Interviewed by Denny Young, O'Leary said of Bratton. "He'll jump in front of the cameras, but he'll take advice." Whatever advice Miller gave Bratton, it was not to stay away from cameras.

I had met Miller in the mid-eighties when I left Police Plaza to open *New York Newsday's* Bronx bureau. Arriving there, I found myself in the middle of a real-life urban adventure tale: the capture and trial of Larry Davis for shooting six police officers. While Davis was still running wild, Bronx district attorney Mario Merola had indicted Raymond Donovan, the U.S. Secretary of Labor, on mob-related corruption charges he was later acquitted of and Merola's spokesman, an old-time newsman named Ed McCarthy, was leaking stories about him to the *Daily News*. When the *News* hesitated to run a story, McCarthy courted me. Late one night, he called me at home, offering me the story the *News* was reluctant to run.

"Call me back," he said, "and let me know if *Newsday* will run it." When my editors gave me the go-ahead, I called him as instructed. But when I opened the *Daily News* the next day, I saw they had the same story I had written. "I used you to get them to do it," McCarthy gloated.

Some weeks later, in what I took as an apology, he offered me a secret report about a cop suspected of murdering his wife, supposedly aided by my old friend Sal Reale. The report was written by a New Jersey law enforcement agency working with Merola's office. McCarthy said he was giving me the "print" exclusive because he'd promised the TV exclusive to a local television reporter. That reporter was Miller.

McCarthy brought us both to his office and allowed us to read the report. His only stipulation was that we, Miller and I, paraphrase, not use direct quotes for our stories. That way, he said, the New Jersey authorities could not pin the leak on him or Merola. Then McCarthy asked me to hold the story for a day because Miller was busy that afternoon on a story on John Gotti. I agreed.

Later that night, after my deadline had passed, McCarthy again called me at home. He said he had received inquiries from the *Daily News* about the Jersey report and had had no choice but to give it to them. When I reminded him he had promised me the "print exclusive," he hung up. He refused to return my subsequent calls. So instead of paraphrasing, I quoted the report. The New Jersey authorities cut off relations with Merola. McCarthy threatened to run me out of the Bronx. Miller never understood why I burned such a valuable source, and I never bothered to explain. And as it turned out, it was McCarthy, not me, who was forced to leave the Bronx.

When I interviewed Miller for the first time as Bratton's deputy commissioner for public information nearly a decade later, neither of us brought up our Bronx tale of McCarthy, which, I suspected, might have been at the back of his mind. Instead, attempting to inject some humor into our conversation, I glanced at Miller's suit and said, "John, I never realized you were such a clotheshorse." He glanced at my suit. Then referring to the veteran reporter and dean of the City Hall press corps, Miller answered "Lenny, you and Gabe Pressman are single-handedly keeping the corduroy industry alive."

vi.

Bratton's most important appointment affirmed his status as a reformer and innovator, unafraid to take risks. As chief of department, the NYPD's highest-ranking uniformed position, he appointed John Timoney, jumping him over sixteen senior officers, including five superchiefs and eleven two-star assistant chiefs, seven of whom were borough commanders. At age forty-five, Timoney became the youngest chief of department in NYPD history.

With his red hair, ruddy complexion, and square jaw, Timoney was Hollywood's image of a tough Irish cop. Born in Dublin, he had grown up in Washington Heights in Upper Manhattan. His father had died at age fifty-four as Timoney entered his senior year at Cardinal Hayes High School in the Bronx, which had been founded for the sons of Catholic immigrants by New York's former cardinal Francis Spellman. A year later, Timoney's mother returned to Ireland with his younger sister, Marie. Timoney and his brother, Ciaran, two years behind him, who would also join the NYPD, refused to go. Instead, they remained in their apartment, a six-story walk-up between Audubon and Amsterdam Avenues, where the rent was $69 a month, while Timoney supported them by driving a Coca-Cola truck and working as a police trainee, answering telephones at the 17th Precinct on the East Side of Manhattan from 4:00 to 10:00 P.M. and from midnights until 8:00 A.M. at $112 every two weeks. There, in the police department, he found a second family.

With his dese, dems, and doses, Timoney's accent was thick with New York City. At the same time, he retained a brogue. That combination, together with his ninety-mile-per-hour delivery, made it virtually impossible at first to comprehend what he was saying. Bratton had to arrange a second meeting to assure himself he'd made the right decision. Timoney's appointment, he said, remained, "a huge roll of the dice for a guy I'd met twice for only forty-five minutes." He might have added "and could barely understand."

What did Timoney sound like? Once when I turned on my TV for a latenight movie, the sound came up a moment before the picture and I thought I heard his voice. It was that of another New York City boy from an equally hardscrabble background—James Cagney.

Timoney, who walked with a Cagney strut, seemed to have absorbed all aspects of NYPD culture. He could recite from memory the seating chart for the top brass at ceremonies at One Police Plaza: On the dais, the police commissioner sits in the middle, all uniformed officers to his right, starting with the four-star chief of department, then the three-star, two-star, and one-star chiefs on his far right flank. On his other side, the civilian commissioners, beginning with the first deputy seated nearest him to his left.

Timoney, however, wasn't blind to the dangers of policing. As a patrolman in the 44th Precinct in the Bronx, he had partnered with Thomas Ryan, known as Nutsy for his wild and mad ways. While Timoney was on vacation, Ryan and another officer arrested a robbery suspect who had fired at them through an apartment door. When they brought the suspect to the precinct, Ryan and others beat him to death. Nutsy became the first cop in twenty years to be convicted of an on-duty homicide. Timoney taught this as a lesson for young cops: When the cuffs go on, the fisticuffs stop.

While the NYPD was the heart of his life, Timoney became an educated man. After obtaining an undergraduate degree, he earned two masters, in American history and in urban affairs. He ran a tutoring school for officers studying for promotional exams and founded a department book club, where officers discussed classics from *The Iliad* to *Crime and Punishment*. Not long after Bratton promoted him to chief of department, Mount Holyoke College's Russian literature department invited him to participate in a seminar. It was billed as "Just the Facts, Mr. Raskolnikov. The NYPD's top cop reflects on Crime and Punishment in Dostoyevsky's classic novel."

Timoney, so far as I could tell, had one professional goal: to head the NYPD. So devoted was he to the job that he would spend more time with his second family than with his own. This would become a source of tragedy. For a time, his daughter was addicted to heroin. His son was convicted of attempting to buy four hundred pounds of marijuana from an undercover agent and sentenced to eighteen months in federal prison.

vii.

As chief of personnel, Bratton promoted the young and idealistic Michael Julian, who had also worked under Kelly. Julian was in his midforties but looked ten years younger. He had ideas about everything, from reforming the pension system to putting cops on bicycles to ridding the city of the ubiquitous squeegee men. Bratton called him his "Chief of Big Ideas."

Julian remained with Bratton only nine months, before taking a job in the private sector. Even his departure reflected Bratton's openness to change, including his attempt to reform the dysfunctional disability pension system, which he had dared me to investigate. On his next-to-last day in office, Julian filed for a disability pension, citing a knee injury he had sustained as a captain while putting down a mini riot in Tompkins Square Park on the Lower East Side. That would have paid him $90,000 annually, tax-free. The next day, however, he withdrew his application. When I asked why, he said he questioned the fairness of a system that allowed him the tax-free benefit when, as he put it, "I am limited but not incapacitated."

The question, he said, "is what is your reputation worth? All I can think of is Chief Johnston. He was a police officer for forty years. He was a great commander. He was chief of department for six years. But to the media, he will be remembered only for having received a disability pension under dubious circumstances."

Then there was the position of first deputy. Bratton needed a black face at the top of the department, and Dave Scott, a Ward protégé and the department's highest-ranking black officer, seemed the perfect fit. Bratton had been impressed with Scott's restraint during the mosque incident. Two weeks later, he promoted him to first deputy. In so doing, he couldn't resist a dig at Kelly. "I intended to make [Scott] the most powerful first deputy in the history of the NYPD," he wrote, "unlike Ray Kelly's first deputy, John Pritchard [also black], who was largely a figurehead."

This, however, turned out to be mere palaver. Just as Lee Brown had cut out Kelly as first deputy, allowing Chief of Department Johnston to report directly to him, Bratton set up a similar chain of command. Timoney, Bratton's chief of department, reported directly to Bratton. Within a year, Scott retired. Bratton promoted Timoney to first deputy to replace him. But the new chief of department reported to Timoney. The line to Bratton went through him.

As chief of patrol, Bratton appointed the ruggedly handsome, quick-witted, and proudly Italian Louis R. Anemone. Anemone was as serious, and as knowledgeable, about crime as Maple, who called him "the most valuable player on the nation's largest police force." As Maple put it, describing Anemone's gung ho style: "Do we really want to live in a world where everybody works seven days a week, 365 days a year? Do we really want everybody to dress like George Patton twenty-four hours a day, even when they go to bed?"

Like Timoney, to whom Anemone reported, Anemone had worked under Kelly. After the Crown Heights riots Kelly named him to the newly created position of disorder-control commander to devise responses for future riots. Many in the department viewed him as the department's first future Italian American police commissioner. With the election of Giuliani, this seemed a real possibility.

The two appeared to be kindred spirits, not merely in their heritage but in the way they viewed fighting crime. "Louie was friendly and loyal to Giuliani," said a chief. "And everyone knew what he wanted."

So exuberant was Louie in fighting crime that even as chief of patrol he loved responding to police jobs. Coming upon a rookie officer, Louie said to him, "Officer, can I walk your post with you?" Arriving at Yankee Stadium to supervise the first of two jam-packed Pink Floyd summer concerts, he got so pumped up he began directing traffic outside the stadium, while shouting, "Where's my chief?" He was referring to Bronx borough commander Rafael Pineiro, who had taken the night off. Although Pineiro wisely showed up for the next night's concert, Anemone never forgave his transgression. When he succeeded Timoney as chief of department a year later he transferred Pineiro to the chiefs' burial ground at headquarters, the Criminal Justice Bureau.

It was Giuliani who secured Louie's position as chief of department. When Bratton moved Timoney up to first deputy, following Dave Scott's retirement, Timoney had suggested that Joe Leake, the black chief at the Harlem mosque incident, succeed him, Bratton agreed, seeking to retain a black presence among the top officials. Leake, however, had upset the mayor by negotiating with, rather than arresting, the members of the mosque. Giuliani vetoed him and told Bratton he wanted Anemone.

"I already told Leake he had the job," Timoney protested to the mayor. "We already made the deal."

"I make the deals around here," Giuliani answered.

Louie then promoted his car. As chief of patrol, he had driven a marked department vehicle with his title, CHIEF OF PATROL, stamped on the side and a license plate with three stars. In his new position, he kept the car, had CHIEF OF DEPARTMENT written on the side, and added a fourth star to the license plate.

Louie also commandeered a former torpedo recovery ship from the navy, the USS *Labrador*. It did eight knots before a following wind and came with a full tank of fuel—ten thousand gallons of gasoline. He had it docked on the Harbor Unit's base on Randalls Island under the Triborough Bridge, had it painted the NYPD colors of blue and white on one side so that people would see it when they drove by it. Then he rechristened it Launch 681. He viewed the boat both as an offshore communications platform and as way of transporting officers in emergencies via water to parts of the city inaccessible by bridges. It was put to unexpected use after TWA Flight 800 went down in the ocean off Long Island. Louie's launch remained out there for five days and served as a command post for divers.

Some viewed Anemone as a tactical genius who had aggressively halted the Crown Heights riots. His instincts were said to be as sharp as Ted Williams's batting eye. When David Willis, a 10th Precinct rookie officer, was struck and killed by a mail truck that broadsided his patrol car on Eleventh Avenue and 30th Street as he and his partner responded to a false 911 call reporting a man with a gun in the Chelsea Houses, Anemone sensed something amiss. Although Willis's death wasn't a homicide, Louie, at Willis's funeral, motioned to a detective on his staff to meet him outside the church. "This case bothers me," Louie whispered. "Something's wrong."

Working outside the normal channels at Detective Bureau and the 10th Precinct's squad commander, the detective, Nick Casale, began examining the 911 tape of the call. When the 911 operator asked the caller to identify himself, he responded, "Hey, baby, I want to be anonymous."

Casale began examining other false 911 calls, searching for Mr. Anonymous. At one point, he played the tapes for a professor of speech pathology at Columbia University, who concluded the caller was a Puerto Rican man, aged twenty-five to thirty, who worked with Jews, probably in the Garment District.

Anemone was so impressed with those details he asked to meet the professor. Casale brought him up to Anemone's office on the thirteenth floor of Police Plaza. Seated on Anemone's couch, the professor repeated all he had told Casale, then added that the caller was probably around five feet seven and weighed 170 pounds. Louie thanked him and escorted him to the door.

Returning to his office, he started screaming at Casale that no one could tell a man's height and weight from his voice. "Get this nut out of the building," he shouted. Casale walked out of Anemone's office, took the professor down the elevator and told him the chief had loved his briefing.

Two months later, Casale found his man. The day Anemone was supposed to go on vacation with his family to Mexico, Casale brought the suspect, a thirty-eight-year-old, unemployed laborer named Manny Perez, to the 10th Precinct squad room. Perez admitted he had made the false calls to increase police protection for his neighborhood. Outside, his ear to the door, stood Louie. He was wearing dungarees and a tank top. His family was outside in the car. He had stopped by the precinct to check on the case en route to the airport.

"Well done" was all he said to Casale. He did not need to articulate what both knew to be the reason Anemone had been so disturbed. The attempt of a young cop to better the city had ended in his death. If an investigation of phony calls had been properly conducted before, he would still be alive.

As for Perez, he did jail time. He also turned out to be the weight and height that the professor had given.

viii.

Before formally taking over as commissioner, Bratton had sized up the department and, according to his autobiography, declared it "basically dysfunctional." Cliques and fiefdoms abounded. Some bureau chiefs did not talk to each other. The Organized Crime Control Bureau didn't talk to the Patrol Bureau and Patrol didn't get along with the Detective Bureau. Nobody talked to Internal Affairs.

Narcotics units worked nine to five. Warrant, auto, and robbery squads had weekends off, as did the six thousand community policing officers. "Essentially," said Bratton, "the whole place took Saturdays and Sundays off."

The NYPD, he wrote, "had people bluffed." Their reputation was smoke and mirrors. He cited as an example the department's policy on gun cases. In 1993, there had been 11,222 arrests for crimes in which a firearm was confiscated. Instead of pursuing the accomplices of those arrested, department policy had been to turn the arrestees into confidential informants, or CIs. In over 11,000 arrests, their efforts had resulted in turning only four arrestees into CIs.

Bratton said nothing publicly about the department's supposed dysfunction. Instead, he used the same Broken Windows approach he and Maple had used in the subways. When they had cracked down on minor crimes like fare beating, they reaped a wider benefit: One of seven arrested fare beaters had an outstanding warrant for a more serious crime. One of twenty-one was carrying a weapon, whether a gun, knife, or box cutter. Bratton's fare-beating crackdown caused criminals to leave their weapons at home, with a subsequent drop in robberies and murders.

He and Giuliani vowed to expand the subway's crime-fighting strategy aboveground, to the streets. They called it "zero tolerance." By mobilizing his police force more effectively, Bratton claimed he would alter criminal behavior. Kelly, who now held a position at New York University, spoke up, doubting whether success in the "closed environment" of the subways would translate aboveground. Undeterred, the NYPD began cracking down on "quality of life" crimes: graffiti, squeegee men, public urinators, low-level drug dealers, pot smokers, and shoplifters. "If they are seen committing a violation, we question them and ask for identification," said Maple. "If they have none, we arrest them. Then we check outstanding warrants. Then we question them about more serious crimes, such as gun violations. Then they give us information about those crimes and we start all over again."

Community policing, the cornerstone of the Dinkins era, was first to go. Giuliani had set the tone, deriding the policy as "social work." Bratton leaked a series of critical departmental memos commissioned by Kelly the year before. One described training for community policing as a "dismal failure." Another cited "minimal arrest activity" of drug dealers after 6:00 P.M., suggesting community-policing officers were working what the *Times* called "bankers' hours." Another memo reported that "no arrests were made on morals charges for 12 consecutive weekends."

Again, Kelly protested, saying those problems had been corrected and that Giuliani was playing politics. "I think he's taking a shot at the previous administration, which is what other mayors have done, and whatever changes take place, he'll claim credit," Kelly said. Of Bratton, he added, "I think he's doing the mayor's bidding."

Next, Bratton and Giuliani took aim at one of the department's most sensitive subjects—police corruption. They scrapped the department's twenty-year-old, post–Knapp Commission policy of preventing local cops and squad detectives from arresting drug dealers. Giuliani's key Hispanic supporter, Herman Badillo, had brought the futility of the department's anticorruption strategy home to the mayor. During the election campaign, Badillo, himself an unsuccessful mayoral candidate twenty years before, had toured a Dominican neighborhood in Washington Heights. The neighborhood was so overrun with drugs, he was told, that a Dominican cartel was franchising street corners for the right to sell crack— including one near the George Washington Bridge, with its access to New Jersey, for $350,000—more than the price of the surrounding apartment buildings. Meanwhile, residents, seeing drugs sold openly, believed the cops were corrupt because they made no arrests. Not everyone, though, thought the police were dishonest. Some believed they were merely incompetent. Whatever their belief, it was neither a positive nor a healthy one for citizens to hold about the New York City Police Department.

To many New Yorkers, the issue of police corruption was such a sensitive subject they would accept only one point of view: You were either for fighting corruption or you were against it. Timoney echoed Badillo's more nuanced view. As he put it, "The number-one issue was always corruption, not crime. It used to drive guys like me and Anemone crazy. We'd both been in Narcotics. We'd both been shot at. Yet you never heard anything from downtown about the arrests you made. Careers were never shortened by a crime. What would stop you dead was corruption."

Because police corruption was such a sensitive issue, this revolutionary change in policy went unheralded and unreported, even by a police commissioner obsessed with publicity. The only time I heard anyone at headquarters even acknowledge the change in priorities was nearly a year later—and then obliquely—when Timoney was sworn in as first deputy. "For the first time in my twenty-five years as a police officer," he said, "the department's first priority is what I joined the NYPD to do: fight crime." Timoney would pay a price for his candor. The year after the Dirty Thirty scandal broke and Timoney criticized prosecutors' actions as a "witch hunt," they would call him "soft on corruption."

Instead, with great fanfare, Bratton and Giuliani turned to the ubiquitous squeegee men, the street people who ruled the bridge and tunnel entrances to Manhattan, cleaning the windshields of stopped cars, then demanding money from helpless drivers. "As minute a problem as that might seem in the overall scope of a city with two thousand murders," said Bratton, "squeegees are of great significance because like fare evasion and the disorder on the subways, it's the type of activity that is generating fear."

It was easy to rid the city of them, and Bratton and Giuliani took credit for their disappearance. Again, no one listened when Kelly insisted *he* had initiated the squeegee push months before. Indeed, he had, in the fall of 1993, after Giuliani made squeegee men a campaign issue. He had assigned the resourceful Mike Julian, the man Bratton later appointed chief of personnel, to address the problem. "We identified seventy squeegee people Manhattan-wide," Julian explained, "and seven locations, all entrances to the city—the Holland, Lincoln, and Midtown tunnels, the George Washington Bridge, Houston and Second Avenue, 56th and Twelfth Avenue, and the FDR Drive at 96th Street." Like the subway fare-beaters, all the squeegee men had outstanding warrants for more serious crimes. Virtually all had criminal records. Half of them had drug convictions. So the police began chasing and warning them. When that didn't work they served them with summonses. But none of them responded. "So we began arresting them," Julian explained. "That was the only thing that worked." Within weeks, they had all disappeared. Kelly had begun the program in October. Two weeks after the election, they were gone.

But Kelly had been politic. Given the climate of the times, with a black mayor and the fact that most squeegee men were black, Kelly felt he needed to address concerns that the department was not acting illegally against a largely nonwhite population. He sought an academic imprimatur. Enter the Broken Window theory cofounder George Kelling, who through Bratton had made a small fortune in consulting contracts from the Transit Authority. With another $25,000 from the Police Foundation, the nonprofit group of wealthy New Yorkers who helped fund the department, Kelling was fed Julian's information. He regurgitated it back as a twenty-nine-page report, *Managing Squeegee*.

Kelling was unable to complete his report before Giuliani dismissed Kelly and designated Bratton as police commissioner. Instead, Giuliani and Bratton took credit for the squeegee men's disappearance without citing Kelly. His protestations were viewed as sour grapes.

Kelling's report, however, did credit Kelly. "Although Police Commissioner designate William Bratton received considerable publicity as a result of the promise to eradicate [squeegee men]" Kelling wrote, "it was former Commissioner Raymond Kelly, after all, who initiated the problem-solving exercise to determine how best to solve the problem." Four years later, in his autobiography, Bratton was equally generous, writing that Kelly and Dinkins had effected the turnaround. "Ironically, Giuliani and I got credit for their initiative," he wrote, somewhat disingenuously. "Only politics prevented David Dinkins and Ray Kelly from receiving their due."

But Bratton included something else in his autobiography that was bound to infuriate Kelly. "I saw the squeegee population as a fitting symbol of the sad situation of the previous NYPD," Bratton wrote. "They had given up." That, of course, was an overstatement. The NYPD could handle the squeegee problem. Still, Bratton had a point.

ix.

Bratton's most innovative, and most publicized, crime initiative was Maple's Compstat, which became the tool and symbol of the NYPD's newfound accountability. In the past, the department had produced quarterly crime reports — not for combating crime but for year-end statistical review. In January, Bratton's first month as commissioner, Maple insisted that every precinct keep pin maps on its walls, reflecting its crime patterns, with separate maps of robberies, burglaries, shootings, narcotics, and gun arrests. That way, he said, commanders could properly deploy their men.

Then Maple demanded crime reports be given to him monthly. By February he wanted them weekly. Then he demanded twice a week, three-hour crime meetings with the department's top commanders. The meetings reviewed the crime stats of each precinct, the precise times that a rape, robbery, or shooting occurred. Each commander was then forced to explain how he planned to combat them. The Compstat meetings began at 7:00 A.M. in the small, second-floor press room with precinct captains, detective squad commanders, and other key personnel. The meetings grew so large they were moved upstairs to the eighth-floor operations room, the NYPD's command center, the "war room," as it was known, with its bank of TV monitors, computer screens, and 115 seats, large enough to hold an entire borough command.

Compstat became a showcase. It was great theater, the interplay between the bosses and commanders, not unlike a dramatic scene from cop movies. Up to two hundred people attended meetings — standing room only — with district attorneys, federal prosecutors, and dignitaries from other states and even from foreign countries. The presenter stood behind a podium. Maple and Anemone sat behind a desk, at center stage. "I'm looking into your eyes, Commander," Maple would say. "This is the Jackster you're talking to now."

Some commanders squirmed and fidgeted. Others were unable to answer the questions. On the street, officers knew instinctively what they had to do and did it. At Compstat, they may have had their crime strategies in their heads. But many panicked at articulating them. "I am dismayed by the treatment some of our members are receiving at the Crime Strategy meetings," William Kelly, the president of the Captains Endowment Association, wrote in its union newsletter. "It is incomprehensible that some leaders of the department who are well-trained in correct personnel principles would stoop to the type of ridicule and sarcasm that have become a feature of these sessions."

Maple's and Anemone's questioning became so raw that fistfights erupted. At one meeting someone threw a chair. After Anemone insulted an assistant district attorney from Brooklyn, his boss, Joe Hynes, wrote a formal letter of complaint to Bratton.

At another meeting, Anemone and Maple accused Chief of Detectives Charles Reuther, who seemed less than enthusiastic after members of his bureau were subjected to Louie's and Jack's taunts of "treason" and "heresy." Timoney made them both apologize, but Reuther soon joined former Bronx borough commander Pineiro in the Criminal Justice Bureau, where, in a display of unwanted and wasted top brass, the two-star Pineiro reported to the three-star Reuther.

At yet another meeting, the newly appointed Brooklyn South borough commander Tosano "Tony" Simonetti explained how he had begun reducing crime. On a screen behind him, Anemone flashed a computerized drawing of Pinocchio with his nose growing. Louie had gone too far. For that insult, he would pay.

x.

Bratton's love of attention also revolutionized the crusty image of the police commissioner, comfortable with only his own kind. Instead, he became a fixture at upscale restaurants, movie openings, and theater premieres. He hobnobbed with reporters. He appeared in the gossip pages. He signed a book contract with Random House to write his autobiography. Academics lauded him. His Broken Windows friend Kelling—who through Bratton had secured half a million dollars in consulting contracts and whom I nicknamed "Six-Figure Kelling"—lauded him in an article for the Manhattan Institute, a right-wing group of intellectuals that fancied itself the police department's intellectual godfathers. "From Plato in Athens to Police Commissioner Bratton in New York," Kelling grandiloquently wrote, "experts on public order have ceaselessly worried over one key problem: how to control the police who maintain that order."

Bratton joined Miller and Maple in dining at Elaine's, the restaurant and saloon on Second Avenue frequented by the literati. Sometimes, Bratton's attorney wife, Cheryl Fiandaca, accompanied him. The daughter of a politically connected official in the Boston court system, Fiandaca liked to say she had been typing search warrants since she was eleven years old. She had graduated from the New England School of Law and done criminal defense work for ten years before placing her career on hold to accompany Bratton to New York. A $75,000 job was arranged for her at John Jay College of Criminal Justice, although she would soon give it up to become a television commentator on the O. J. Simpson trial, which began that summer. Then she would give up the law altogether, becoming a full-time television reporter.

Sometimes Miller would bring along Giuliani's press secretary, Cristyne Lategano. Because she was inexperienced in dealing with the media, he was supposedly tutoring her and introducing her to his sources. He said they had developed a "casual relationship." Others said it was anything but casual.

Bratton's table also included Maple's and Miller's *Daily News* tough guy–columnist friends, Michael Daly and Mike McAlary. In "The Confidential," I began referring to Elaine's as Police Plaza North.

Bratton had grown up in a coldwater flat in Dorchester, a poor section of Boston. Like Maple, his father had been a postal clerk. Like Maple, he had big dreams. Elaine's became his Oak Bar. As he rose through the ranks of the Boston Police Department he began to meet what he described in his autobiography as "notable and important people." "These were people I had read about in the newspapers, seen on the news and in the society pages," he wrote. "For a Dorchester boy who didn't have hot water plumbing in his home until he was 14, this was heady stuff."

If that was heady stuff, consider him at Elaine's. He was like a starving man at a banquet. He sat at a large round table, amid staff and friends, the center of attention and fascination, his eyes drinking in all the diners. Celebrities—actors, writers, entertainers, fancy criminal lawyers, wealthy businessmen, many of them strangers—would approach his table either to glance at him or to shake his hand. Bestselling novelist Tom Wolfe stopped by. One night Bratton and Cheryl were introduced to Shirley MacLaine. Media-savvy criminal attorney Edward Hayes became Bratton's literary agent and began referring to him as "the most significant law enforcement leader of our time." Bratton himself had become a celebrity. A star. A *Daily News* poll confirmed his popularity. He had a favorable rating of 62 percent, 9 points above Giuliani's. The story's headline read: "Rudy Takes Back Seat to Bratton in New Poll."

He also allowed James Lardner, a writer for *The New Yorker*, to follow him about for months. Lardner was the grandson of the sportswriter and satirist Ring Lardner. His article would appear the following February. It turned out to be so laudatory of Bratton, it nearly cost him his job.

xi.

Meanwhile, a story was developing in Boston that would estrange me from Bratton. Because he had moved around so much, his twenty-one-year police career in Massachusetts had been divided among three agencies. Only two of them, the Boston Police Department, where he had begun and ended his career, and the Metropolitan Police Department, fell under the city-state pension system. The third, the Massachusetts Bay Transit Authority, where Bratton spent three years, had a separate retirement plan. Therefore, those three years did not count in the city-state pension system. Because he'd left each of his jobs early, Bratton was two years shy of earning the twenty-year pension.

I had been tipped off he was seeking legislation for a private bill that would include those lost three years. If successful, he would obtain an annual pension of $40,000 when he turned fifty-five. If the purpose of my column was to get behind the scenes and the headlines, here was a perfect backstory.

Bratton confirmed to me he was seeking the bill but insisted similar legislation had been passed before. I didn't buy it and took the train up to Boston. Bratton's bill, I learned, had to be passed by both the Boston City Council and the Massachusetts State Legislature. The state bill had been filed by Representative Emanuel Serra of East Boston, a friend of Bratton's father-in-law, Joseph Fiandaca.

The Boston City Council president James M. Kelly had filed a separate bill in the council, but few supported it. Kelly, I learned, had advised Bratton to come up to Boston and lobby. City Councillor Daniel Connelly opposed the bill. His chief of staff, Alex Geourntas, told me Bratton had telephoned Connelly but said, "We haven't called him back." Councillor Maureen Feeney, who would chair the hearings, said she had "serious reservations" about the bill. "By writing a special bill for him we're opening a Pandora's box," she said. "I know of ten or twelve other officers from the MBTA who are eligible. God knows how many other city employees also qualify and never applied."

As I made my rounds, I realized Bratton wasn't as popular back home as he was in New York. The mayor, Thomas Menino, still smarted over Bratton's crack that if he didn't get the New York job then heading the Boston Police Department was a good consolation prize. No one could remember another example of a city employee trying to pass a private pension bill.

"How frequently can you get laws written for you?" said Michael Travaglini, the executive officer of the State-Boston Retirement Fund. "Maybe it's more frequent in New York than in Boston."

I wrote my story, detailing the controversy. The bill went nowhere, although some years later, after joining a dozen others who had spent more than twenty years with different Massachusetts police agencies, Bratton did receive his pension. By then, I was not Bratton's favorite reporter. In Lardner's *New Yorker* article, Bratton would grouse that *Newsday* had been "particularly hostile" toward him. He derided it as "a Long Island newspaper owned by a Los Angeles firm that was losing ground in circulation in the city." He described "The Confidential" as a gossip column, not real news.

"Let me ask you something," I said to Maple when I read that description. "What would you call Bratton's attempt to get a private pension bill passed through the Boston City Council and Massachusetts State Legislature? Would you call it gossip or real news?"

Maple, in his bow tie and striped shirt, with a three-peaked handkerchief in his breast pocket and wearing his spectator shoes, merely smiled.

xii.

Back in New York, things were going so well for Bratton that Miller thought he could pull a fast one with the news. It began with a column by McAlary in late April that debunked a rape in Brooklyn's Prospect Park. A twenty-seven-year-old black woman reported that while walking home, carrying groceries, a man had grabbed her from behind, choked her, pulled her up a hill, and raped her under a tree.

The next day, Miller told the in-house reporters at Police Plaza that investigators doubted her account. Detectives, he said, had found no witnesses to corroborate her story and no physical evidence—no sperm, no vaginal bruises or other injuries. Miller spoke on background, on condition of anonymity, supposedly as a caution to reporters to alert their desks in how they played the story. That was how DCPI operated, with behind-the-scenes nods. That was one way the police department controlled the news.

I had missed Miller's briefing and only learned of the rape when McAlary's column appeared the next day in the *Daily News.* It ran under the headline: "Rape hoax the real crime." McAlary described the woman's account as "an outrageous story," adding, "In Brooklyn, you have a woman who cried wolf."

He wrote that the police had found no drag marks up the hill and no groceries she might have dropped. He added that the woman was planning to speak about the rape at a Gay and Lesbian Anti-Violence rally, suggesting a political motive for her supposedly false claim. "Scaring a whole city," he wrote, "won't help anyone's cause."

The story created the predictable outcry as the department struggled to get its facts straight. In his first mention, Bratton apologized for the remarks of the anonymous police official in McAlary's column, whose identity he maintained he did not know. "We don't know who leaked the information, whether it was the investigating officers or somebody who might have information," he said. He then ordered Chief of Detectives Joseph Borrelli to find him.

Meanwhile another story in the *News* quoted an unnamed Brooklyn detective who defended the woman. Speaking anonymously, the detective told the *News* that detectives who had questioned her believed her story. "There is no officer here who ever doubted this woman," the *News* quoted the detective as saying. And the department added a further detail to the story. They said a second laboratory analysis, administered the day before, had found semen in the woman's vagina and on her running shorts.

The *News* stuck by McAlary. "Mike McAlary has a long track record of solid authoritative reporting and we stand by his column," the paper said.

I, too, was familiar with McAlary's reporting. I had worked with him at

Newsday before he left for the *News* to begin his column. At his best, he approached Jimmy Breslin. Some at the *News* considered him Breslin's heir apparent. Breslin, though, had no equal. He had created a world of low characters around the Queens courthouse that spoke to all human frailties. His columns from Vietnam and a decade later from the Middle East were brilliant. McAlary, a terrific reporter, stylist, and showman, confined himself to the NYPD. Only there, on a smaller stage, did he resemble Breslin.

While at *Newsday*, he had conducted a last fateful interview with Brian O'Regan, a young and tortured cop from Brooklyn's scandalized 77th Precinct, which would become the subject of McAlary's first book, *The Buddy Boys*. Believing he was about to be arrested on corruption charges, O'Regan had telephoned McAlary, who had driven out to a diner in Brooklyn to take down his story. A few days later, O'Regan was discovered in a Long Island motel, where he'd ended his life. Nearby lay a copy of *Newsday*, open to McAlary's interview.

Soon after, McAlary left *Newsday* for the *News* and began his column. When the drug-dealing Brooklyn cop Michael Dowd was arrested by police on Long Island in 1992, McAlary turned up Sergeant Joseph Tromboli, who, like Serpico, had gone to the authorities years before but had been ignored. Mac's stories about him helped pressure Dinkins into appointing the Mollen Commission.

A year after joining the *News*, McAlary jumped to the *New York Post* for more money, then back to the *News* for even more, then back to the *Post* for even more than that. At the same time, his success proved to be his downfall. He was living wildly and dangerously, and there were times, I felt, that his columns were as out of control as his life. While driving home to Brooklyn late one night, he crashed on a rain-slicked stretch of the FDR Drive. He was rushed to the hospital, barely alive. There were rumors of drinking, of speeding, and of drugs. He couldn't work for months, and no one was certain he'd make it back. But he did, weakened by the crash, thinner, and seemingly physically shorter, yet at the same time, larger than ever. He returned to the *News* for a third time, writing that while in the hospital he hadn't heard from the *Post*'s owner, Rupert Murdoch, while he'd received a card from President William J. Clinton.

The day he returned, he came out to Brooklyn, where I was covering a trial in federal court. There had been stories about him in the papers and on television, and as we walked across the street to have lunch, strangers approached to wish him well. When I began "The Confidential," he was the first to offer congratulations.

But he wasn't the same McAlary. Perhaps he was trying too hard to be, as his reporting on the Prospect Park rape story suggested. He had gone out too far and was in trouble. A year later, the victim would sue him for libel, and although she would lose her case, it exacted a toll.

And Mac wasn't the only person in trouble over the rape story. So was his friend, and apparently his source, Miller. Initially, Miller tried to brazen it out. "I'm not going to discuss it. It's an ongoing case. All I can say is that I wasn't McAlary's source."

The following week, Bratton again acknowledged that forensic evidence indicated the woman had been raped. This didn't slow down Mac. He wrote another column, disputing the forensics.

Yet again, Bratton maintained the woman had been raped and again apologized to her. He explained there had actually been two lab reports, adding that the second had been necessary because Chief of Detectives Borrelli had been "confused" by the medical jargon in the first. Suffering a biological meltdown, he had apparently confused semen with sperm, which is sometimes not present in semen. As for who had leaked the information to McAlary, Bratton still wasn't saying. He said he was no longer interested.

I, too, was trying to sort it out. McAlary had obviously taken the lead of the unnamed top police official—in my mind, Miller, who was taking his cues from the confused Borrelli. But Borrelli's Detective Bureau supported the victim. This discrepancy was another perfect backstory for me.

Hearing I was knocking around, McAlary telephoned me at *Newsday*. Without preamble, he told me his source had been Borrelli. Reporters never reveal their sources, certainly not to other reporters—certainly not to reporters at rival newspapers. "Mike, get serious," I answered. Then I called Borrelli. "Are you nuts?" he shouted. "When was the last time you heard of a reporter giving up a source? I haven't spoken to McAlary in I don't know how many years."

Borrelli must have then called Miller, who apparently called McAlary, because minutes later McAlary called back. "What I said was a joke," he said. "Borrelli wasn't the source."

"Mike," I said, "you must be crazy. Like this whole story."

And it became crazier. Another reporter, a freelancer named Gabriel Rotello, happened to have written about the rape case for *Newsday*'s op-ed page. His article said that after the attacks on his first column, McAlary had panicked and begged Miller to help him. "Can you bail me out?" Rotello quoted Miller as saying McAlary had asked him: "Can you knock this story down?"

So I called back McAlary. "Now *you* sound crazy," he said, denying he had said anything like that to Miller.

I called back Miller. He, too, denied saying anything like that to Rotello. "I actually didn't say any of those things to him because no such calls occurred and I don't know where he got that or how he extrapolated it from the conversation I had with him," Miller said.

Okay, now I was totally confused. I called Rotello and told him of McAlary's and Miller's denials. And guess what? Rotello said he had tape-recorded his conversation with Miller.

"Can I hear it?"

"Sure," he said. He came into *New York Newsday* and played me the tape. Sure enough, on it was everything he had quoted Miller as having said.

Poor Miller. Talk about being caught with your pants down. He was forced to publicly apologize, first to Rotello for "mischaracterizing" their conversation and "challenging his credibility," then to McAlary for challenging *his*. The situation was comical except that it was no joke. For a spokesman, Miller had committed the unpardonable. He had been caught in a lie—actually more than one lie. In so doing, he had compromised both his and the department's credibility. Either Bratton or Giuliani could have fired him. Bratton didn't want to. Neither did Giuliani. At least not yet.

Had I pushed the story, had I continued writing about it, Miller might not have been able to remain at the NYPD. But I didn't. I liked John. He was flamboyant and he was fun and he provided plenty of newsworthy entertainment. I wrote only one more column on the subject, quoting his DCPI predecessor McGillion. Low-key and wise, she had plenty to teach him. "The spokesman's voice reflects the credibility of the department," she said. "Telling the truth, or being perceived as telling the truth, is elementary to the job."

The NYPD had come a long way since the days of Lincoln Steffens and Jacob Riis, who had been skeptical of virtually everything the police said and did. A century later, DCPI was skillful enough that McGillion had been able to charm the entire in-house press corps into not running the story of the deputy commissioner's son. Now, a decade later, I, too, had been charmed, by Miller, and allowed the story to die.

Considering what was to befall him, I'm not sure I did him any favor.

FOUR

The Dirty Thirty

i.

In a split second, police officer Jorge Alvarez proved he was willing to die for his partner. But as his partner, Randy Vazquez, would discover, Alvarez was no hero.

The two worked the midnight tour in West Harlem's 30th Precinct, which had one of the most active drug trades in the city. Hard by the George Washington Bridge and its access to New Jersey and points south and west, the Three-Oh, as it was called, was a desolate spot, with empty storefronts and rotting tenements, ideal for dealers to move their drugs. In April 1993, tensions erupted into a midnight gun fight between dealers on West 151st Street. Alvarez and Vazquez found themselves in the middle of it. As they leapt from their patrol car, one of the dealers fired at them. Alvarez and Vazquez fired back, hitting him. As Vazquez reloaded, the wounded dealer staggered to his knees and aimed straight at him. Reflexively, Alvarez dived in front of Vazquez and shot the dealer, killing him and saving his partner's life.

His bravery's glow lasted just three months—until his past caught up with him. Tipped that 30th Precinct cops on the midnight tour had become part of the drug trade, investigators from the office of Manhattan district attorney Robert Morgenthau had conducted a sting. In July, they secretly videotaped Alvarez searching a dealer's car. Discovering packets of money, he was caught on video stuffing them into his clothes. The tape showed him seated in the driver's seat, leaning over to reach the glove compartment as a packet of cash fell down his leg onto the car floor. Alvarez scooped it up and stuffed it inside his pants, then shoveled the overflow into his sock.

That September, Morgenthau's investigators confronted Alvarez with the videotape. Facing seven years in prison, he turned on the partner whose life he had saved in April. Alvarez confessed that he and Vazquez had been robbing drug dealers and selling the drugs to competitors. Then he went further. He agreed to wear a "wire," a concealed recording device, to trap other crooked 30th Precinct cops. For the next seven months, Morgenthau's prosecutors allowed him to keep his gun and continue working in the station house, keeping his purpose, and his disgrace, a secret.

But the tensions of the double life unnerved him. Normally outgoing and chatty, he became sullen, and began drinking. Cops grew suspicious. In February 1994, amid rumors that the midnight tour's drug dealing was about to be exposed, police officer Stephen Morrissey taunted him, accusing him of wearing a wire. He and Alvarez began to scuffle at the station house's front desk. Alvarez drew his revolver and shot Morrissey in the foot. Unwilling to reveal their hand, prosecutors hid the extent of the shooting from even the top police brass.

Two months later, in April 1994, the scandal, dubbed the Dirty Thirty, exploded. A dozen cops on the midnight shift were busted for drug-related crimes. But it wasn't the Manhattan district attorney who made the arrests. It was the rival feds—the United States Attorney's Office for New York's Southern District. Federal prosecutors had been in league with investigators from the Mollen Commission, the mayoral panel investigating allegations of police corruption. Like the Knapp Commission of two decades before, the commission, with its small staff of investigators, would discover major corruption that the NYPD, with all its resources, had failed to uncover. The heart of it lay inside the 30th Precinct.

The Knapp Commission may have rid the department of the systemic and organized corruption that then existed even at the highest levels, but it hadn't eliminated the problem. Instead, the nature of police corruption had mutated.

Now, two decades after the Knapp Commission, it existed in pockets, in poverty-stricken, high-crime precincts with an active drug trade. Within those pockets the corruption was worse than anything in the past. No longer was it confined to accepting payoffs from bookmakers to ignore gambling. No longer was there a distinction between "grass-eaters," the minor offenders, and the "meat-eaters," the serious ones. Instead, within these pockets cops had become criminals. In the 30th Precinct, the corrupt cops on the midnight tour had become carnivores.

On the surface, these cops appeared to be model officers. Virtually all of them were raised in modest circumstances. Alvarez was born in Havana, Cuba, and raised in the Bronx, where his father was a building superintendent. He had graduated from Power Memorial Academy, a Catholic high school, in 1979, worked for the United Parcel Service and as a banquet waiter at the Waldorf-Astoria before joining the police department in 1982. In fact, his background reminded me of Timoney's. He, too, was an immigrant. Like Alvarez, he had come to New York with his parents as a child, lived in Upper Manhattan, and graduated from a Catholic high school. Before joining the police department, he had driven a Coca-Cola truck. Yet in the generation since Timoney joined the force, the department, as well as the world outside it, had changed. For a young cop like Alvarez, far from the college track, a high-crime pocket like the 30th Precinct was a place to score. By robbing drug dealers instead of arresting them, he could rationalize he was pocketing cash while meting out street justice.

At the same time, at least one facet of the police culture had not changed, the code of personal courage: Witness Alvarez's risking his life for Vazquez. But in giving up his partner, Alvarez appeared to have violated another department code: He had breached the blue wall of silence. And he was not alone. Under pressure from prosecutors, the blue wall in the 30th Precinct broke apart whenever a cop was caught. Confronted with long prison terms, a third of those arrested in the Dirty Thirty scandal became informers.

Assistant United States Attorney Michael Horowitz, who prosecuted most of them, explained that the key lay in making strong cases. "You have to know where their bank accounts are, where they've hidden their money. Then you have to let them know you have the goods. Cops won't volunteer anything. You have to let them know you aren't bluffing. When you lay it on the line and tell them what will happen if they don't cooperate, they'll think long and hard."

Twenty years before, when Serpico had come forward, no one had listened to him. Every step he took to fight police corruption he had taken alone. Neither the police department nor any outside law enforcement agency had helped him. In fact, the department's systemic corruption had literally occurred for decades under the revered nose of Morgenthau's predecessor, the longtime district attorney Frank Hogan, who was known as Mr. District Attorney. Hogan had had friends in the top levels of the police department. His closest friend was said to be First Deputy Commissioner John Walsh, who, as the Knapp Commission revealed, had stonewalled the feds investigating corrupt NYPD cops.

City Hall had also turned Serpico away, supposedly because Mayor Lindsay feared a long hot summer of riots and needed the police on his side. Then there was the question of what a corruption scandal might expose. It was like opening a Pandora's box. Who knew what trouble lay inside? No mayor, or police commissioner for that matter, cared to find out.

The Knapp Commission would change the dynamic between the police department and the outside world. It would make police corruption part of the city's political dialogue. Unlike Hogan, state and federal prosecutors now saw police corruption as an opportunity. Take Giuliani. As an assistant U.S. attorney in the Southern District in the mid-1970s, he made a reputation by supposedly "handling" Robert Leuci, a crooked NYPD narcotics cop and pathological liar who cooperated with authorities in the Prince of the City case, the title of Robert Daley's bestselling book. Although Giuliani's role with Leuci remains unclear, he nevertheless touted himself as an expert on police corruption. Like most prosecutors familiar with the NYPD, he maintained the department couldn't be trusted to police itself.

Morgenthau also believed the department couldn't police itself. Besides Alvarez, his office was investigating another corrupt 30th Precinct cop, thirty-one-year-old George Nova, who was to break open the scandal. Nova, like Timoney, had grown up just north of the 30th Precinct, in Washington Heights. He had dropped out of George Washington High School and held odd jobs, at pharmacies and as a youth counselor, before joining the police department. In 1987 he was assigned to the 30th Precinct. Like Alvarez, he appeared to be personally brave. He belonged to the precinct's elite anticrime team and had received seventeen citations for numerous gun and drug arrests, including one where he recovered $100,000. After another seizure of drugs and $43,000 in cash from a car he stopped that had run a red light, he was given a special department commendation.

At the same time, he had more than two dozen civilian complaints, most of them from drug dealers. He had allegedly broken into their dens, stolen their drugs and money, then sold the drugs at discounted prices to rivals. In August 1993, he allegedly stole drugs valued at $16,000, then sold them for $7,000 to another dealer. He purportedly stole so much that Morgenthau's investigators began tailing him. They tailed him for the next two years.

The Mollen Commission was also tailing Nova. Its investigators learned he was shaking down dealers for $2,000 a month in protection money that he picked up at a bodega on Amsterdam Avenue. The bodega's owner left the money in an empty coffee container inside a brown paper bag. Mollen investigators discovered the bodega owner was also involved in a food stamp scam. Food stamps are a federal program, run by the Department of Agriculture. Ignoring Morgenthau, Mollen notified Giuliani's old outfit, the U.S. Attorney's Office for the Southern District.

"We got involved because [the Mollen Commission] needed someone to prosecute a food stamp case," Horowitz explained. Pressured by the feds, the bodega owner agreed to wear a wire. "That," said Horowitz, "got us Nova." The feds arrested him before Morgenthau did.

"Morgenthau had been investigating Nova for two years," said Mollen, explaining his decision to take his case to federal authorities. "But he hadn't come up with enough to make an arrest."

On September 23, 1993, the feds arrested Nova. "They told me enough to know I was dead," he said. In return for a reduced sentence he agreed to give up *his* partner and to wear a wire. Later, federal prosecutors would say that after Nova, the arrests came like falling dominoes.

Morgenthau never forgave Mollen for poaching his case. Fighting police corruption may have been his stated job as a prosecutor; fighting off rivals was an unstated part. It would take him two years to exact his revenge. Once again, the noble cause of fighting corruption would take another turn. This time prosecutors would fight each other. The results would be tragic.

ii.

One person nowhere to be found during the 30th Precinct corruption scandal was Mayor Rudolph Giuliani. As a prosecutor he had relished the spotlight of the Prince of the City corruption case. As mayor, he touted himself as a police expert and involved himself in every aspect of the department. But he vanished from public view when the Dirty Thirty scandal broke. It would be the only time in his eight years as mayor that he would become invisible during a police crisis. It was easy to speculate why. No doubt, like everyone in the police department, he was uncertain where the scandal might lead and whether it would be confined to the 30th Precinct. But his disappearance was so seamless no one noticed. No official spoke of it. No reporter wrote of it.

And he had Bratton. For perhaps the only time in his mayoralty, he welcomed Bratton to provide cover. His absence left Bratton an open field. Realizing the scandal reflected on the Dinkins administration—not on him—Bratton turned it into another public relations gambol. The night the first dozen cops were arrested in the spring of 1994 he staged a midnight appearance at the 30th Precinct and had reporters tipped off. When I arrived at 11:30 P.M., the place was rocking. Bands of cops stood outside on the street, wearing windbreakers with the names or insignias of their investigating agencies—Manhattan District Attorney, United States Attorney, Mollen Commission, and the NYPD's Internal Affairs Division. You couldn't make out all the letters, though, because over their jackets they wore bulletproof vests. Authorities were afraid the arrested officers might resist and pull their guns.

Just as I arrived, a van of Mollen Commission investigators appeared. A few minutes later, Bratton arrived with Miller. As they entered the station house, I followed. Because of the turmoil, I was able to walk in right behind them. Suddenly, officers in plainclothes rushed inside. Others, wearing windbreakers with "Internal Affairs" on them, took positions inside the precinct's front door. The first officers surrounded a slight, young Hispanic cop, also in plainclothes. The officers did not draw their guns. They spoke to the young cop so softly that although I stood just a few feet away, I couldn't hear a word. Then, in what seemed a slow-motion pantomime, I saw the young cop loosen his gun belt. It fell around his ankles to the floor.

The officers pushed him out a side door to the precinct parking lot and into the backseat of an unmarked patrol car. A crowd had gathered. Moments later, they brought out another officer, a large, stocky man, also in plainclothes, and placed him inside the patrol car next to the first. The crowd began to taunt them. "Put your head up," someone shouted. "Be a man," someone else called out. "Now you're going to get yours."

As the car passed through the crowd and departed the precinct, both officers ducked down on the floor and covered their faces. Watching them, cowering and afraid, I felt embarrassed not only for them but for the police department. I felt I had witnessed a department humiliation that no civilian should see.

iii.

At the next day's press conference announcing the arrests, Mollen, Morgenthau, and U.S. Attorney Mary Jo White took center stage. But this portrait of law enforcement unity had a crack. When Morgenthau and Mollen, both white-haired septuagenarians, passed each other, each appeared to give the other a shove. They weren't friendly shoves. The petite Mary Jo White, barely five feet tall, had to step in to separate them.

Standing on the sidelines, Maple and Timoney began to laugh. The Morgenthau-Mollen go-round inspired Maple to coin a new word, based on the term describing how police officers lie when testifying on the witness stand—"testilying." Maple's term for the press conference's charade of law enforcement unity was "prestilying."

Meanwhile, the cameras turned to Bratton. In what appeared to be a gesture of spontaneous anger, the normally composed police commissioner hurled the tin shields of the two arrested officers into a garbage pail. Teeth clenched, he said he was sending a message to other cops. "I am retiring their badges," he announced, "so that no cop will have to wear a disgraced number again." Unbeknownst to the public, a cop had placed the pail there as a prop before Bratton started his press conference. "Believe me," said a chief, "there was nothing spontaneous about any of it."

Prop or not, Bratton's gesture didn't ring true. Cops needed no further message from him about corruption. Seeing two fellow cops dragged out of a station house in the middle of the night was message enough. Tossing the shields was merely good television.

Bratton's showmanship, while effective with others, was starting to wear on me. I was haunted by the scene of that slight Hispanic cop, surrounded and forced to drop his gun belt, then pushed into a police car as the crowd jeered him. The same scene was repeated with the second officer. By then I had learned their names and ages, Jose Rivera, thirty-two, and Alfonso Compres, thirty-three. They, too, had come from hardscrabble backgrounds. Compres was born in the Dominican Republic and immigrated with his family to New York when he was twelve. His father had worked as a sewing machine operator in the Garment District. After graduating in 1979 from George Washington, the same high school Nova hadn't finished, he worked for ten years on a factory assembly line and in a photo print shop. In 1990 at age twenty-nine, he joined the department.

Rivera had grown up in the Bronx and graduated in 1979 from All Hallows, another Catholic high school. He had attended John Jay College of Criminal Justice but dropped out; he joined the Marine Corps, and was discharged as a corporal. He then worked as a security guard in San Diego before joining the police department in 1987.

As a harbinger of all that was to go wrong for him, Rivera had overextended himself financially. In 1990, he bought a house in New City, forty miles north of the city, that left him with a $183,000 mortgage and $2,399 in monthly payments. Later that year the Internal Revenue Service placed a lien on the house for $5,447 in back taxes. To bring in extra money, his wife, Jana, babysat neighborhood children. In February 1993, their mortgage holder sued for nonpayment. That summer their house was foreclosed and they moved to an apartment in New Rochelle. He and his wife separated. Meanwhile, the state placed a tax lien on him for $4,053. Before "turning" Nova, the feds had considered making a run at Rivera, and began tailing both of them. While Nova returned home to his family after work, Rivera partied at clubs. The feds decided against trying to turn him.

As it turned out, my sympathy was misguided. Rivera was charged with taking payoffs from drug dealers in return for protection. Compres was worse. His nickname on the street was *"Abusador,"* the Abuser. If dealers refused to pay, he beat them. He once snuck up behind a dealer waiting for an elevator, hit him in the head, shot him in the side, then stole his cocaine. He was charged with robbery, assault, intimidating a witness, tampering with physical evidence, narcotics conspiracy, violation of civil rights resulting in bodily injury, and taking $10,000 from drug dealers on West 139th Street over several months. Facing twenty years in prison, he had become so hardened that, according to the complaint against him, he bragged that he could "spend five years in jail and come out with money."

iv.

Standard operating procedure in criminal investigations calls for starting with small crooks, turning them, and working up to bigger crooks. The 30th Precinct corruption scandal didn't work that way. Here prosecutors made deals with the worst offenders, then sent the crooks back into the precinct, still carrying their guns, to trap cops in lesser offenses. They had made deals to reduce the sentences of the meat-eaters in order to trap the grass-eaters.

No one outside the police department picked up on this inversion of investigatory procedure. The newspapers measured success by the mere number of arrests. Reporters, myself included, failed to recognize how these tactics sowed the seeds of tragedy.

Six months after Alvarez shot Morrissey, Joseph Walsh, another crooked cop, was nearly shot. He was one of eight officers known as Nannery's Raiders, named after their crooked sergeant, Kevin Nannery. Their official mission had been to confiscate drugs, guns, and cash. Instead, their modus operandi appeared to be "key jobs"—stealing drug dealers' door keys—and "booming"—breaking down—drug dealers' apartment doors without warrants. Instead of vouchering the drugs, guns and cash that they confiscated at the precinct, they lied about it.

Nannery stole so much money in this way, he bought a new car and house in upstate Newburgh. Cops in the precinct wondered how he did it, what with his wife not working and caring for their baby. I scrounged up his address and drove up to see for myself. There it sat, a large new home at the end of a cul-de-sac in a just-completed development.

Walsh, meanwhile, allegedly helped Nannery steal railroad ties from a Bronx storage garage to use in Nannery's backyard. After Nannery hurt his back lifting the ties, Walsh filed a false report in which he claimed to have seen Nannery injure his back while on duty, so that he could receive a disability pension.

On October 28, 1992, Walsh and two other cops responded to a radio call at 546 West 146th Street and learned shots had been fired in an upstairs apartment. Arriving there, Walsh heard a gunshot. A child opened the door and told Walsh his mother had been shot. From another room, Walsh heard a baby crying. He kicked in the door and saw, beside the baby, a man and a woman dead on the floor, with a gun at the man's feet. "Having risked his life to ensure the children's security," wrote Assistant U.S. Attorney Horowitz in his complaint, Walsh then stole $100 in cash he found in the room.

On November 9, 1993, Walsh and Nannery arrested several people at 530 West 152nd Street. There Walsh allegedly stole $4,000, which he shared with Nannery and two other cops, Kevin Kay and Thomas Giovanniello. On December 2, Walsh purportedly had someone place a false 911 call, stating shots had been fired at 61 Hamilton Place, a drug location. Walsh, his partner, and two other cops responded to the building. Through a back window they spotted cocaine inside an apartment. Entering it, they found a pound of coke, a gun, and bundles of cash. Without telling the other officers, Walsh allegedly stole three bundles, totaling $13,000, and tossed a few hundred dollars to Nannery.

On June 6, 1994, Walsh was arrested at his home and, as Horowitz delicately said of him, he "was provided an opportunity to cooperate." Walsh, too, agreed to wear a wire. Four days later, prosecutors persuaded him to attend a Mets game at Shea Stadium with Kay and Giovanniello. They fitted Walsh with a recording device and gave him a beeper transmitter so he could call them if there was trouble.

Although instructed not to drink alcohol, Walsh got drunk with Kay and Giovanniello in the parking lot. Entering the stadium, the two discovered Walsh's beeper transmitter in his pocket. To allay their concerns, Walsh tossed it in the garbage, while keeping the recorder hidden. He didn't realize it was recording.

Later, after leaving the stadium and returning to the car. Kay placed his gun on the dashboard. He and Giovanniello asked Walsh if he was cooperating with the feds. After a silence, Kay said that what Walsh had done was far worse than anything he and Giovanniello had. Walsh panicked. He bolted from the car and ran away across the parking lot. Frightened investigators searched for him for two hours before he turned up, still drunk, where they had been waiting to debrief him. Because of his recording, Kay and Giovanniello were arrested. They, too, agreed to cooperate.

Just as they had covered up Alvarez's shooting Morrissey inside the 30th

Precinct station house, prosecutors covered up the Shea Stadium incident. I learned of it from one of the cops' attorneys. Only then did prosecutors acknowledge what had occurred. Both dramas heightened tensions inside the precinct to tragic levels. In July, Captain Terrence Tunnock, a twenty-eight-year veteran, walked into the bedroom of his Bronx home and, while his wife made breakfast, shot himself in the head with his off-duty revolver. Tunnock, who knew many of those involved in the scandal, was not involved himself. Rather, he seemed caught between conflicting forces—his conscience and the department's code of silence.

What had happened to cause him to take his life? The previous August, he had responded to a call about a cocaine storehouse at 180 Edgecomb Avenue where he found money, crack vials, and a gun. Minutes later, Nannery and his Raiders arrived, along with Compres. Nannery assured Tunnock that Compres would voucher the items. When Compres was arrested the following April, Tunnock contacted Nannery and asked if Compres had properly vouchered the items from the previous August. Nannery assured him Compres had. Then, in July, Tunnock learned Nannery was under investigation. He decided to check the 30th Precinct property index himself. Leafing through it, he discovered Compres had not vouchered the property. Nannery had lied to him, and Tunnock reported him to Internal Affairs. But Tunnock was of the old school. The department's code of silence apparently weighed enough on him that he couldn't live with himself for having turned in his fellow officers.

As if his story weren't tragic enough, someone at *Newsday* made a terrible error in the story I wrote about the suicide. The headline mistakenly implicated Tunnock in the 30th Precinct corruption. When I read it, my stomach dropped.

Most cops despised *New York Newsday* because of its tough police coverage. A few years before, PBA president Phil Caruso had urged its members not to buy the paper. But *Newsday* was an honorable shop. Although it was small comfort to Tunnock's family, the paper immediately acknowledged its error and ran a correction two days later.

"A story in Sunday's editions may have incorrectly suggested that Captain Terrence Tunnock was forced by prosecutors to cooperate with the 30th Precinct corruption investigation," it read. "Tunnock came forward voluntarily and offered evidence of possible corruption." The noble cause of fighting police corruption had cost another victim.

v.

That fall, a second suicide rocked the precinct. This one was among Nannery's Raiders. Rookie cop Stephen Laski was placed on modified assignment and knew he would soon be arrested. Three weeks later, he killed himself.

Still another rookie locked himself in the station house bathroom and threatened to blow his brains out. He had worked but a single tour with another corrupt cop, Michael Walsh, who was cooperating with prosecutors and wearing a wire. Fearing Walsh had falsely implicated him, the rookie panicked. The precinct's desk lieutenant called Timoney at headquarters. "The kid has locked himself in the bathroom with his gun in his mouth."

Bratton had never viewed the scandal personally, but the three dozen arrests and two suicides had pierced Timoney to his NYPD core. He raced up to the precinct. Reporters had gotten wind of the rookie's situation and were camped outside when he arrived. By then the lieutenant had talked the kid out of the bathroom and whisked him out a side entrance. But for Timoney the breaking point had been reached. Two suicides, a near suicide, a shooting inside the precinct, another threatened shooting at Shea Stadium—and no end in sight. "The danger with the 30th Precinct cases," he said in retrospect, "was that the prosecutors were in competition. Nobody was speaking up for the cops. We were eating our own."

Later that night he returned to the precinct with Maple, Miller, and Anemone to meet with the "good cops"—those remaining on the midnight tour who had not been indicted. Then Timoney, Maple, Miller, and Anemone began an extraordinary seven-hour, no-holds-barred session. So intense did it become that Timoney allowed it to continue through the night, replacing the entire midnight tour of officers with an outside force.

"People were crying. They were red with anger," said Timoney. "They were in shock over the last suicide attempt. They accused me and the other top brass of tearing people and the precinct apart. They accused the prosecutors of dragging out the investigation, leaving guys hanging for months. They were especially critical of allowing cops like Alvarez and Nova to keep their guns and secretly tape-record others to trap them in minor violations."

The next day, Timoney began telephoning prosecutors, pleading with them to finish their investigation before another cop tried to kill himself. "You're getting your names and faces on television," he said, "while playing a numbers game over cops' lives." His efforts backfired. Prosecutors, several of whom he regarded as friends, turned on him. A whispering campaign against him began, accusing him of being "soft" on corruption. Given the department's history, it was a tough accusation to overcome. "There's a lot of hypocrisy here," a prosecutor warned. "These cops knew what was going on and never came forward. I guarantee some of them complaining the loudest will end up getting arrested later on."

An under-the-radar war now raged between prosecutors and the police department. The first casualty was Timoney protégé Captain Lewis Manetta, the 30th Precinct's former executive officer, or second in command. Timoney had recently promoted Manetta to head the newly created 33rd Precinct in Harlem, which had been carved out of the northern portion of the 30th. The following year, in the first step toward his promotion to deputy inspector, the department's top brass rated him first of all NYPD captains.

But with the 30th Precinct arrests, corruption allegations against him surfaced. The first came from Nannery, who had been charged with breaking into apartments, stealing money, taking payoffs, and lying under oath. As part of a plea bargain to lower his sentence, he claimed Manetta had encouraged his Raiders to "boom" drug dealers' doors. Another arrested Raider, police officer Thomas Nolan, also pleaded guilty to a reduced charge of perjury. To lower *his* sentence, he accused Manetta of authorizing "key jobs" to illegally enter drug dealers' apartments. At his sentencing, Nolan's attorney stated that Manetta "took rookie cops out . . . to a building that he told them was a drug location and he proceeded to tell them . . . how you kick down doors and you go like gangbusters and you find whatever there is to be found and then you make up your story."

Federal prosecutors issued Manetta an "invitation" to testify before a federal grand jury. His lawyer wouldn't allow him to appear because prosecutors refused to grant him immunity. Shortly afterward, he retired from the department.

Explaining the circumstances of his retirement to Nolan's sentencing judge, Loretta Preska of the Southern District, Horowitz wrote that while his office and Morgenthau's did not have enough evidence to prosecute Manetta, the NYPD had been prepared to charge him with administrative violations. "When Manetta was informed of the possible administrative charges," Horowitz wrote, "he left the NYPD."

But that wasn't quite true. Manetta, said Timoney, was "an honest, tough, unpolished diamond in the rough. Louie's a tough guy, not a thief. He epitomizes the type of commandeer I'd want. He gives 110 percent every day of the year."

Explaining Manetta's retirement, Timoney said, "We couldn't get any sense of how these prosecutors were going. I said to him, 'They could come after you. It's clear you're not going to get promoted, even though you are the number-one-ranked guy.'" Said another department official: "We told him it was time to go. He had been beaten up so much, it was better for everybody."

vi.

Of all the prosecutors, Timoney was most angered by the department's own— the civilian deputy commissioner for internal affairs, Walter Mack. To Timoney, Mack was a zealot, an elite, white-shoe prosecutor, who represented "them," the outside agencies that did not understand the department and the realities of being a cop. He and Mack appeared to be polar opposites. The tall, blond-haired Mack was a graduate of Milton Academy, Harvard College, and Columbia Law School. He seemed a cross between a prep school headmaster and a minister. In his own words, he was "alien" to the NYPD.

Yet he and Timoney had more in common than either realized. No less than Timoney, Mack was independent and principled. As a marine captain, he had seen combat in Vietnam. He became so disillusioned that, upon returning home, he joined the Vietnam Veterans Against the War. Later, as an assistant U.S. attorney in the Southern District, he worked for a decade prosecuting organized crime cases—until he was forced to quit after suggesting publicly that his new boss was taking credit for investigations begun by his predecessor. That new boss was Rudy Giuliani.

"He wanted me to succumb," Mack said. "I refused." Years later, Timoney would find himself in a similar position.

Since his appointment in 1993, Mack had envisioned the Internal Affairs Division as "hard and aggressive . . . so respected that it would become an official corruption unit available to agencies beyond the NYPD." In the 30th Precinct, Mack viewed his mandate as removing every corrupt officer on the midnight tour. To him, prosecuting dirty cops was no different than going after mobsters.

"You treat corrupt cops like drug dealers or organized crime figures," he said—like ordinary criminals. "We had to demonstrate that the department could bring them all to justice. Do you take his weapon? Do you put a guy back on the street? I called every shot."

Federal prosecutor Michael Horowitz praised Mack's hard-line approach. "They were willing to put an officer with a gun wearing a wire back inside the precinct for seven months. How often does that happen? It takes someone committed to getting to the bottom because that involves a lot of risk."

Like Guido, the only person in the department's history to successfully run Internal Affairs, Mack felt that his strength lay in his alien status. Upon retiring in 1985, Guido's parting remark to me had been, "Five years after I am gone, there will be a major corruption scandal." The 30th Precinct scandal proved him right. When Kelly appointed Mack in 1993, I called Guido. "He doesn't understand the police culture," he said of Mack. "He'll never last." That, too, proved right.

Mack was so much an outsider that Bratton, an outsider himself, distrusted him as much as Timoney did. Mack furthered their distrust by refusing to inform them about key 30th Precinct developments. This included Alvarez's shooting of Morrissey. Timoney was infuriated when he learned of it from prosecutors outside the department.

Timoney was further incensed by another 30th Precinct sting Morgenthau had conducted. It occurred inside an apartment, where an Internal Affairs undercover was disguised as a drug dealer. A rookie cop and his partner, a PBA delegate, arrived to search for drugs. Disgusted at finding none, the delegate kneed the undercover and was arrested for brutality. Prosecutors, who had secretly videotaped the confrontation, charged the rookie with covering up the incident because he didn't file it in his memo book. Timoney protested the minor charge against the rookie to Mack. "This is outrageous," Timoney said. "What would you expect the rookie to have done? His partner was a union delegate."

"I agree," Mack told him, "but there is nothing I can do about it."

Mack's run-ins with Timoney only hardened Mack's resolve. To him, Bratton, Timoney, and the others in Bratton's inner circle had what he termed "a paranoid view of prosecutors."

"We had a fundamental disagreement. I was not in their clique. I was Ray's boy," he said, referring to Kelly, who had appointed him. "I was someone to be tolerated. They were not sophisticated enough to understand my role. Who better to duke it out with prosecutors to protect the department than me? Instead, they were biding their time to get rid of me."

What finished Mack was an informant the Mollen Commission had developed inside the 30th Precinct. Back in the 1970s the Knapp Commission had used a corrupt cop, William Phillips, to guide it through the layers of departmental corruption. The Mollen guide was an IAD undercover named Barry Brown, who had been placed inside the precinct years before. Judge Mollen, however, did not realize that, like Phillips, Brown came with baggage.

So embedded was Brown that for a time he was Nova's partner on the midnight tour. Despite Mollen's denials, many suspected it was Brown who had tipped off his investigators to Nova and the bodega owner. At the commission's public hearings in the fall of 1993, Brown testified with a black hood covering his face, giving his name as "Officer Otto." Only two people knew his true identity—then police commissioner Kelly and his newly appointed civilian head of Internal Affairs, Mack.

Meanwhile, in his plea deal with prosecutors, Nova promised to come clean about a former partner who, Nova said, had committed perjury at trials leading to the convictions of at least two drug dealers. That former partner was Barry Brown. Nova had no idea that Brown was the Mollen Commission's secret informant, Officer Otto. Neither did Bratton, Timoney, or Maple, who had become Brown's new boss in the warrant squad.

Only when Morgenthau prepared to indict Brown for perjury did Mack inform Bratton that Brown and Officer Otto were one. Bratton, said Timoney, was dumbstruck. Maple was furious at Mack for remaining silent when Brown was transferred into his squad. Mack, on the other hand, believed he had been acting honorably. "I know about loyalty from the Marine Corps," he said. "I had given him [Brown] my personal promise, as had Kelly."

Bratton, saying Mack had kept him "out of the loop," fired him. Minutes later, Mack received a call from Giuliani. "He wanted me to know he had nothing to do with it," Mack said.

Brown, meanwhile, was permitted to resign from the police department in exchange for Morganthau's dropping his investigation of Brown. Morgenthau trumpeted that the Mollen Commission had done as much harm as good. Morgenthau had waited two years, but he had exacted his revenge.

Years later Brown would say that after his identity was revealed by the D.A., he had to resign from the department. "I had already received death threats. I was afraid for my life. I was afraid I would be the next Serpico and get shot by another officer. I had pushed this investigation for more than seven years but they made me out to be a corrupt cop."

Brown's story wasn't quite finished. His attorney, Richard Emery, arranged interviews with *The New York Times*, the *New York Post*, and CBS television's *60 Minutes*, which portrayed Brown as a hero for breaking the blue wall and informing on corrupt cops for the Mollen Commission. Emery then sold an option for Brown's story to Hollywood Pictures, a subsidiary of Walt Disney Studios. Meanwhile, Brown came up with an unlikely defender—John Miller, who by then had left the department and said Brown had done more to fight corruption than Serpico had.

Miller was apparently not speaking for the police department or for Bratton. When a group called the Concerned Alliance for Professional Policing honored Brown, saying its award "was being presented with the approval of Police Commissioner William Bratton," Bratton threatened to sue. "I am putting each of you and your organization on notice that the above quoted statement is false in its entirety," he wrote them. "I have certainly not approved an award of any kind to be presented to Detective Brown. I strongly urge your organization to publicly retract your reference to me and I advise you I am considering legal action." Years later Brown would say that after his identity was revealed by the D.A., he had to resign from the department. "I had already received death threats. I was afraid for my life. I was afraid I would be the next Serpico and get shot by another officer. I had pushed this investigation for more than seven years but they made me out to be a corrupt cop."

Unlike Serpico, no movie about Brown was made. Thirty-three cops from the 30th Precinct were convicted of corruption, a sixth of its 191 officers. Only four served more than a year in prison. Some of the worst offenders received only probation. Alvarez pleaded guilty to a reduced charge of third-degree grand larceny. In May 1997, he received probation. Vazquez pleaded guilty to reduced charges of conspiracy to sell drugs in the second degree and second-degree assault. On January 31, 1996, he was sentenced to six months in prison. Nova pleaded guilty to one count of narcotics distribution and one count of conspiracy to violate civil rights. On September 26, 1996, he was sentenced to a year in prison. Joseph Walsh pleaded guilty to perjury, tax evasion, and civil rights and conspiracy charges and the authorities apparently agreed not to pursue other charges. He was sentenced to six months in prison. Compres, the infamous *Abusador*, pleaded guilty to a reduced charge of extortion in exchange for them dropping the other charges. On

November 21, 1995, he was sentenced to five years in prison. Nannery, one of two sergeants in the corruption scandal, pleaded guilty in federal court to civil rights violations and income tax evasion in return for dropping other charges. Because of his cooperation, a federal judge granted him probation. On June 16, 1997, he pleaded guilty in state court to first-degree perjury and was sentenced to one to three years. "You represent the worst of everything I have seen in this corruption situation," Justice Leslie Crocker Snyder told him.

True, the Mollen Commission had cleaned up the 30th Precinct. But after all the headlines and tragedies, the suicides and betrayals, what in the long run had it accomplished? Like King Charles I of England, of whom it was written that nothing in his life became him like the leaving of it, nothing that the Mollen Commission did equaled the eloquence of its final report. Echoing the Knapp Commission's warning twenty years earlier, it described a police culture that valued "loyalty over integrity" and blamed "willfully blind supervisors who fear the consequences of a scandal more than the scandal itself." It quoted former police commissioner Kelly as saying that only outside oversight "keeps the Department's feet to the fire."

"If history proves anything," its report concluded, "it is that when the glare of scrutiny shines on the Department, it can and will successfully police itself. History also proves that left to its own devices, the Department will backslide and its commitment to integrity will erode. It is no coincidence that the only two times in the past 20 years that fighting corruption has been a priority in the Department was when an independent commission publicly reviewed and disclosed the Department's failure to keep its own house in order."

With that the commission made two recommendations and passed into history. The first was the establishment of a permanent corruption monitor outside the police department. The second was that the monitor have subpoena power to investigate police corruption on its own. Mayor Giuliani rejected both recommendations. In his first public statement on the scandal, the mayor took a position antithetical to what he had maintained for years as a prosecutor. "The most effective way to investigate police misconduct is to do it through the police department," he said, "because they have the investigators who have the capacity to understand the police department. The more independent you make the review process and investigatory process, the less chance it has of success."

For the eight years of his mayoralty and the next eight of his successor, Michael Bloomberg, the police department would be left to police itself.

FIVE

The Fall of Bill Bratton

i.

In just the first months after Giuliani became mayor and Bratton police commissioner, the city seemed to have changed. The signs were everywhere. The
most visible concerned the NYPD. For the first time in a generation, the department seemed to have gotten its hands around crime, which was dropping in
record numbers. Preliminary figures for the first five months of 1994 showed an
11 percent drop, with reductions of 25 percent in high crime precincts like the
75th, Brooklyn's toughest, where Bratton and Maple were pouring in extra officers. By year's end, the drop would be so dramatic it became the cornerstone of
a national decline in major felonies. Although New York City comprised only 3
percent of the U.S. population, its crime drop accounted for one-third of the nation's. Even criminologists who had initially attributed the declines to factors
other than policing were crediting Bratton and the NYPD.

But the more Bratton succeeded, the more contentious his relationship with
Giuliani became. Success may have many fathers, but Bratton and Giuliani
seemed unable to share the credit. Bratton never learned the lesson of his first
week: To Giuliani, favorable publicity was a zero-sum game. In Churchill's wartime cadence, Bratton had announced, "We will fight for every house in this
city. We will fight for every street. We will fight for every borough. We will win."

Yet his victory would be a Pyrrhic one. The higher he rose in the public's esteem, the more inevitable it became that he would fall.

The Vera Wang incident, which should have been an occasion for backslapping camaraderie between Police Plaza and City Hall, represented instead all that went wrong between Bratton and Giuliani. On March, 23, 1994, three months after Bratton and Giuliani took office, two men in jackets and ties rang the doorbell of the Vera Wang Bridal House inside the Carlyle Hotel on Madison Avenue. Both the Carlyle and Vera Wang were famous names. Vera Wang was a favorite of altar-bound socialites, Hollywood celebrities, and anyone else who could afford her five- and six-figure gowns. Her flagship store was inside a building well known to potential customers. The Carlyle, on Madison Avenue and 77th Street, was in the heart of the city's Upper East Side. For years it was home to the smooth jazz of Bobby Short; before that, to the smooth talk of John F. Kennedy when as president he visited the city.

The two well-dressed men mumbled something about a wedding dress to the receptionist, who led them up the stairs to Vera Wang's showroom on the second floor. Suddenly, one of them pulled out a small-caliber, silver revolver and shoved it against the receptionist's back. They confronted customers Gerald and Edith Schaeffer, of Potomac, Maryland, whose twenty-two-year-old daughter Alisa was trying on a wedding gown while their fifteen-year-old daughter Jennifer watched.

The two men zeroed in on Edith Schaeffer's $60,000 diamond ring. "Give up the ring," one of them shouted. He yanked it from Mrs. Schaeffer so violently, he broke her finger. When, frozen in fear, she didn't move quickly enough, the gunman shot her in the abdomen. As her husband rushed to protect her, the gunman shot him in the abdomen as well.

The robbers escaped with the ring. Paramedics rushed the Schaeffers to nearby Cornell Medical Center, where their wounds required two weeks of care. Their brush with death resonated throughout the city. The robbers had struck in broad daylight, inside the city's wealthiest enclave. It was the kind of random violence that stereotyped New York City as out of control, a reminder of the darkest days of the Dinkins administration. The robbery recalled the 1990 subway attack on another out-of-town family—the stabbing death of twenty-two-year-old Brian Watkins, who had died protecting his mother.

Most unnerving for Rudy Giuliani were the words of the would-be bride's fifteen-year-old sister Jennifer. They epitomized all he had promised to repair and resurrect in New York. Sobbing hysterically, as her mother was wheeled into an ambulance, the girl had cried out, "I hate this city."

The manhunt for the two armed robbers became a top priority for the NYPD. Police linked them to a string of Upper East Side stickups the previous winter, targeting well-heeled women. Casing upscale restaurants, the robbers tailed their victims, then forced them to turn over their diamond rings and other jewelry on the street, in the lobbies of buildings, in a private club, even in the stall of a women's room. As at Vera Wang, the robbers had not hesitated to use force at the slightest sign of resistance.

After three months of dead ends, detectives caught a break, although their sloppiness nearly cost them the evidence. In late June, the gunman and his partner held up a couple from Texas as they entered the lobby of the Peninsular Hotel on Fifth Avenue and 55th Street. When precinct detectives failed to immediately question the couple, a friend of theirs called an officer on Bratton's staff, mentioning that one of the robbers had pulled a silver revolver. Bratton's detectives rushed to the hotel to examine the surveillance camera in the lobby. They were lucky to have arrived in time as the surveillance tape automatically recorded over itself every forty-eight hours. Discovering the silver revolver on the tape, they recognized the person holding it as thirty-eight-year-old Randy Caggiano, who had served seven years in prison for the murder of his brother. Two weeks later, an anonymous tip led police to a Queens pool hall, where detectives arrested him and his partner, thirty-nine-year-old Robert Segal. Both were convicted in the robbery.

The police department always trumpets high-profile arrests, and the Vera Wang case was a natural for its full-court press conference treatment. Miller scheduled it for late Saturday afternoon, the day after the arrests were made. Problem was, he could not reach Giuliani. Rudy, a passionate Yankee fan, was at Yankee Stadium with Lategano and other staffers, but no one was answering Miller's pages. In New York to identify the suspects, the Schaeffers had let Miller talk them into appearing before the cameras. But they were growing restless. They wanted to return home. It would be impossible to delay the news conference indefinitely.

As more reporters and camera crews arrived at Police Plaza, Miller kept trying to raise someone on Giuliani's staff. By the time he made contact, it was just fifteen minutes until start time—too short a time for Giuliani to make it downtown from the Bronx. After some back-and-forthing on the telephone, Miller and Bratton began the news conference without him.

Later that evening, Miller received an SOS from Giuliani's counsel Denny Young, summoning him to Gracie Mansion, the mayor's official residence on the Upper East Side. Miller braced himself for a dressing-down but maintained a poker face during the drive uptown. Said Detective Jimmy Motto, who drove him, "John was the kind of guy who believed in never letting anyone see you sweat."

Young was waiting for them on the mansion's back porch. He urged Miller to apologize and forget trying to explain the communications breakdown. "Please," Young said, "I know some of this may be true. But I wouldn't argue with the mayor about this. He's very angry. I would just say, 'Sir, it went wrong and it's not going to happen again.'"

Miller knew Young better than he knew the mayor. He considered him one of the saner people on Giuliani's staff. At least he listened when you talked to him. But what he was saying now made no sense. City Hall's communications system was supposed to be maintained so that the mayor could be reached at all times. While ostensibly meant to defuse Giuliani's anger, Young's advice sounded like a bureaucratic cover-up for a staff blunder.

Minutes later, the mayor arrived. Motto saw him slam his car door and heard him shout, "Where's Miller?" Whatever explanation Miller offered, Motto realized Miller was in for a rough time.

Motto ran inside the mansion through the kitchen to warn him. But he was too late. The mayor had gone around the front and was already screaming at Miller, "What the fuck happened?"

For once, the loquacious Miller found himself at a loss for words. He didn't want to blame the mayor's staff for not answering their pagers. He was especially protective of Lategano, who was spending much of the summer with him at his beach house at the end of Long Island. Giuliani harangued him about the importance of solving the Vera Wang case, how the arrests were vital to improving the city's image, and how he as mayor had a right and a duty to announce the good news. In a harbinger of the trouble to come, the mayor said to Miller, "I have the distinct impression that someone over there is putting someone else's agenda ahead of mine."

ii.

To synchronize their agendas, Bratton's and Giuliani's staffs began meeting weekly. Every Thursday afternoon, Bratton and his crew—Timoney, Maple, La-Porte, and Miller—would troop across Police Plaza to City Hall. There they would engage Giuliani and *his* crew—Powers, Denny Young, and Lategano. The meetings came to be known as the "One-on-One." Ostensibly, they were to discuss Giuliani's and Bratton's war on crime. Instead, they became staff free-for-alls. The One-on-One had been constructed so that Bratton and Giuliani never confronted each other. As their relationship deteriorated, this arrangement allowed each to say disingenuously, "There was never a cross word between us."

A visionary in fighting crime, Bratton was myopic in dealing with Giuliani. At the One-on-One, he gave Miller and LaPorte, his thirty-year-old chief-of-staff, specific assignments. Of LaPorte, who was dating Giuliani's secretary, Bratton said, "He was my shield against the mind-numbing games and machinations continually flowing out of the Hall." He assigned LaPorte to "neutralize" Powers and Denny Young, men twenty years his senior.

Miller's assignment was to neutralize Lategano. Lategano may have lacked a journalism degree, but she proved more than Miller's equal. Indeed, her résumé before joining the mayor's staff was thin. A Rutgers College graduate, she had worked a year in Washington at the Republican National Committee and as a spokeswoman for a Maryland congresswoman before joining Giuliani's mayoral campaign as a press assistant. Saucy and stylish, with cascading shoulder-length hair, she compensated for her lack of experience by her enthusiasm, long work hours, and devotion to Giuliani. So confident in her was the mayor that in his first week in office following the Harlem mosque incident, he had had her read Miller the riot act for Bratton's front-page spread in the *Daily News.*

To Giuliani, it didn't matter that Bratton created the successful anticrime strategies, such as zero tolerance or Compstat. Giuliani wanted top billing. But was this so unreasonable for a politician? Was it so different from any politician who worries about reelection, especially as a Republican in a Democratic town? In his autobiography, however, Bratton sounded slighted that Giuliani wanted to be seen as the city's savior and wanted *him* to be seen as his subordinate. "No matter who created the concepts or was going to run the operation," he wrote, "the public unveiling of any and all police strategies had to come from the mayor."

Bratton was also piqued that Giuliani wanted to control the timing and publicity of his new and innovative police strategies. Bratton's auto theft strategy—his plan to aid gypsy taxi drivers who were the victims of robberies—was ready for months before City Hall allowed him to schedule a press conference to announce its launch. Ditto his gun control strategy. As for his drug strategy, the mayor delayed it for more than a year, only green-lighting it when he forced Bratton from office.

Bratton further complained that City Hall forbade him from trumpeting his greatest success—the 1994 crime statistics. The year-end figures had come in, and they were impressive: overall crime down by 12.3 percent; shootings down by 16.4 percent; murders down 18.8 percent, which he claimed was the largest decrease in history, with 385 fewer victims than the previous year. Robberies were down approximately 10,000. Car thefts had declined 14 percent; burglaries 9 percent, to the lowest in twenty-five years.

But Giuliani could not prevent Bratton from leaking stories to the newspapers, especially *The New York Times*. Bratton viewed the *Times*, the paper of record with its national audience, as his ideal platform. Of the paper he had "intended to marry," he wrote, "I wanted the paper of record to tell our story, and I went out of my way to make the *Times* understand what we were doing." A result was the 2,225-word piece on November 19 by its police bureau chief Clifford Krauss that ran under the headline, "Bratton Builds His Image as He Rebuilds the Police." As Bratton proudly noted, the article "ran almost a full page inside and was both a profile of me and my team."

Top police brass, police commissioners included, are bureaucrats, not rebels. They accept and obey the dictates of City Hall. Not Bratton. He and his crew made fun of City Hall, calling it, "the black hole of law enforcement." So painful had the weekly One-on-One become that Miller devised a joke—to rank how many phone books they should wear under their pants to cushion the blows. A reprimand by the mayor's staff was a "white page" meeting. A complete dressing-down ranked as a "double phone book" or a "yellow and white page" meeting.

Maple hypothesized the mayor was overcompensating for his childhood. He suggested that schoolyard bullies had probably picked on the overweight and nonathletic Giuliani. Said Maple: "Rudy was the kid whose lunch money I used to steal."

Maple meant to be amusing, but I'd long wondered about Giuliani's childhood. In his book *Rudy! An Investigative Biography*, journalist Wayne Barrett discovered that Giuliani's father, Harold, had been a mob enforcer and served time in prison for armed robbery. He was said to be a leg breaker, a violent man, who, according to an account in *Newsweek*, thanked Rudy's teacher at Bishop Loughlin Memorial High School for slugging his son to keep him in line. Although Giuliani has had only praise for his father in public, one has to wonder what went on inside his childhood home.

iii.

By overshadowing Giuliani, Bratton sabotaged both his police reforms and himself. As obvious as this was to everyone else, Bratton never publicly acknowledged it. Years later, after he had left New York and moved to Los Angeles to become its police chief, I asked him whether, in retrospect, he felt any responsibility for his rift with Giuliani. He said he didn't. Of Giuliani's attempts to manage the police department and control its publicity, Bratton said, "I just don't operate that way." That ended our discussion.

Indeed, when it came to publicity, Bratton seemed unable to restrain himself. By the fall of 1994, he focused on preparing to celebrate the 150th anniversary of the NYPD the following October. He planned a ticker-tape "police parade," led by himself and the mayor.

Giuliani had gone along, until he discovered that the date Bratton had selected for the parade — Saturday, October 6 — happened to fall on Bratton's forty-eighth birthday. Bratton had neglected to tell the mayor but could not shut his mouth before the cameras. Interviewed on a television talk show, he announced that he was going to have "one of the biggest birthday celebrations in history."

When that quote appeared in "The Confidential," Giuliani retaliated. Just as Bratton had never informed him about his birthday coincidence, Giuliani never informed Bratton the parade was history. Instead, it was Lategano who leaked the news that the mayor had canceled it. When Miller telephoned her to protest, they began to argue. "The mayor got on the phone and screamed at Miller for criticizing Lategano, then hung up on him," Bratton related in his autobiography. "Peter Powers called back to warn Miller he was in trouble, he'd better watch himself."

Still, Bratton didn't get it. Or if he did, he didn't care. He tried to rebound with another big idea. This one was Maple's brainstorm. To capitalize on their success fighting drugs, Maple wanted to move 10,000 cops—a quarter of the force—into the Narcotics Division. Maple argued that this wasn't as far-fetched as it appeared. If 30 percent of the city's crimes were drug-related, why were only 1,600 officers— or 4 percent of the force—in narcotics? Maple called his plan "the Surge." But the 10,000-man transfer was too radical even for Bratton. He had Maple scale it down, to a borough at a time. They selected Queens. Eight hundred cops would pour into the Narcotics Bureau there to jump-start 1995. Bratton and Maple became so excited they renamed the plan "the Normandy Invasion."

In December, Bratton tried to sell his invasion to Giuliani by staging a two-hour multimedia, Compstat-like presentation. He set up Compstat's eighth-floor command center, amid its banks of TV monitors and computer screens. Maple and Anemone began the program with a review of the city's narcotics history and the NYPD's response. They showed a war movie interspliced with scenes of drug use to a background of stirring music. Images of cops flashed across the screen, breaking down drug-den doors and leading away perps in handcuffs. Then the screen switched to pictures of New Yorkers walking along clean streets amid men and women wearing NYPD windbreakers. In a follow-up presentation at City Hall, Maple brought maps and charts, and he and Bratton plotted an attack plan for the city. By then "the Normandy Invasion" didn't sound grandiose enough. Bratton and Maple renamed it Operation Juggernaut.

Again the mayor went along—until the details of Operation Juggernaut appeared on page one of the *Daily News*. Even that leak might not have squashed the plan because it had merit. But the *News*'s headline sealed its doom, proclaiming in bold letters "Bratton's Juggernaut." Worse, Bratton's picture filled a quarter of the page. So ended Operation Juggernaut, at least for the time being. Bratton had outflanked Giuliani, then Giuliani outflanked Bratton. Their personal antagonism had trumped effective policing.

Operation Juggernaut would have its day. But not under Bratton.

iv.

By early 1995, relations between Bratton and Giuliani had become so strained that even Timoney's promotion to first deputy degenerated into a confrontation. Again, control over publicity destroyed what should have been a celebration. Timoney and a half dozen of the top brass arrived at City Hall for the ceremony. As was customary, he entered the mayor's office to thank Giuliani and pose for pictures. He then walked into the Blue Room, where Giuliani and Bratton formally announced his promotion to the media.

The trouble began after the ceremony had ended. As Timoney started to leave, the Associated Press's veteran City Hall bureau chief, Jack Shanahan, approached, saying, "Chief, can I ask you something? You epitomize the police department. What will it feel like to take off the uniform?" A promotion to first deputy meant that Timoney would be a civilian member of the force for the first time.

Timoney returned to the podium. "I love the uniform," he began. "A year and a half ago, I was a one-star deputy chief. To get the four-star chief rank and now first deputy, it's a pretty heavy experience and I am grateful to Commissioner Bratton for it." With that he left the room, returned to the mayor's office, thanked Giuliani again, and walked back to Police Plaza. There he bumped into LaPorte. He, too, had attended the ceremony.

"Did you feel an edge in the room?" LaPorte asked. "I was watching Cristyne. She didn't seem pleased."

Timoney had no idea what LaPorte was talking about. He had no idea anything was wrong. Preoccupied by the keynote speech he was to give that night at a formal dinner of the Friendly Sons of St. Patrick, an Irish fraternal organization, he rushed to his office to shower. (A perk of the chief of department is a private shower.) Then the phone rang.

"It's Denny Young," Timoney's assistant called to him. "He wants to talk to you."

"Tell him I'm in the shower," Timoney shouted back. "I'll call him back."

"He wants to talk to you now."

"Tell him I'll call him back."

Timoney put on his tuxedo, cummerbund, and a red bow tie. Then he called Denny Young. "We have a problem," Denny said. "You made a faux pas."

"I what?"

"You didn't thank the mayor."

"What do you mean I didn't thank the mayor? I shook his hand. I thanked him before the news conference in his office. I thanked him after the news conference."

"But when the guy stopped you and you went back to the microphone, you thanked Bratton. You didn't thank the mayor. That is serious. You have to come over to City Hall now."

"Well, that is not happening. I can come by after my speech."

"Hold on," said Young. A moment later he was back. "What time is your speech over?"

"Nine thirty, ten o'clock."

"Okay," said Young. "Come to Gracie Mansion."

Timoney called Bratton to alert him. He was having dinner with Miller and Maple at Campagnola, another of their Upper East Side haunts. "Stop by and we'll talk," said Bratton. "I'll ride up there with you."

Arriving at the mansion, they were ushered by the mayor's security detail to the basement. They sat down at a table. Young and Powers joined them.

"You didn't thank the guy who gave you the job," Powers began.

"I thanked him and shook his hand before the press conference," Timoney said. "I thanked him and shook his hand after the press conference."

"Yes, but when the TV cameras were on, you didn't do it."

"What are you, nuts?" said Timoney.

"You don't understand," said Powers. He and Timoney were friendly. Of all the mayor's staffers, Timoney felt most comfortable with him. "We all owe our jobs to him," Powers continued. "You didn't thank him in front of the press."

"Are you people all crazy?" Timoney shouted. Then Bratton jumped in, like a manager protecting his player. "I resent your reaching out to my first deputy and bringing him up here behind my back," Bratton said.

"We've already had this conversation," Powers shot back. He was referring to their confrontation a year ago after the mosque standoff, Bratton's first week as police commissioner. A year later, the issue still burned.

The four of them went at it. "The idea that they would try to intimidate my most powerful aide was more than a little troubling," Bratton would write years later. "This was clearly a broadside at my authority."

Young tried to act as peacemaker. "I'm glad we got to iron this out," he said. "Iron what out?" said Timoney. "You people *are* all crazy."

v.

For Timoney, it only grew worse. Next time, it involved Giuliani directly. That conflict erupted over the volunteer Hatzolah ambulance service, which served the city's Hasidic community and used private station wagons as ambulances. Because the Orthodox Jewish community had political clout, Hatzolah had lobbied for legislation recognizing their station wagons as licensed emergency vehicles. This would allow them to use lights and sirens and speed through red lights.

But the police department was already fed up with Hatzolah and refused to license them. Just months before, Mike Julian, then a newly appointed three-star chief, had chased a speeding Hatzolah station wagon, siren blaring at twice the decibel level of licensed ambulances. The ambulance had blown through red lights all the way from Manhattan into Brooklyn. The driver also failed to pay the toll at the Brooklyn Battery tunnel, then shot onto the Gowanus Expressway, into the Prospect Expressway, exiting at Church Avenue in Borough Park, a Hasidic enclave. There he ignored four more red lights. Making a sudden U-turn, he pulled to the curb and ran up the steps of a house. Julian called a patrol supervisor, ordering him to knock on the door and arrest the driver for reckless endangerment. The driver argued he had done nothing wrong—that he had sped home to care for his sick child. The truth, as Julian learned, was that the driver had argued with his wife and rushed home to confront her. Later that night, Julian received a telephone call from a local rabbi he knew. The rabbi told Julian he would handle the incident if the matter ended there. Julian refused. Instead, he confiscated the driver's vehicle's license plate.

Because Giuliani had ties to the Orthodox Jewish community, Hatzolah had begun pressuring him to change the police department's ban on their licensing. At the One-on-One, Denny Young and Giuliani's chief of staff Randy Mastro tried to change Timoney's mind.

"They've been a headache since day one," Timoney responded. "They blow lights, their sirens are twice as loud as licensed ambulances and fire trucks, and they have caused tensions in the neighboring black communities. Licensing Hatzolah would make them a law unto themselves."

"The mayor is very concerned about this," said Young. "The state's director of motor vehicles has written an opinion stating these station wagons are classified as ambulances."

"Fine," said Timoney. "Let the director of motor vehicles license them!"

For weeks they went back and forth. Finally, they told Timoney the mayor wanted to see him—on a Sunday afternoon at City Hall. That also infuriated Timoney. They had chosen Sunday afternoon, he thought, just to break his chops, as if none of them had a life outside Rudy. To ensure they weren't trapping him over a legal issue, Timoney brought along the department's counsel, George Grasso. But before they saw the mayor, Young and Mastro intercepted them. They asked Timoney if he had changed his mind.

"No way," he said.

They all sat down inside the mayor's office. "Mr. Mayor, you've got to trust me on this," Timoney began, deciding to preempt Young and Mastro. He risked irritating Giuliani, but Timoney wasn't about to let others sway the mayor. "The department is your best friend on this issue," he continued. "Licensing Hatzolah can only hurt you."

When Timoney finished, the mayor turned to Young and Mastro. "I think I agree with John on this," he said. For a moment Timoney felt relieved. He had, he felt, quashed a measure that could have damaged both the mayor and the police department. But his relief lasted but a few seconds. He noticed that the mayor was angry, and thought at first Giuliani was angry at Mastro and Young for having placed Giuliani in an embarrassing confrontation. Then Timoney realized the mayor was angry at *him*. Not for what he had said but that he had been unafraid to speak out to Giuliani as an equal. Worse for Timoney, he had done so in front of Giuliani's staff.

"Until then," recalled Timoney, "I had believed that loyalty and hard work would be recognized and rewarded." A year later, he discovered something else: His candor had ended whatever chance he had to succeed Bratton as commissioner of the New York City Police Department.

vi.

A month later the roof fell in on Miller. The underlying cause was Bratton's excessive publicity, for which the mayor blamed Miller. But the proximate cause was something more personal. It involved Miller's relationship with Cristyne Lategano.

After summering at his beach house at the end of Long Island, he and Lategano had trained together for that fall's New York City Marathon. They were close enough that whenever she spotted him at City Hall, she would rush toward him, fling herself into his arms and wrap her legs around him. Bratton's crew laughed themselves silly over these displays of affection because they so upset Giuliani, who watched in silent fury.

But by the end of the year, Miller had cooled toward her. For New Years' Eve, he had another date for dinner, then continued on to Times Square with Bratton and his wife, Cheryl Fiandaca, and Maple and his inamorata, Transit Lieutenant Brigid O'Connor. "The word was already out around City Hall that Cristyne wanted more from John," said longtime City Hall spokesman, Tom Kelly, then of the Department of Correction.

But Lategano was not to be left easily. Two days before Christmas, she again leapt into Miller's arms. This time she did it inside the City Hall rotunda in front of Giuliani. Miller played into it, spinning her in the air twice around before setting her down a few feet from the mayor.

Kelly happened to walk into the rotunda as "the Famous Embrace," as *Vanity Fair* writer Jennet Conant called it, was ending. As Kelly put it, "I arrived for the dismount." Returning to his office at the Correction Department, he told his assistant, Tom Antenen, that Miller had to be out of his mind. "I said this guy will soon be out of work. Everybody knew, or thought, that Giuliani and Cristyne were very friendly. Compound that with the fact that what Miller did was totally inappropriate. You don't do that in City Hall. A returning war hero may get a woman to do that, but not a deputy police commissioner, and not in front of the mayor."

Kelly also found himself wondering about something else. By instigating the embrace, was Lategano getting back at Miller? With their breakup imminent, was she trying to get him in trouble with the mayor? "I wondered," Kelly said. "Was her embrace as fresh and innocent as it seemed, or was it a calculated move?"

Kelly, who had served as Koch's deputy press secretary and was valued enough that he had managed to remain in city government under both Dinkins and Giuliani, knew how Lategano operated—specifically, how she affected the mayor. "If Cristyne liked you, if she explained something to the mayor with a smile, he would accept it. If she phrased it in another way . . ." He knew this from personal experience. After he had a run-in with her, the mayor had ignored him for days. "He acted like he didn't even see me, even when I was standing next to him. It was like I was dead."

Her leaping into Miller's arms, Kelly suspected, had been no innocent, loving gesture. To him, it looked like a woman trying to make another man jealous. "She knew," said Kelly, "that this was going to sink Miller."

Lategano was shrewd enough to sense something else: Sinking Miller played into Giuliani's agenda. It might also lead to sinking Bratton.

vii.

The fuse was lighted two months later, in February 1995, when James Lardner's profile of Bratton appeared in the February 6 issue of *The New Yorker*. Titled "The C.E.O. Cop," the article praised Giuliani but made a star of Bratton. Lardner, whom Bratton had allowed to follow him around for months, inadvertently struck the match when he observed that morale among the police had soared. "Their feeling," he wrote, "is partly due to the election of Giuliani, the city's first mayor in four decades with a law enforcement background. . . . But Bratton himself may be a bigger factor." The city's police officers, he continued, "have nothing but good things to say about him—an unprecedented phenomenon in the modern history of this chronically disgruntled organization."

Just a few days after the magazine article appeared, the mayor struck. Bratton was too popular for a frontal attack. Instead, Giuliani attacked his flank—Miller. And he tapped an eager Lategano to do his dirty work. Behind Giuliani's in-your-face tough talk was a cunning Machiavelli.

At City Hall, Lategano announced to reporters that Miller's press office suffered from "bloat." The public, she said, would be better served if DCPI's cops were out on the street and their jobs performed by civilians. I imagined her satisfaction. The ingénue was publicly insulting her ex-boyfriend-tutor who had dumped her.

Giuliani gave Miller an ultimatum. Denny Young conveyed it to Bratton's chief of staff LaPorte. Miller had to fire his entire thirty-five-person staff by sundown. Furthermore, the mayor demanded a list of everyone in the office and where each of them would be assigned. Miller would be allowed to have a new press staff of only seventeen—one less than the mayor's.

Bratton sent Timoney over to City Hall to stop the massacre. "We're talking about people's careers here," Timoney told Giuliani officials. "These are loyal cops. You're not just going to dump them out somewhere. That's not how we do business here." I could testify to how loyal some of them were. I had known Sergeant John Clifford and Captain Tom Fahey—both of whom had returned to DCPI under Miller—since they had worked for Alice McGillion more than ten years earlier. Fahey had two daughters who were police officers.

At one point Timoney met with Giuliani's chief of staff Randy Mastro but got nowhere. "There's nothing more to talk about," Mastro told a fuming Timoney, who stormed out.

Bratton, too, saw where this was going. On Friday morning, February 10, he called a meeting in his office on the fourteenth floor of his top staff—Timoney, Maple, LaPorte, and Miller. "If they push this Miller thing, I'm going to resign," he said, according to his autobiography. "I'm not going to take this. I run this department."

"We should all resign," said Timoney. "We should go over to City Hall en masse and resign." Their plan called for all five of them—Bratton, Miller, Timoney, LaPorte, and Maple—to walk across to City Hall and resign together. Timoney's willingness to join Bratton when viewed as his heir apparent further cemented their friendship. They had not even known each other when Bratton became commissioner a year before. Here, Timoney was willing to give up his career for him. LaPorte got on the phone with his contacts at City Hall. They told him the mayor would be more than willing to accept Bratton's resignation. He had even selected a replacement: Howard Safir, the city's fire commissioner and a former federal marshal whom Giuliani had known from his days as a federal prosecutor in Washington.

It was then that Miller slipped out of the meeting. Without a word, he walked down a flight of stairs to his office below on the thirteenth floor and summoned the in-house press from the Shack. He said he had an important announcement. He also called the city's all-news cable television station, New

York 1. With the reporters assembled and New York 1's camera rolling, Miller announced he was resigning as Bratton's spokesman.

He began by attacking City Hall. "They said that because of what's been in the papers, the people here couldn't be trusted," Miller said. "They were going to ask me to throw everybody out of here. Now loyalty is important. I'm loyal to the mayor. I'm loyal to the police commissioner. But there were loyal Nazis too. So what do they say: the captain is supposed to go down with the ship?" Here Miller's voice broke.

Watching him, I couldn't believe what I was seeing. I couldn't believe what I was hearing. Miller was publicly comparing Giuliani's staff to the Nazis. He was implicitly comparing the mayor to Hitler. "So I'm not moving the cops out to downsize the office," he continued, "and I'm not moving the others out to go along with this ridiculous request based on somebody's idea of what loyalty's about. I'm not moving anybody out. I assume they will come for my badge and they can have it. I think I work for the greatest police commissioner there ever was. I want to thank the police commissioner for giving me the greatest year, or fourteen months, of my life." With that he broke down again. He then left the room and walked back upstairs to Bratton's office.

There, stupefied, the others had watched him resign on television. In his fevered state, Timoney said, "They're going to be showing this in journalism school for the next hundred years." Bratton, more somberly, realized what Miller had done. He had demonstrated his loyalty, sacrificing himself to stop them from all resigning. He had fallen on his sword to save them.

viii.

Two weeks later, Giuliani turned up the heat. Having gotten rid of Miller, he went after Bratton. Again he tapped the eager Lategano. Alerted that something was up at City Hall, I wandered over from One Police Plaza. There, in the rotunda, surrounded by reporters, she stood. With no preamble, she began railing to all within earshot about Bratton.

"Public relations was put before any kind of substance," she began. "When you put glamour over fighting crime, it leads to serious problems. . . . Now it is the time to get serious. This is a reality check."

Incredible, I found myself thinking again. Giuliani was having his press secretary publicly attack his best-known and most successful appointment.

"We're here to fight crime, not to be Hollywood stars," she continued. "This is real-life cops, not *NYPD Blue*. This job is not a stepping-stone to something later in life. If police officers would rather be on TV or on the covers of magazines instead of fighting crime, then their priorities need to be straightened out."

That was quite a mouthful from a thirty-year-old, and one with virtually no experience in government. Her theme was clear enough. Public relations before substance: *NYPD Blue*, Hollywood stars, the covers of magazines, the latter, I suspected, an elliptical reference to Bratton's profile in *The New Yorker*. I was certain Giuliani had been infuriated by the article's line that Bratton was more important than he was in the NYPD firmament.

Later, Lategano would maintain Giuliani had never read the *New Yorker* profile. I doubted it, although she sounded a list of grievances toward Bratton that had been accumulated long before the article. Although I looked askance at Giuliani's methods of revenge, I could appreciate his resentment. Whatever Bratton's success in turning around the NYPD, he could not have achieved it without Giuliani. Without Giuliani's imprimatur, there would have been no all-out fight on crime—no jettisoning of community policing and the anticorruption priorities of the Knapp Commission that enabled uniformed patrol officers to go after drug dealers. Even Timoney's remarks at his promotion ceremony to first deputy—that for the first time in his twenty-eight years as a police officer, the NYPD's top priority was fighting crime—were a testament to Giuliani. Yet the *New Yorker* article, the first major story in a national magazine about the NYPD's turnaround, had praised only Bratton. Once again, Bratton had outmaneuvered him. He had allowed the writer to follow him around for nine months— a neat trick if he had kept it from the mayor. And a neater one if he had obtained the mayor's permission.

At the same time, I asked myself yet again, why was Giuliani unable to share credit? Why, as Mayor Koch would suggest, was he incapable of stepping back and basking in Bratton's reflected glory. What character flaw prevented him from doing so? What was it about Bratton that made Giuliani crazed with jealousy—so much so that he was willing, as in the case of Operation Juggernaut, to sabotage his own policies?

Lategano soldiered on, telling reporters that the rules of engagement at Police

Plaza were now changed. Bratton, she said, would no longer be able to call news conferences at whim—no more Vera Wangs. Now he would have to clear all news conferences with City Hall. He "will be permitted to hold 'in-house' press briefings at One Police Plaza," she continued, referring to his informal meetings with the Shack's reporters. "He doesn't have to clear *that* with the mayor."

But, she said, Bratton could no longer hold other kinds of press conferences. "All interagency press conferences and the release of strategy position papers will be done out of City Hall. That was always past policy—policies that were in place," she maintained, though how seriously anyone at City Hall took them was open to question. She added pointedly, those rules "were not adhered to and not respected."

There was a final indignity, but this one Lategano didn't announce. It was rumored that Giuliani had warned Bratton to stay out of Elaine's. Both Giuliani and Bratton denied the mayor had done so and Bratton said he had no intention of avoiding his favorite restaurant. Later that month, he, Maple, Miller, and La-Porte celebrated his Cheryl's birthday there. Soon after her penne arrived, so did the newspaper photographers.

It was Lategano, parted forever from Miller and now in another man's orbit, who no longer dined there.

ix.

Lategano's public tongue-lashing of Bratton drew a retort from another quarter—Ed Koch. "You cannot have people around the mayor embarrass your police commissioner in public," Koch said. "His press secretary does not have the right or responsibility to publicly chastise the police commissioner. To humble, to seek to humble the police commissioner is to me incredible." Koch said he was concerned enough about Giuliani's attack on Bratton that he wanted to amend a bet he had made, that Bratton would resign by the year's end. Now, said Koch, he was betting Bratton would leave "long before the end of the year."

"It looks like Rudy is driving him out," Koch added. "Whether intentionally or not, it's having that effect. Bratton is a proud and able man who's done a wonderful job. I cannot believe he will accept micromanagement from City Hall for any length of time." Giuliani didn't seem to care. Koch told his former press secretary George Arzt that when he asked the mayor who would run the police department if Bratton resigned, Giuliani answered, "I will."

But Bratton did not resign. Unlike Miller, who joined ABC and went on to famously interview Osama bin Laden in Afghanistan before 9/11, Bratton had no other job offer. In New York only a year, he had limited contacts. Indeed, it would be a brave New Yorker willing to incur Giuliani's wrath by hiring him.

More important, Bratton had no savings. In Boston, his peripatetic existence, including two moves to New York, had cost him his Bay State pension. There were no offers back home in Massachusetts. With his crack that the Boston Police Department was a "consolation prize," he had burned his bridges. In short, he was in no position to resign. He couldn't afford to.

So he hung on, under even tighter City Hall strictures. Now he could not even pick his own spokesman. The mayor announced he sought approval over Miller's replacement. "Bratton will make proposals to me," Giuliani said. "If we don't agree, we'll look for a different person. That's the way it's traditionally been."

Again, Koch spoke up for Bratton. "The idea that he [the mayor] decides on a press secretary for his police commissioner is ridiculous," Koch said. "The NYPD is a special agency. The police commissioner should have the final decision." Koch cited Alice McGillion. She had been a former press aide to Koch's rival, Mario Cuomo, but she had been the choice of Koch's first police commissioner, Robert McGuire, to head DCPI. "I wouldn't have hired her myself," Koch said, "but I didn't stop McGuire." Nor did Koch interfere when McGuire's successor, Ben Ward, decided to keep her. "He and I never even talked about it," Koch said. "It never came up."

To replace Miller, Bratton again turned to Al O'Leary of the Transit Police, whom he had tried to hire before Miller. Again, the mayor vetoed him. No longtime friend of Bratton was getting that job. Instead, the mayor settled for the City Hall veteran Tom Kelly, whose credentials no one could question. Kelly knew and loved the NYPD. After graduating from Newtown High in Queens, he had applied to become a cop but was rejected because of stomach problems. He figured if he couldn't become one, he could at least write about them. So he became a reporter, working seventeen years at the Associated Press, before joining Koch as his deputy press secretary.

At City Hall, Kelly specialized in law enforcement issues. He had been the first mayoral official to arrive at the Palm Sunday Massacre that rainy night in

1984, and it was he who had tried to explain away to me Ward's absence with the bizarre observation, "*You* say he was unreachable. We don't." Even mouthing such nonsense, he kept a straight face. He was only following orders.

Kelly had been the Correction Department's spokesman when Giuliani tapped him for the DCPI job. Giuliani had done so, Kelly believed, on the recommendation of the newly appointed deputy correction commissioner, a third-grade police detective who, while off duty, had chauffeured and guarded Giuliani during his mayoral campaign—Bernard Kerik. "I wouldn't have ended up there at the NYPD if not for him," Kelly said.

Kelly had had no idea of Kerik's importance when Kerik joined the Department of Correction in the summer of 1994, but he soon found out. Kelly had been there just two weeks when he received a call from reporter Dan Janison of the *New York Post.* The Correction Department had conducted a sweep of the city's jails and come up with scores of weapons. Kelly asked the correction commissioner, Tony Schembri, whether that was true. Schembri told him it was.

"'Okay,' I said to Schembri," Kelly recalled. "'You have to be careful. When you speak to Janison, you have to tell him you knew all about it, that you weren't surprised, got it?' 'I got it,' he says." Kelly got Janison on the phone. "The next thing I know, Schembri is telling him how shocked he was at the amount of weapons they had recovered." Kelly couldn't believe it. Well, he thought, I can only do what I can do.

The day the *Post* story hit, the mayor's office called. "They were furious. They were screaming at me, 'How can you be so stupid? We put you over there because of all your experience.' Well, that call rattled me. I was convinced it was my last day, that I would be out of work." Then Kerik entered. He had been with Schembri when Kelly had told Schembri what to say. "Did you explain to the mayor what happened?" Kerik asked Kelly. Kelly told Kerik he hadn't had a chance.

"A half hour later, I get another call from Denny Young," Kelly continued. "He said, 'Don't worry about it,' that I should have spoken up. As I was on the phone, Kerik came in. It dawned on me he must have said something to the mayor. 'Holy fuck, did you call the mayor?' I said to him. He just smiled. He stood there with this look. That's when I realized he was someone special."

While not his choice, Bratton warmed to Kelly, who also had Timoney's backing. As it turned out, it was a wise choice, as Kelly helped prolong Bratton's stay. Unlike Miller, he would not become Bratton's crony. As Bratton's first choice, O'Leary, said of Kelly, "There was less testosterone and more reality."

Having orchestrated his appointment, Giuliani nonetheless feared Kelly might become a Bratton ally. The mayor's insecurity was apparent at the City Hall news conference announcing his appointment. After Bratton expressed delight in having Kelly as his new deputy commissioner for public information, the mayor returned to the microphone and announced that Kelly was only going to be the acting deputy commissioner. After the news conference, Bratton asked Kelly, "Did the mayor mention anything to you about being an 'acting'?"

"No, he didn't," Kelly said.

Bratton laughed. "He didn't mention it to me either."

"Nobody talked to me because I was perceived as Giuliani's guy," Kelly said of his first week at Police Plaza. "Then Bratton held a meeting to say I was his pick and that Timoney had recommended me. That broke the ice."

Kelly discovered some unexpected allies: chiefs who resented Miller for sticking his nose into their departments. "Some of the bosses Miller had alienated started coming to my office," said Kelly. The chiefs appreciated something else. Unlike Miller, Kelly acted like a civilian and didn't carry a gun.

Still, Kelly was presiding over a diminished operation. Not only was he working for a police commissioner Giuliani had embarrassed, but Lategano was now importing untrained civilians from City Hall to work in DCPI. No one knew their qualifications, how they were selected, or where their loyalties lay—whether to the department or to the mayor. With the transfer of DCPI's entire staff—some, like Fahey or Clifford, with institutional memory and histories of dealing with reporters and editors—who would teach the newcomers the job?

These difficulties became apparent with Lategano's first appointee, twenty-eight-year-old Bradford Billet. Billet had been the chief financial officer for his family's oil and gas-exploration company, where, according to his résumé, his job had been to "negotiate multi-million-dollar contracts with the USSR and West African countries." He had also made two minor contributions totaling $285 to Giuliani's 1993 election campaign. For reasons I couldn't fathom, he had given up his lofty-sounding job and joined the Giuliani administration as a $69,000-a-year associate executive director at the city's Emergency Medical Services.

Why Lategano had transferred him from EMS to Police Plaza, I didn't know, either. After spending his first morning puttering about DCPI's thirteenth-floor office, he skipped out to the department's first-floor auditorium for its annual Irish heritage celebration, where the mayor was speaking, and plopped himself down in a first-row seat next to Lategano. As the mayor described the sacred legacy of Irish-American police officers who had risked their lives and made the ultimate sacrifice to protect the city, Bradford joked and fidgeted. LaPorte saw him acting like a two-year-old. After the ceremony, he yanked Billet away, thwarting my attempt to interview DCPI's newest member.

A few minutes later, LaPorte returned, red-faced and shaken. "I just chewed that guy's ass out," he said. "I was sitting right behind him during the ceremony. I didn't know who he was, but I saw he was bored with it. He was making fun of it. They were singing Irish songs and talking about Irish cops killed in the line of duty and he was rolling his eyes. He may not be of that ethnic group but he has an obligation to be respectful. I was shocked and offended at his behavior. I told him he had no business in this building if this is the way he is conducting himself."

The next day, City Hall transferred Bradford Billet back to EMS. He had lasted just two days at DCPI, the shortest career in memory.

x.

Still, City Hall continued to turn up the pressure on Bratton and his staff. When a subway train crashed on the Williamsburg Bridge in June, Kelly, off that day, came in to handle the media. The Transit Authority wanted to hold a news briefing. Kelly checked with City Hall. Told the mayor wasn't coming to the crash site, he went ahead with the briefing. That prompted a furious call from Lategano for not clearing it with her. She later acknowledged to her staff that she had overreacted. But she never called Kelly to apologize.

Still, she had reason to smile. Giuliani had recently promoted her, with a $25,000 raise, to the newly created position of communications director, at a salary of $103,000. Giuliani justified the promotion, saying, "Cristyne has been doing at least two jobs. Since she has been performing both roles so well, it made sense to recognize it with the promotion." Six months later he raised her salary to $123,000.

In her new position, she no longer dealt with reporters but was responsible for what Giuliani described as "developing a communications strategy for the administration." Now responsible for Giuliani's public scheduling, she scheduled herself—"more or less," as she put it—so that she accompanied the mayor to evening functions. She spent so much time with Giuliani, even traveling with him to Israel for a terrorism conference in March 1996, that it appeared she had usurped the position of his closest and oldest confidant, Peter Powers, who then left the administration. When Giuliani's political adviser David Garth warned Giuliani to drop Lategano, Giuliani instead dropped Garth. As Miller related to Jennet Conant in her *Vanity Fair* article, "The Ghost and Mr. Giuliani," in September 1997: "When the smoke clears, I'm dead. Garth is dead. Bratton is dead. Powers is dead. . . . You look at this pile of bodies and Cristyne is still standing."

Appearing so often with the mayor, Lategano also appeared to usurp the position of first lady. Members of Bratton's inner circle clued me into the new realities of the Giuliani household: Giuliani's wife, Donna Hanover, an actress and former television reporter, refused to attend public functions with the mayor if Lategano was within sight. "Check it out," one of them said to me. "When was the last time you saw Donna with the mayor when Cristyne was there?"

And so I did. Admittedly, this was somewhat beyond my police sphere, unless you accepted Giuliani as the de facto police commissioner. I picked up stories of him and Cristyne having late-night dinners at Jim McMullen's restaurant on the East Side, of their traveling together in the back of the mayor's official vehicle, a Chevy suburban SUV with tinted windows. At the King David Hotel in Jerusalem, where Giuliani had stayed at the terrorism conference, a guest spotted her leaving the mayor's room at 2:30 A.M. Saturday afternoons, officials told me the mayor and Lategano could be found in her basement office, which was connected to his, supposedly watching college football.

I was also told that one day, a fed-up Donna went to City Hall. When she arrived, aides made her wait in an office, telling her Giuliani was in a meeting. When he emerged, she was in a rage. Supposedly, it was Bernie Kerik who acted as peacemaker.

Lategano maintained that her relationship with Giuliani was purely professional. "If I were a man who spent all that time with the mayor, you wouldn't be asking these questions," she told me. One need hardly imagine the questions reporters would be asking had a male press secretary been seen leaving Giuliani's hotel room in Jerusalem at two thirty in the morning.

I was hardly the only reporter to note their closeness. In Room 9—City Hall's version of the Shack—their relationship was a source of gossip. Still hardly a word appeared in any newspaper. About the furthest anyone had gone were *Newsday* writers Michael Shain and Tony Scaduto, who reported that she and Giuliani had spent a Sunday shopping for a dress so she could attend an event with him that evening.

Describing their relationship two years later, *Vanity Fair* writer Conant wrote that Giuliani had "all but silenced the irascible New York press corps through intimidation." To me, the New York press corps was less irascible than pliant. But I did agree with her further observation: "Insiders make the point that in New York the presses are owned by businessmen with substantial real estate interests—and they concede that Giuliani is notoriously vindictive."

In June 1995, I wrote a column that described Lategano's growing influence with the mayor. I started with her screaming fit at Kelly over the subway crash press conference on the Williamsburg Bridge and detailed her closeness to Giuliani and her promotion to communications director. Then I wrote the line: "Her promotion also merited a newly converted basement office that is connected to the mayor's office through an inner door." Describing an office renovation provided an outlet for the whispers. Despite their denials, I wondered whether I had outed them with interior design.

xi.

No column I had written created such a stir. Unfortunately, it came as *New York Newsday* was crumbling. Circulation was down, and the publisher had made the mistake of announcing the paper was losing $8 million a year. His candor came amid a shake-up at the company's corporate headquarters in Los Angeles. The new CEO publicly questioned *New York Newsday*'s viability. I made Bratton a bet as to who would last longer in New York City, he or *New York Newsday*. Bratton won, but it was again a Pyrrhic victory. Less than a year later, he, too, would be gone.

In July 1995, a month after my Lategano basement office story, *New York Newsday* announced it was folding, although through a bizarre set of circumstances, it hung on for another decade as a small-scale city edition of a larger Long Island entity. The day of the announcement I received a chilling phone message. "You got what you deserved," said the caller, "for what you wrote about Terry Tunnock." Tunnock was, of course, the captain who had killed himself amid the 30th Precinct scandal. The caller was obviously referring to the headline that had mistakenly implied he had been part of the corruption. No matter that *Newsday* had a run correction as soon as I'd caught it. These were hard times and these were hard people.

Meanwhile, I was preoccupied with a more selfish question, Could "The Confidential" survive? The outlook wasn't promising. The day after *Newsday*'s announcement, I received a call from Art Browne, the *Daily News*'s metropolitan editor, whom I'd known since he'd headed the *News*'s City Hall bureau more than a decade before. I met with him and the *News*'s editor in chief, Martin Dunn, who seemed interested only in my column on Lategano. Neither offered me a job.

Back at Police Plaza, it wasn't going much better. The following week, when I questioned Bratton at an in-house news conference, he answered, "Lenny, now that *New York Newsday* has folded, we don't read you anymore."

When I returned to the Shack, my phone was ringing. It was Tom Kelly. "Bratton didn't mean that," he said. "He was just breaking your balls." Though kind of Kelly, it was small consolation. Later that afternoon, as I walked to City Hall, I happened to pass an empty, locked patrol car parked under the arches of the city's Municipal Building. Glancing inside, I saw a copy of *Newsday* spread across the dashboard. It was opened to "The Confidential." My first thought was to call *Newsday* for a photographer as the picture would make a terrific promotional ad. It took me a moment to realize those days were gone. No one at *Newsday* was interested any longer in promoting the city edition, much less "The Confidential."

xii.

Like me, Bratton was down. Like me, he wasn't ready to quit. Although crippled, he still had fight. He went about his business as though no ill wind were blowing from across the street at City Hall. He seemed oblivious to his living on borrowed time—or maybe he no longer cared. At in-house news conferences, he continued to talk of his successes. The crime drop was so steep that he ruminated out loud about retiring. "I've been very adept at leaving a winner at all the jobs I've ever been in, but I also leave at an appropriate time when the gains have been cemented in," he said. "When I leave, it will be at the top of my form."

Rumors flew he was going to Chemical Bank or Citibank or to Disney/Cap Cities/ABC at a salary of near $500,000. Bratton denied it all but said he liked the sound of the amounts because, each time, his price went up. "They started at $340,000, and last week it was up to $480,000," he said. "When it reaches $1 million I'm gone."

He added that he had no interest in working for the federal government. He knew the Clintons. Bill was then president; Hillary not yet a senator. He also maintained he had no interest in elective office, which, as it turned out, was not completely true. "I want to go out and run companies," he said. "I like making decisions." Of the NYPD he said, "I have a $2.5 billion company here with 40,000 employees. When I leave I don't want to go out as a consultant. I don't want to go out as Joe Blow the security director."

He even began talking up Timoney as his successor, saying that wherever he went, his "number two" followed him. "The practice has been in every department I've been in that my number two has always moved up, with my strong urging and support." That, of course, was nonsense, on the same level as Giuliani's claim that it was his prerogative to select the police commissioner's spokesman. Bratton had never stayed in any job long enough to pick a successor. As for Timoney, Bratton's support was a kiss of death.

Meanwhile, with City Hall proscribing his meetings with the local media, Bratton pitched himself to the international press. "Let the word go forth," LaPorte announced to the *Times*, explaining that he—rather than Tom Kelly—was Bratton's liaison with the national and international community. Bratton's face began appearing in newsmagazines and newspapers and on television in England, Japan, Norway, Italy, and Brazil. Correspondents from China, Hungary, Germany, Switzerland, Portugal, the Netherlands, and Israel all visited the now twice-weekly Compstat meetings, which were also filmed by television crews from *America's Most Wanted*, *Dateline*, and *48 Hours*. In addition, Bratton began hosting officials from around the world, including a Saudi prince. The British magazine *The Economist* said Bratton "has brought a new lexicon to law enforce-ment" and compared him to Theodore Roosevelt. *The Sunday Times* of London wrote: "In a city famous for its murders, muggings, ghetto gunfights, subway anarchy, drug gangs, junkies, rapists, winos, pickpockets and every other form of seething urban desperado, Bratton is turning the tide."

Bratton also hit the road to tout his crime-fighting strategies, making speeches in Boston, Washington, and Bermuda. In London he participated on a panel entitled "The Future of the Cities." Accompanying him was his wife and his Boston-based friend Robert Johnson, who owned a private armed-guard service called First Security Services Corporation. Bratton had recently named him chair-man of an "Integrity and Respect Committee." Why he selected someone from Boston rather than from New York was unclear. Bratton's aides scotched specu-lation Bratton was considering joining Johnson's firm.

He also delivered a paper at a conference of the National Institute of Justice in Washington. He attended a *Business Week* seminar in Palm Springs, Califor-nia, where he was seen schmoozing with its keynote speaker, Colin Powell. He seemed to have a message tailored to each publication. *Business Week*, whose re-porter was treated to a Compstat session, quoted him saying, "I equate profit with reduced crime." The week of the Oklahoma City bombing of a government of-fice, which killed 168 people and injured over 800 and was, until 9/11, the dead-liest act of terrorism on U.S. soil, Bratton was in Orlando, lecturing to the Police Executive Research Forum. Some speculated that in the pre-Giuliani feud days, news of the bombing would have caused Bratton to cut his Florida trip short to return to New York. Some said he should have returned anyway. How did Bratton get away with all his trips? With most jaunts, he waited until the last minute to inform City Hall. *The New York Times* quoted an aide—who sounded like LaPorte—saying, "We don't send things over in a timely fashion."

Bratton and Cheryl also began taking weekend vacations as guests of Wall Street financier Henry Kravis and his wife. He flew away from his problems on the billionaire's private jet to his homes in Colorado and the Dominican Re-public. Did Bratton do so to taunt Giuliani, to show he had a rich and powerful friend in New York City? Was he trying to escape his troubles in the police de-partment? Whatever his reasons, there would be repercussions.

xiii.

Just as *The New Yorker* had hastened Miller's exit, a *Time* article hastened Bratton's. In January 1996, *Time* senior writer Eric Pooley telephoned Tom Kelly with an urgent request. A new editor had been appointed and wanted a "package" on the nation's falling crime rate. He wanted to include a feature on Bratton in New York City. Pooley had just a week to pull the whole thing together.

Pooley knew the NYPD. At his previous job at *New York* magazine, he had spent a month preparing a profile of Ray Kelly. "I was a big fan of Kelly," Pooley said. "I felt he didn't deserve to get canned." He had also covered Giuliani's 1993 mayoral campaign and his first eighteen months at City Hall. In the summer of 1995, after joining *Time*, he had written a tough article about Giuliani for *The Washington Post*. In it he referred to the mayor's "inquisitions" and "politics of aggression." He also quoted Koch, who compared Giuliani to a Frankenstein monster.

Bratton's first reaction to Pooley's call was to ensure that his spokesman, Tom Kelly, alert City Hall. Kelly informed Lategano's first in command, the new press secretary, Colleen Roche, who had come over from Morgenthau's office and who passed the information up the line. "At the beginning," said Kelly, "it seemed like a small story inside *Time* magazine." Nonetheless, he made certain Pooley receive Police Plaza's royal treatment. That meant admittance to a 7:00 A.M. Compstat meeting and a tête-à-tête with the ever-poetic Maple.

"Pooley seemed fascinated. He was asking all sorts of questions," Kelly said. Pooley then requested interviews with Bratton and Giuliani. Again Kelly called over to City Hall. This time he cleared it with Lategano.

Next, *Time* wanted pictures of Bratton and Giuliani. "They were bringing in their own photographer, some hot shot," said Kelly. The story seemed to be getting some life. Kelly arranged a photo shoot the following Friday afternoon on the Brooklyn side of the Brooklyn Bridge, a five-minute drive from Police Plaza and City Hall.

Again, Kelly alerted City Hall. Apparently, the Giuliani interview with another *Time* reporter had not gone well because the mayor's people seemed uninterested in the shoot. As Kelly put it, "They told me the mayor was not that thrilled." By then Pooley had finished his reporting at Police Plaza. Where the story would be placed in the magazine was not his call. But he told Kelly it seemed to be growing.

"I told Bratton and Maple and Timoney, the guy sounds enthusiastic," Kelly said. "I told them, 'Don't be out of touch this weekend. If they have questions, I need to find you.'"

That night Pooley called Kelly again. Depending on what news broke worldwide that week, there was a chance the story might become a cover. Yet again, Kelly alerted City Hall. Again, the mayor's people seemed uninterested.

The photo shoot had been arranged for Friday afternoon at three o'clock. But at one o'clock, Giuliani summoned Bratton, Timoney, and Maple to City Hall. There they sat and sat and sat waiting for the mayor. Kelly, who was beneath the Brooklyn Bridge with the photographer, tried to reach Bratton. "I was trying to get him down to the shoot. Giuliani himself is not doing it. At 3:00 P.M. I call the Hall. Giuliani is keeping Bratton there until dark. We all knew what that was about. This was his way of killing the picture."

Then *Time*'s picture editor telephoned Kelly. "She said she was calling because the shoot hadn't come off by three. She said, 'I don't want to be stuck for a picture if this is the cover.' I assured her she'd get her picture as soon as I could deliver Bratton."

At four o'clock, Kelly called City Hall again. They were still there. Outside, it was freezing and growing dark. He and the photographer had been waiting under the Brooklyn Bridge for hours. At one point the photographer had gathered up his equipment, but Kelly wouldn't let him leave. "We could put yellow tape around your car and say there was a suspicious package inside," he joked. "You could be here for two or three days."

It was nearly five when Giuliani let Bratton go. By the time he reached the Brooklyn side of the bridge, it was dark. They shot the picture under the bridge with Bratton in his trench coat, an icy wind at his back and the lights from a police car and two emergency service trucks flashing against a backdrop of the city skyline and the World Trade Center. Bratton was excited. "If it's a cover, I want you to wake me," he told Kelly. Then he smiled. "If it turns out to be the cover, it will be our asses. We'll all be out of work."

Later, back at Police Plaza, *Time*'s picture editor called Kelly again. If nothing came in over the weekend, she said, Bratton would be the cover.

"If it's the cover, I need to know," Kelly told her. He gave her his home phone number. At 2:00 A.M. Saturday morning, she called him. "It's a go," she said.

And that was how Bratton made the cover of *Time* magazine. There he stood on the January 15 issue. "New York's Commissioner William Bratton," the magazine heralded him. The headline of the story said it all. In capital letters it read: "POLICE COMMISSIONER WILLIAM BRATTON SET OUT TO PROVE THAT COPS REALLY CAN CUT CRIME. THE EXPERTS SCOFFED—BUT FELONY RATES HAVE DROPPED SO FAR, SO FAST, THAT NO OTHER EXPLANATION MAKES SENSE." In a delicious twist of irony, a cover caption in smaller lettering described Bratton as "a leading advocate of community policing."

Afterward, Bratton, Maple, and Timoney asked Kelly what the reaction had been at City Hall. "City Hall never called," Kelly said. Years later, he said, "I didn't worry. I felt comfortable. I had notified the Hall. I had told Lategano. Nobody ever complained."

At least not to him.

xiv.

The mayor never mentioned the *Time* cover to Bratton, maintaining he'd never read it. "Nice trench coat" was all he said. Instead, Bratton wrote in his autobiography, the mayor killed him with a thousand cuts. Bratton omitted the fact that at least one of them was self-inflicted. It began the following month when he signed a $350,000 book deal with the publisher Random House to write his autobiography. The deal was brokered by his lawyer-agent Ed Hayes, who was now calling Bratton "the most significant law enforcement leader of our time and perhaps the twentieth century. He's bigger than J. Edgar Hoover."

Random House told the *Times* that the book would chronicle how the son of a postal clerk ascended to the highest job in policing and developed strategies that dropped violent crime to levels not seen since the late 1960s. "This is one of the rare times when you have such a positive story about such a negative issue," declared Random House's editorial director and the book's editor, Ann Godoff.

She added that she would press Bratton on providing a backstage look at his relationship with Giuliani. Once again, Bratton appeared to have outflanked the mayor.

Giuliani professed little enthusiasm for Bratton's literary aspirations. But instead of confronting him, the mayor went public. "What I'm concerned about is that it follow the ethical and legal guidelines that are set for this," he told the *Times.* He had a point. Not only would Bratton be writing the book while serving in the most demanding of jobs, he would also be earning more than twice as much money from it as from his job as police commissioner. Giuliani instructed Bratton to meet with Denny Young before he started the book. The mayor insisted that Young and the city's chief lawyer, corporation counsel Paul Crotty, review the contract, ostensibly to clear it with the city's Conflict of Interest Board for what Giuliani termed possible ethical violations.

Bratton resisted. These tactics are "clearly an attempt to embarrass me by questioning my ethics," he said. "[F]or the mayor to imply publicly that I might have stepped outside the law was an insult apparently intended to impugn my character." Giuliani, he added, could dismiss him anytime he wanted. "[H]e didn't need to read the fine print on my contract to know that; this public handwringing seemed calculated."

So began the endgame. City Hall tried yet another round of controls over the police department. First they demanded approval of Bratton's lists of discretionary promotions—to first- and second-grade detectives. Then they demanded input on senior-level transfers. Such political interference had been a staple of New York City into the 1950s. Modern mayors, whether Lindsay, Koch, or Dinkins, had left their police commissioners alone to run the department, if for nothing else than to avoid the appearance of political interference. Giuliani announced that he viewed his role differently. His experience as a prosecutor had given him a law enforcement expertise other mayors lacked, he told the *Times.* He failed to mention that such expertise had led him to render himself invisible during the Dirty Thirty corruption scandal.

The mayor then rejected two of Bratton's top-level transfers. The first was that of Bronx Borough Commander Rafael Pineiro to the backwater of the Housing Bureau, in part as punishment for his no-show at the crowded Pink Floyd concert at Yankee Stadium. City Hall stopped it, supposedly in response to the concerns of Bronx Hispanic officials. Instead, Pineiro ended up at the

Criminal Justice Bureau. Although his rank remained the same, it was, called in NYPD parlance, "a lateral transfer with a dip."

Next, City Hall blocked the promotion of Jules Martin to Brooklyn North Borough commander. According to Bratton, Denny Young had labeled Martin, who was black and had headed Dinkins's security detail, a "Dinkins guy." When Timoney tried to explain that chiefs in the NYPD are loyal to whoever occupies City Hall, Young asked, "Has he [Martin] made any public utterances in favor of the mayor?"

City Hall also embarrassed Bratton over his formal reappointment. By law, the police commissioner's term runs for five years. The term Bratton was completing—which was begun in 1991 by Lee Brown and continued by Ray Kelly—expired on February 21, 1996. By March, Giuliani had still not reappointed him. He blamed Bratton's book deal and his refusal to show City Hall his contract. Rather than fuel another week's headlines, Bratton submitted the contract for review. "Give them what they want, I don't care," his lawyer Ed Hayes quoted Bratton as saying.

But agreeing to the review created another set of problems for Bratton. At the mayor's request, he met with Crotty. Instead of discussing the book contract, Crotty came armed with a list of every out-of-town trip Bratton had made as police commissioner. Crotty told him some were unauthorized. He zeroed in on the two flights Bratton had taken with Henry Kravis to Colorado and the Dominican Republic. Within days, Crotty's questions appeared in the newspapers and City Hall was whispering about Section 104.3 of the NYPD *Patrol Guide Manual*, which prohibited department officials from accepting "any reward, gratuity, gift or other compensation for any service performed as a result of or in connection with their duties as public servants."

Next, City Hall began criticizing Bratton to the media. *Newsweek* magazine quoted Randy Mastro as saying that Bratton was about to "cash in" on job offers. Defending himself, Bratton released a list of seven private trips he'd taken, including those with Kravis, and announced he had reimbursed his hosts for all of them.

It was too late. Even the *Times* had turned against him. Its March 26 editorial was headlined "Time to Move On." It sounded like an obituary. Bratton, the *Times* wrote, "has let it be known for some time that he was looking for a way out, preferably into a lucrative job in private business. Along the way, he has made significant errors of judgment. He signed a book contract with Random House, reportedly in the six-figure range, raising questions about his willingness to use his public office for private gain. He has also taken trips paid for by private groups and individuals, including some who might well be in a position to employ him when the time comes to leave. . . . His long-term attention is now so focused on what to do next that he is damaging the Police Department's morale and weakening his own usefulness as Commissioner."

The day the editorial appeared, Bratton announced his resignation. In perhaps his most candid assessment, he explained in his autobiography: "It is very difficult to work effectively when you have lost the confidence of the people you work for." Giuliani, he continued, "had made it clear whose police department he thought it was. He had also made it abundantly clear that I would not be allowed to run it." At the time, however, neither he nor Giuliani offered a credible explanation for his resignation. Instead, the next day's *Daily News* headlines told the story:

"Why Police Commissioner Quit," read its front page. "City Hall planned new out-of-town probe." On page three: "Bratton Is Out Amid Probe," with the subhead: "Feared inquiry would taint him."

As for landing a lucrative offer in business, Bratton's only offer came from his Boston friend Robert Johnson of First Security Services. Bratton dressed it up as First Security Consulting, implying it had something to do with stocks or bonds but Security still meant security. It was a private armed-guard service. In the end, it was the Joe Blow security job Bratton vowed he'd never accept.

SIX

Get on the Train or Get Under It

i.

It was an inauguration of such pageantry that it rivaled Rudolph Giuliani's own. There in City Hall Plaza on a sparkling spring day, amid bagpipers, a marching band and bunting flapping in the April breeze, the mayor had assembled four hundred dignitaries, including the city's district attorneys, the state's chief judge, and four previous police commissioners, including the out-of-favor Ray Kelly. The gala event was to swear in the city's new police commissioner, Howard Safir, a testy, taciturn, six-foot three-inch ex-federal marshal, who looked as though he'd bitten into a lemon.

This was Safir's day only in name. The mayor had produced and choreographed this extravaganza to display to the world that Bill Bratton's departure was but a blip on Giuliani's crime-fighting screen, that past successes would seamlessly continue because he, Giuliani, remained in charge. Having completed two unremarkable years as the city's fire commissioner, Safir was but a prop and, it turned out, an afterthought. As the television cameras rolled, the mayor presented him with Theodore Roosevelt's gold police shield, an honor he had never accorded Bratton. Yet Safir was nearly denied his turn at the podium. After introducing him, Giuliani's master of ceremonies Denny Young became so carried away in praising another Giuliani aide that he called on the chaplain to give the benediction, ending the ceremony without calling on Safir to speak.

Young caught his slip and Safir managed to get in a few words. Watching this, I wondered whether Young had made an innocent mistake and forgotten that Safir might actually have something to say at his own swearing-in or whether he was unconsciously acting out Giuliani's desires: After two years of Bill Bratton, the mayor was willing to allow his new police commissioner to be seen but not heard.

"I've heard about City Hall control, but this is ridiculous," Safir began as the crowd tittered in relief that an embarrassment had been avoided. He was brief, speaking for only four minutes, no doubt aware of Giuliani's reluctance to share the spotlight. The *Times* took notice, writing that the length of his speech was but a third of Giuliani's.

It was an awkward but telling start for a police commissioner who had just been derided as a "lightweight" by outgoing first deputy Timoney. Smarting from Giuliani's having passed him over for the top job, Timoney's insult, nevertheless, rang true. Born in the Bronx, raised in East Meadow, Long Island, Safir had graduated from Hofstra College, then washed out of the Marine Corps Officer Candidate School. He spent eighteen months at Brooklyn Law School before dropping out there as well. After a turn as a federal drug agent, he landed at the Justice Department's Marshals Service in Washington. There he met Giuliani, a rising federal prosecutor. When President Ronald Reagan was shot, Giuliani, number three at the Justice Department, turned to Safir to guard the shooter, John Hinckley.

The apex of Safir's career had him heading the U.S. Marshals' Witness Security Program, a misnamed fugitive-hunting team that may have violated laws by trying to kidnap people all over the world. Hunting such criminals as Watergate financier Robert Vesco and the Asian drug lord, the Khun Sa, Safir tried to turn his experience into a book and movie deal. This, too, turned out badly. The project ended when a Maryland court ordered Safir to pay his ghostwriter $17,500 for failing to reveal that a dozen publishing houses had previously rejected his story.

Safir did, however, attract attention. Interviewed on *60 Minutes* in 1991, he sounded like a character from a juvenile adventure tale. "There is no hunting like the hunting of armed men," he intoned, "and those who have hunted armed men long enough and like it never wish to do anything else thereafter."

When *60 Minutes* correspondent Steve Kroft asked him whether such kidnappings violated the law, Safir responded, "The kind of things that I did are not exactly what diplomats do."

Kroft persisted. Were there objections from the State Department and the FBI? "They're politicians," scoffed Safir. "That's what they do is worry about official repercussions. I'm not a politician. I'm a cop."

Disdainful of the law, oblivious to how his attitude appeared to the public, this was the person Giuliani had chosen over Timoney as the thirty-ninth police commissioner of New York City. In his solipsistic way, the mayor had never given Timoney a courtesy call about Safir's selection. Only after Timoney discovered it on his own and announced that he planned to retire did Giuliani make an eleventh-hour bid to keep him. Just before announcing Safir's appointment, the mayor asked Timoney to come to City Hall.

"I went into the mayor's office," Timoney recalled, "and the mayor said something like, 'I need Howard at this point in time. However I understand you are upset and have indicated you will leave.' He then went on to stroke me, regarding the reasons I should stay. I said absolutely nothing. I just sat there staring at him. After he finished, I got up and left."

Timoney went to lunch at the South Street Seaport, where he knocked down a couple of beers. When McAlary called him there, Timoney let loose. "I won't be part of propping up Howard Safir," he told McAlary. "I can't prop up something I don't believe in. He's a lightweight. This whole thing is false and I won't go along. Rudy is the smartest man I ever met. He may be the greatest mayor in the city's history. But Rudy is screwed up. There's something wrong there."

The *Daily News* blared Timoney's words across the next day's front page under the banner headline: "Mayor's Man Gets NYPD Top Job. Snubbed Deputy Rips Appointment." The headline on McAlary's column read: "No, Timoney Won't Stay to Groom Rudy Yes-man."

Giuliani was furious. "A police officer should have the discipline and the professionalism not to make comments like that," he said. Was the mayor angrier at being called "screwed up" or at the "lightweight" crack about Safir? Giuliani never specified. Instead, he ordered Timoney out of Police Plaza. Timoney had just enough time to file retirement papers and secure his $64,000-a-year pension, based on half his last year's salary as first deputy. Then, at a previously scheduled officers' promotion ceremony, he received a thunderous standing ovation from both the top brass and the rank and file. The *News*'s headline next day caught the moment: "Timoney Quits, Beats Rudy's Ax."

Giuliani wouldn't let it rest; he ordered city lawyers to find a way to demote Timoney to the lower-paying rank of captain, which would slash his pension to $46,000-a-year. Timoney was so popular that the police unions, hardly advocates for the top brass, intervened. PBA President Lou Matarazzo cautioned the mayor about unspecified "trouble" if Timoney were demoted, delivering his warning through Staten Island borough president Guy Molinari.

"There was a great concern among all the police unions," said Molinari. "It took them some time to get me that evening and I reached the mayor somewhere around eleven that night." Giuliani backed down. Timoney kept his rank but was gone by evening, though he later sneaked back into the building for a final picture with his command staff.

I tried to inject some humor about this melodrama into "The Confidential" by taking off on Timoney's "screwed up" crack and asking some shrinks what many at Police Plaza wondered: whether the mayor could use psychiatric help. (The verdict was mixed.)

City Hall was not amused. "Your suggestion is very insulting," said Colleen Roche, Lategano's successor as press secretary when Lategano became communications director. "This is not funny. Our relationship with you is over."

I captioned her remarks in the next week's "Confidential": "Rudy Sane, Says Aide."

Whatever the clinical diagnosis, Giuliani got what he wanted in Safir: a police department that reflected Giuliani and his values, which was to reduce crime to the exclusion of all else. Building on Bratton's Compstat reforms, Safir would drive crime farther down. While the number of murders had fallen dramatically under Bratton, they fell even more under Safir. By the end of 1996, Safir's first year, murders slipped below 1,000, to 983. The next year, the number fell to 770, and 1998 saw the lowest homicide total in thirty-five years: 633. Giuliani would rightly claim these historic declines as his legacy. As a dig at Bratton, he would call Safir "the greatest police commissioner in the history of New York City."

But with no one to restrain them, Giuliani and Safir would foster a culture that turned police officers into cowboys. As in the westerns, they shot first and asked questions later. In their rush to reduce crime, they seemed oblivious to the concerns of nonwhite New Yorkers. Smug and self-righteous, they appeared unconcerned about exacerbating tensions and further polarizing the city, ripping its fabric—fragile in the best of times—along racial lines. Take the case of Patrick Dorismond. The twenty-six-year-old unarmed black security guard had been standing with a friend on Eighth Avenue and 37th Street in midtown Manhattan on March 16, 2000, when a stranger offered to sell him drugs. Dorismond refused and a fight broke out. The stranger turned out to be an undercover police officer. His backup rushed in and shot and killed Dorismond.

Giuliani sought public support for the cops' actions. Citing "the public's right to know," he ordered Safir to release Dorismond's criminal record, which included arrests for robbery, assault, attempted robbery, and criminal possession of a weapon, although his only conviction had been for disorderly conduct. The disclosure violated a long-standing, unwritten department policy in which only prior arrests leading to convictions are released, and only if the arrests are relevant to an issue at hand.

Dorismond's record also included a sealed 1987 juvenile arrest when he was thirteen years old. Giuliani ordered Safir to release that as well. "People do act in conformity very often with their prior behavior," the mayor said, suggesting that Dorismond's "pattern of behavior" contributed to his death. The news media, he continued, "would not want a picture presented of an altar boy, when in fact, maybe it isn't an altar boy."

In fact, as his juvenile record showed, Dorismond had been an altar boy. Over three thousand mourners attended his funeral. Escorting his body, many shouted anti-Giuliani slogans and fought with police. Eventually, the city paid his family $2.25 million.

ii.

Like Giuliani, Safir selected as staff people who wouldn't overshadow him. That meant Maple, the architect of Compstat, had to go. The rumor was that with Timoney out, he had asked for the first deputy's job. But after meeting with Safir, he announced his resignation.

"Jack Hits the Road," the *News* headlined its front page the next day, displaying a picture of the Jackster in a white suit with stripes, a Homburg, and his black and white Spectators. I caught up with him in his office later that day. Resplendent in a red, white, and blue bow tie and a powder blue shirt, he was busy signing autographs of the *News*'s front page but invited me to share a last cup of espresso. When I asked about his departure, he offered a typically jaunty reply. "I have to go home with the guy I went to the dance with." He also refused to discuss the first deputy rumors, saying only, "My conversations with Safir are private."

That left only Anemone from Bratton's high command. Initially, it appeared Safir might need Louie, who knew the NYPD from bottom to top through his advance from beat cop to chief of department. Without Maple, he was also the undisputed king of Compstat. To help curb his aggressiveness, he had been trying to improve his image with private lessons from a female corporate communications consultant. Her charm school seemed to work, up to a point. On the surface, Louie seemed kinder, gentler. He smiled at reporters, made jokes at which people actually laughed, and was even seen shaking hands with someone he despised. He also took to wearing glasses. "Softens the image," he said.

Many police officials, Anemone included, believed Giuliani was grooming him as the department's first Italian American police commissioner. The mayor seemed to encourage this. The month before appointing Safir, he had included Anemone among his City Hall and political cronies who were invited to Israel for a terrorism conference. Louie so impressed the Israelis that they feted him at a farewell dinner with a Middle Eastern fish delicacy. A couple of years later, when the Israelis visited New York, Anemone reciprocated by hosting a breakfast for them. It was at Ratner's, a kosher deli on the Lower East Side, where *he* ordered the fish—gefilte fish, a traditional Eastern European Jewish dish of poached patties made from a mixture of deboned fish. The Israelis had never tasted it. "Where did it come from?" they asked. "It's an East River fish," said Louie, ignoring the fact that no sane person had eaten a fish from the East River in the past fifty years.

Unlike the mayor, Safir never seemed comfortable with Anemone and thwarted his ambitions. Instead, he elevated the butt of Anemone's Pinocchio joke, Chief Tosano Simonetti, to first deputy. Louie reported to him.

Safir's key civilian appointees knew even less about the NYPD than he did. He recruited them from the fire department but, apparently not wanting to be upstaged, bypassed its top chiefs and hard chargers. For his chief of staff, with the imposing title of deputy commissioner of administration, Safir named the amiable Richie Sheirer, nicknamed "Bumper" for his girth. Sheirer had been a lowly fire dispatcher before Safir made him his personal aide at the FDNY. Sheirer called Safir "the kindest, bravest, most wonderful human being I've ever met in my life."

As Safir's spokeswoman and the public face of the department, Safir appointed his longtime assistant, blond, blue-eyed Marilyn Mode. A graduate of the elite Connecticut College for Women, Mode, like Lategano, had no formal journalism training. She had served as Safir's spokeswoman at the fire department and their ties went back to the Marshals Service, where, under Safir, she arranged new lives for mafia turncoats. Mode described her previous job to me as a "kind of social worker for the mob." One mobster was Jimmy "the Weasel" Fratiano, author of *The Last Mafioso*, a "tell-all" about the mob. Mode said she took care of his "domestic arrangements."

"I arranged his book tour, helped with his disguises, and learned his recipes," she said. "He's a terrific cook, like many mobsters. He has some secrets about meatballs, how to make them stick together without losing their taste."

Unable to fit into the NYPD's military-style culture, Mode seemed continually exasperated, as out of place at One Police Plaza as Dorothy and Toto in Oz. In fact, Mode, too, had a dog, a small, white terrier named Lil, that Mode insisted on taking with her wherever she went at headquarters, sweeping through the halls, tugging her on a leash.

Up on the thirteenth floor, Lil roamed about DCPI, cadging cops' lunches and nipping a female sergeant in the foot and drawing blood. Mode even brought Lil to a raid on a gang of Latin Kings in Brooklyn, where she remained inside a police van yipping. At least one person complained about Lil to the city's Department of Health. "I am a police officer," lamented the anonymous writer, who sent copies of his complaint to the mayor, the police commissioner, and me. "The problem is Marilyn Mode, the deputy commissioner of public information who brings her dog to the office every day. This is not only unprofessional but a violation of the health code, yet nothing is done about it because the police commissioner allows her to do it. I am not the only person in the office or on the thirteenth floor who is bothered by this but everyone is afraid to speak up . . . I know lots of people who love their pets but can you imagine what it would be like if everyone was allowed to bring them to the workplace?"

Despite her ridicule, Safir did not order Mode to keep her dog at home. After the unhappy officer's complaint appeared in "The Confidential," he defended

Mode, announcing, "We don't have a policy on bringing dogs. There is no pro-hibition in the city health code." After I ran his quote, *Daily News* reporter Mike Claffey took Safir at his word and walked into One Police Plaza with his dog, a Wheaton terrier mix named Mugsy. Stopped at the security desk, he and Mugsy were permitted entry after Claffey produced "The Confidential" with Safir's quotes and cops checked with the department's Legal Bureau. The department then announced that, in the future, visiting dogs would be treated on a case by case basis. "We won't allow pit bulls or Dobermans," an officer explained. "We will allow small dogs like poodles or Chihuahuas."

Just as Safir protected Mode, she thought she was protecting him by turning petulant toward anyone who criticized him. After his inauguration, Giuliani be-gan marketing Safir as the city's first Jewish police commissioner. During a ten-day period, Giuliani took him to a flurry of Jewish-related events: a Sunday morning breakfast at Gracie Mansion honoring Jerusalem mayor Ehud Olmert; a Monday afternoon news conference at City Hall for Tel Aviv mayor Roni Milo; a Tuesday evening celebration at Battery Park City commemorating Jerusalem's three thousandth anniversary; and a Wednesday night meeting at Gracie Man-sion about the Israeli Day parade.

I noted in "The Confidential" that Giuliani had made no such claim of Safir's Jewishness when he was fire commissioner. In fact, members of the fire department's Jewish fraternal organization, Ner Tamid—meaning in Hebrew, Keeper of the Flame—complained that while Safir had attended Emerald and Columbia Association functions for Irish and Italian firefighters, he never ap-peared at Ner Tamid's annual dinner dance and memorial service. When I wrote about this, Mode accused me of being "a self-hating Jew." I suggested to Mode her description seemed more applicable to Safir.

It was Mode who instigated Safir's first brouhaha with the media when she came up with the idea of barring the *Daily News*'s police bureau chief John Marzulli from Safir's initial in-house news briefing. Marzulli had offended her by doing nothing more than his job. Reporting Simonetti's promotion to first deputy, he had written, "Simonetti would replace former First Deputy Com-missioner John Timoney, who labeled Safir a 'lightweight' when he was named top cop."

Mode was unfamiliar with newspaper reporting and apparently with the First Amendment. No one could remember the last time, if ever, that a police reporter had been barred from attending a police commissioner's news briefing. Mode, though, maintained that barring Marzulli was not censorship. "A representative of the *Daily News* was invited and did not attend," she explained.

Safir backed Mode. "There is no requirement that I invite everybody who is a reporter to interview me in my conference room," he said. "I have always been able to choose who can interview me from which newspaper."

Giuliani backed Safir. "Nobody has a constitutional right to be invited into Safir's office," said the mayor. Standing at his side, Safir added that he didn't believe anything he read in the newspapers anyway.

The *News* issued a statement calling Safir's actions "ridiculous and absurd." The paper added, "It's not the place of a city official to dictate who covers the news. We will not be dictated to over who covers the police." A few weeks later, the *News*'s owner, Mortimer Zuckerman, who sometimes interjected himself into police department affairs, announced that Giuliani and Safir had privately assured him that barring Marzulli had been a "mistake." Zuckerman, however, neglected to share this information with his staff. No doubt, this explained why nothing about it appeared in the *News*.

Mayoral spokeswoman Roche suggested Zuckerman had made it all up. She insisted that since barring Marzulli, "The mayor never had a conversation with Mort Zuckerman." So had Zuckerman invented Giuliani's and Safir's admission of a "mistake"? When I reached him, he amended his remarks. "What I said was that Giuliani spoke to *us*, meaning the *Daily News*. I didn't mean me personally."

Zuckerman may have been many things: billionaire publisher, real estate baron, philanthropist, and occasional diplomat. A newsman he was not.

As for Safir, after the Marzulli incident he did not hold another news conference for a year.

Just as Giuliani had used Lategano to do his dirty work, Safir used Mode to do his. Like Lategano, she was eager and too inexperienced to realize she was being compromised. Apparently at Safir's behest, Mode performed an old-fashioned hatchet job on a Bronx limousine driver who had tipped off the *Daily News* to a traffic light the police had rigged. After receiving a $125 ticket for running a red light on Fordham Road near the Bronx Zoo, the driver, James Schillaci, videotaped the cops manipulating a sensor that caused the flashing yellow light to turn quickly to red. Armed with this video, the *Daily News*'s front page of August 26, 1997, trumpeted: "Gotcha!"

Hours later, police arrested Schillaci at his house on a thirteen-year-old traffic warrant over the objections of the Bronx borough commander, Assistant Chief John Scanlon, who thought the warrant was too old. A judge agreed and dismissed it. Mode then leaked Schillaci's rap sheet to *Daily News* reporter Michael Finnegan, including his arrest in 1975 for sodomizing his girlfriend, a charge that was dismissed. As in Dorismond's case, Mode's action violated the department's long-standing unwritten policy. Not only had the sodomy charge been dismissed, but there was no relevance in releasing the criminal record of someone involved in a nonviolent traffic dispute, especially one thirteen years old. The only purpose was to discredit Schillaci.

As Mode explained it: "I told Mr. Finnegan [that] Mr. Schillaci had a very lengthy criminal record dating back to the seventies. I told him he had been arrested for burglary, sodomy, drug possession." She added that she had listed the arrests, rather than convictions, because "the convictions' column—the rap sheet—was so lengthy I couldn't follow what happens in each case in this short period of time."

I was struck by Mode's naïveté—not merely in mistakenly including the sodomy arrest that had been dismissed but in personally leaking the information. Had a pro like Alice McGillion decided to leak such sensitive material, as she did on the rarest of occasions, she would have assigned a subordinate who left no fingerprints—certainly not her own.

Giuliani, however, seemed pleased with Mode's work. At a news conference, he waved Schillaci's arrest record about, crowing that the *Daily News* had been duped. "The public is entitled to know all this when police officers are accused," the mayor said.

In the end, though, it was Schillaci who crowed the loudest. He sued the police department for harassment. Rather than go to trial, the city paid him $290,000.

iii.

Safir and Giuliani seemed to bring out the worst in each other. They seemed to egg each other on, to out-tough-guy the other. Safir's first words to the troops at

Police Plaza set the tone for the next four years. "Get on the train," he said, "or get under it."

The first to feel Safir's wrath were Timoney's friends. Two of his assistants were transferred from the first deputy's office to lesser posts. A third was Inspector Jim McShane, who had organized Timoney's retirement dinner at the Hilton Hotel. In the NYPD, such dinners, especially for the top brass, are a big deal. At Ray Kelly's, a decade before, the cast of *NYPD Blue* had performed. For organizing Timoney's retirement dinner, McShane was buried so deep in an obscure traffic enforcement unit that the phone rang thirty-five times before anyone picked it up. He remained there for the next four years.

Because the mayor traveled with a contingent of detectives, Safir did, too. He had them stride a few yards ahead of him down the corridors of Police Plaza, yipping commands into handheld walkie-talkies while clearing the corridors of people as they passed. When repairs sidelined his private elevator, Safir commandeered the freight elevator to avoid riding with hoi polloi. Two uniformed officers were assigned to guard it and accompany him as he went up and down. A new sign was posted on its door to reflect the new reality: "Absolutely no freight on the freight elevator."

Safir and Giuliani seemed especially to enjoy taunting the media. While Giuliani disdained reporters, Safir baited them. At a Police Foundation dinner, he introduced two *New York Times* reporters to a guest as "slime." At news conferences, Safir began calling reporters' questions "stupid" or responded, "None of your business."

Routine questions went unanswered, like the number of officers on patrol in a precinct. The department released nothing but the barest information without a formalized freedom of information request, which took months to process. It edited the quarterly list of overtime earners—public record for decades—to avoid revealing that the highest earners were the detectives guarding Giuliani. Another unanswered question was the number of officers in DCPI. Mode refused to give a figure, so I counted them myself. At one point they numbered thirty-eight, exceeding the number under Bratton before the Miller Massacre.

Mode seemed to delight in providing misleading information. She exaggerated the credentials of her new "press director," Lenny Alcivar, another Lategano hire, boasting in a news release of his "extensive background in police matters." Alcivar was twenty-four years old.

Sometimes, she seemed to just make up facts as she went along. At the 1998 parade in Lower Manhattan celebrating the Yankees' World Series victory, DCPI estimated the crowd at "well over 3½ million." When reporters questioned the figure, officials tensed. Manhattan South Borough Chief Allan Hoehl, the department's expert on crowd estimates, said it wasn't his number. The DCPI lieutenant who released the estimate refused to specify its source. So did Mode. Cops in her office whispered she had used the same crowd count at the Yankee victory parade two years before.

Meanwhile, Safir used the police to conduct what amounted to private investigations. When Geoffrey Chazen, a thirty-nine-year-old doctor, disappeared after leaving a suicide note, Safir dispatched fifty detectives, police dogs, and a police helicopter to search for him. Because suicides don't often involve foul play, they rarely merit a massive police response. But Chazen was related to Safir's friend, the celebrity lawyer Raoul Felder, who represented Safir and his wife, Carol, in various civil suits. Despite Safir's denials, it appeared that he was using the department's resources to return a favor. Felder had given the Safirs a discounted rate on his customary $450-an-hour fee for handling a messy civil suit involving Safir's sister-in-law—his wife's sister—who alleged the Safirs owed her $88,000 from the sale of a Long Island beach house. When reporters asked about this, Safir gave his customary none-of-your-business reply. But it was the public's business. Section 104.3 of the NYPD's *Patrol Guide* prohibits gifts to city officials of more than fifty dollars. The city's Conflict of Interest Board, which Giuliani had insisted probe Bratton's book deal, made no attempt to investigate this apparent ethical breach.

Safir's lack of candor also created embarrassments for him. On January 31, 1997, Carol Safir was rear-ended while driving on the Queensboro Bridge. Two years later, she filed a $1.5 million lawsuit against the driver, claiming the accident had caused her "loss of consortium"—in English, that the accident had made it too painful to have sexual relations with her husband. Safir was also named in the suit because of *his* loss of consortium with his injured wife. He sought $250,000. Questioned by reporters, he professed ignorance of the lawsuit, maintaining his wife had filed it "without my knowledge."

Because his explanation was so preposterous, at his next news briefing, I brought a Bible. Before Safir began to speak, I asked him to place his hand on it and swear to tell the truth. His face turned red. "The only one who lies here, Mr. Levitt," he sputtered, "is you."

His perceived animosity toward me reached mythic proportions. Not long after the Bible incident, I happened to be chatting with an officer from Staten Island at a retirement dinner when Safir walked past. The next day, the officer was transferred to Queens. Within the department, it was rumored that the officer's transfer had resulted from Safir's seeing him talking to me. While I never learned whether there were valid reasons for the transfer, such rumors had the ring of truth because Giuliani and Safir often acted out of vindictiveness rather than sound policy. When state comptroller H. Carl McCall asked to audit the department's citywide crime statistics, Giuliani refused to release them to him, insisting McCall wanted to hurt him politically. When Gene Russianoff, chairman of the Straphangers Campaign, a subway watchdog group, wanted Safir's fax number to request transit crime data, his aides refused to divulge it, saying it was "classified."

Highest on Giuliani's and Safir's enemies list was Bratton. Neither could shake free of his shadow. Two months after Safir's swearing-in, a weeklong, one-man crime wave swept the city, leaving a woman dead on Park Avenue and three other women beaten bloody. Police found the killer because prints at the murder scene matched those on file from his lone arrest: jumping a subway turnstile two months before the killing. Targeting fare beaters had been the cornerstone of Bratton and Maple's Broken Window theory, a fact Bratton was quick to point out to reporters.

Safir was so obsessed with Bratton he tried to prevent Bratton's wife, TV reporter Cheryl Fiandaca, from attending weekly news briefings at Police Plaza. Mode sent a message to Fiandaca's bosses that Safir was "uncomfortable" around her. When that didn't work, Safir and Giuliani tried to hurt Bratton another way—by barring him from an NYPD-sponsored Compstat conference. Their problem was that they had accepted Bratton's $385 registration fee. Not only did they refund it to keep him out, they were also forced to refund $7,700 from twenty other private security firms that had signed up.

Their biggest shot at Bratton was also their most public. Safir bad-mouthed him to a *New York Times* reporter who had been allowed to sit in on the "One-on-One" at City Hall. Safir compared Bratton to showman P. T. Barnum, then described him as "some airport cop in Boston." Referring to Police Plaza, Safir said, "Bratton didn't know what the hell was going on in this building. I'm not there for press releases. I'm here to reduce crime." Then, apparently referring to his days in the U.S. Marshals Service, Safir added "I did things Bill Bratton couldn't even dream of. I went after the Khun Sa."

When I caught up with Bratton, he pronounced himself puzzled by Safir's remarks. "What is sad," he said, "is that there has always been a certain collegiality among commissioners. We might disagree with a policy, but we don't speak negatively in public about each other. There is no need to. Most of Howard's senior staff are people I moved up. There is no one in Howard's inner circle who wasn't basically part of mine."

I had mocked Bratton when he was commissioner for his love of media attention. Yet in contrast to Safir, there was nothing mean or spiteful about him. He had genuinely enjoyed ogling celebrities at Elaine's and being ogled in return. His happiness at Elaine's combined pure exuberance with a certain astonishment at his good fortune. True, his love of the spotlight may have annoyed, even infuriated Giuliani. But it was a harmless affectation, a peccadillo, which did not affect how he performed as police commissioner. Contrast that with Safir, whose meanness and spite seemed part of his inner being. And they did affect how he performed.

Bratton also had a sense of humor, something Safir lacked. When I asked Bratton about Safir's "airport cop" crack, he said mischievously, "I think Howard is confusing the airport with the subways. I wasn't dealing on the international scene, flying around the world, chasing [the] Khun Sa, who, I believe, was never caught."

Then he provided the coup de grâce. "I can understand Howard's frustration," he added. "Like Rodney Dangerfield, he doesn't get any respect."

Bratton was not the only high-profile figure Giuliani and Safir went out of their way to insult. Another was Vice President Albert A. Gore. Giuliani and Safir were to honor Gore when he visited Police Plaza to present the department with an award for Compstat, this one a framed hammer meant to symbolize the defeat of overspending and government waste. The plan had called for Safir and Giuliani to host a Compstat meeting of Bronx commanders for Gore, with reporters and photographers present. At the last minute, though, Giuliani yanked the red carpet, nixing the award ceremony, canceling all press coverage, even barring the police department's own photographer. Gore attended the Compstat meeting, but Giuliani even altered the seating chart. He placed himself between Gore and Safir so that he, rather than Gore, appeared at center stage.

Mode's explanation for the publicity blackout was "a lack of adequate space." When reporters questioned Lategano, she blamed Gore. "The mayor would have been delighted for [the police department] to receive a meaningful award," she said. "But a sledgehammer is not an appropriate award for this police department and this commissioner. The purpose of the meeting was for the vice president to attend a very serious law enforcement event, not a partisan political photo op."

Marzulli reported in the *News* that Gore's deputy chief of staff, Patricia Ewing, greeted Lategano's remarks "with stunned silence. 'Do they always operate like that?' she asked."

The Gore fiasco also claimed a low-level police victim: Compstat's nuts-and-bolts man, John Yohe. Yohe made the mistake of correcting a remark about Compstat statistics that Safir made to the vice president. The next day, Safir transferred him.

"Chief Anemone called me," Yohe recalled. "He said, 'I have good news and bad news for you. The good news is it's a nice day outside.'"

Giuliani and Safir even managed to offend an entire nation—the Dominican Republic. That imbroglio began after Safir announced a plan to capture fugitives from New York City by stationing NYPD officers in Santo Domingo, the nation's capital. But he and Giuliani failed to lay the groundwork with Dominican officials before a story appeared in the *Post* under a front-page headline: "Rudy to the Rescue," with a subhead blaring: "Rudy to Seal Deal for NYPD's Drug Outpost."

Dominican politicians denounced the plan as an affront to their sovereignty. The island's Roman Catholic cardinal, Nicolás de Jesús López Rodrígues, criticized the gringo outpost in a Sunday homily. Safir's Dominican plan died. Apparently blind to the cardinal's position as the island's spiritual leader, Safir blamed "criminal elements" and "irresponsible politicians." As usual, he also threw in the media, claiming they had fallen for a public relations offensive by Dominican drug lords.

Mode added to the contretemps, saying the country's president, Leonel Fernández, "may not fully understand the problem." That prompted an angry response from the NYPD's normally docile Hispanic Society. Its president, Robert Maldonado, demanded Safir apologize for Mode's remarks. "The obvious implication," said Maldonado, "is that President Fernández is not sophisticated enough to understand what Safir wanted to do."

Finally, there was the Wall Street police substation, a plan both absurd and disturbing. To me it epitomized much of Safir's tour as police commissioner. With no public discussion he arranged for a two-hundred-officer substation to open near Wall Street, an area having one of the city's lowest crime rates. In return for the facility, a local fat-cat business group agreed to fund Safir's pet project, a police museum on Lower Broadway, with his wife, Carol, as chairwoman.

The Wall Street substation opened, but the police museum had trouble getting off the ground. My articles attracted enough attention that Giuliani severed the link between the two projects. That meant the Safirs had to raise funds for the museum separately. So each of them visited a couple of Wall Street firms. With the help of PaineWebber's head of security, a retired NYPD chief, Safir met with the company's chief executive, Donald Marron. According to a company spokesman, Marron asked Safir, "What can we do to help the police?" Safir's answer was Carol's museum. Soon afterward, PaineWebber received a formal solicitation letter from the police museum's executive vice president, Kathy Donahue, asking for a six-figure contribution.

Safir also took Carol to a meeting at Merrill Lynch, arranged by *its* head of security, a retired NYPD captain. Safir met with Merrill Lynch's general counsel, Stephen Hammerman, and its charitable foundation head, Paul Critchlow, who the year before had awarded $31 million in grants to various organizations. Soon afterward, Merrill Lynch also received a formal, six-figure solicitation from Donahue.

In the end, neither Wall Street house contributed to the police museum, offended, perhaps, by the Safirs' arm-twisting. Giuliani then awarded the museum a $1 million grant from the Department of Cultural Affairs. The money, however, was contingent on a $3 million "challenge grant" the museum had to raise privately. When it failed to reach that goal, Giuliani changed the rules and gave the museum $1 million anyway. Meanwhile, Safir assigned six cops to the museum, full-time. For six months they sat, guarding an empty building.

When the New York City Police Museum finally opened months later, few people visited it. By then Safir had raised the number of officers assigned to it to twenty-six.

iv.

In February 1997, less than a year after Safir entered office, *The New Yorker* threw a party to celebrate its new issue, "Crime and Punishment." Although Safir had been police commissioner for nearly a year, the issue ignored him and instead profiled Bratton and his crew, featuring Maple as "the Crime Buster."

Maple stood at the magazine's party at the New York City Bar Association, the same building in which twenty-six years before, the Knapp Commission had held its hearings on police corruption, a short, rotund figure in a yellow-and-black-striped bow tie, homburg, black and white spectator shoes and a gray-black stubble of a beard. Celebrating with him were Bratton, Miller, and Timoney.

Safir wasn't there. The department said he had not been invited. A *New Yorker* spokeswoman said he had been.

Whatever the truth, the party went swimmingly without him. In a panel discussion, held under a massive blue and gold "Crime and Punishment" banner, Bratton squared off against Norman Siegel of the New York Civil Liberties Union, who cited rising civilian complaints as a sign that the police department was becoming too aggressive. From the audience, Timoney spoke up, supporting Bratton and attacking the accuracy of Siegel's figures. As former officials, he and Bratton could have demurred when Siegel attacked the NYPD. Rather, the *New Yorker* party was their final performance together, a victory lap in recognition of Bratton's NYPD in exile. At least for this night, they remained in command.

Despite the tributes, there seemed a sense of sadness to that evening. Out of power, Bratton and his team all seemed adrift. The department's unofficial official historian, Tom Reppetto, called them the "Wild Geese." The reference was to the seventeenth-century Irish patriots exiled during British rule after the Battle of Limerick in 1631 and forced to wander as mercenaries through Europe, never to return.

Timoney's exile took him to Philadelphia, where two years after his banishment from Police Plaza, he was sworn in as police commissioner. By then he had apologized to Safir for his "lightweight" remark, though he never apologized to Giuliani. By then, too, Timoney had been recognized as a national law enforcement figure. He traveled to Ireland, where he advised the government on its national police force. Philadelphia's mayor Edward Rendell, a New York City native, had selected Timoney not merely for his crime-fighting expertise but for his relationships with minority officers and minority communities. In 2000, *Esquire* magazine would profile him in a cover story headlined "America's Best Cop."

A high-powered crowd of New Yorkers who were Timoney's friends attended his swearing-in at Philadelphia's City Hall, including Bratton, former commissioner Ben Ward, and the writer Tom Wolfe. While Timoney now headed a major police department, Bratton was still doing private security work and was bored by it. The previous year, he had considered making a run against Giuliani for mayor. Former Mayor Koch encouraged him. The two had dinner, together with Maple. But in the end Koch backed off, stating he would not back Bratton in a Democratic primary. "They asked me if I would become one of his supporters," Koch explained. "I said no. There was no reason to pick Bratton over the others." Bratton gave up the idea.

Scores of officers from the NYPD also attended the swearing-in but asked that their names not be printed because of Giuliani's and Safir's dislike of Timoney. "You print my name and you can say good-bye to your career," said one officer. A chief said he didn't mind if I mentioned his name. "This is America, isn't it?" he said. For safety's sake, I omitted it.

"Well," said a beaming Timoney, surveying the crowd, "I finally made it." Demonstrating he had learned from Bratton's mistakes, he praised Mayor Rendell both at the beginning and end of his speech. Then addressing Philadelphia's Hispanic residents, hit hard by drug-related crime, he surprised the crowd by speaking for three minutes in Spanish—which some joked was easier to understand than his English.

Timoney credited a total immersion Spanish course the NYPD had sent him to twenty-five years before. Graduating first in his class, he had recited his valedictory speech in Spanish back then. He was, he said, following another cop with an Irish name who had also been valedictorian two years before him and who also attended his swearing-in—Ray Kelly.

v.

Safir and Giuliani's first—and only—priority, it seemed, was to reduce crime. They threw themselves into the task in their typically direct and forceful, albeit often unthinking, way. Take the Northern Manhattan Initiative, Safir's plan to curtail Dominican drug trafficking in Washington Heights, with its proximity to the George Washington Bridge and New Jersey. His plan was to bring in a hundred Border Patrol agents from the federal government, supposedly to arrest illegal immigrants who commit crimes, as though New York and New Jersey were separate countries. Explaining his rationale to top police officials in his office, Safir said of the Border Patrol, "They all speak two languages and they can shoot the black out of a target." His letter to the Justice Department, formally requesting the agents, went unanswered.

The department's most effective tactic in reducing crime, Safir believed, was getting guns off the streets. This was largely the work of the department's 138-member Street Crime Unit. Safir credited them with removing 40 percent of the illegal guns confiscated by police across the city. He was so taken with the unit that he said, "I wish I could bottle their enthusiasm and make everyone take a drink of it."

No question, Street Crime was elite. Its officers worked in plainclothes and out of their own building on Randalls Island, free from precinct supervision. Their esprit was such that they called themselves "The Best of the Finest." They also had a provocative slogan: "We Own the Night."

Its commanders liked to say that Street Crime cops had a sixth sense about knowing whether a person was armed. "I can't tell you how many times we took away guns without shots being fired," explained the unit's commander, Captain Richard Savage. "You'd see a bulge. You'd see a guy go into his pocket. He may be looking to dump the gun. In that split second he has the gun in his hand, you'd be justified in shooting. If we fired every time we were justified, the streets would be littered with people."

Savage personally interviewed every cop he hired. "I used the selection process as a secret tool," he said. "I looked at arrest activity. They had to be highly recommended by their commanding officer. I also looked for warning signs: I wanted people with no departmental charges in the police trial room, no prior shootings, and no civilian complaints."

The unit represented the best of the NYPD—except for one problem. It was virtually all white. Worse, the suspects stopped and frisked for guns were virtually all black and Hispanic, although, despite persistent claims of "racial profiling," the race of people the police stopped correlated fairly closely with descriptions given by robbery victims. But despite Safir's and Giuliani's claim that the Street Crime Unit had potentially saved the lives of hundreds of black and Hispanic New Yorkers, many black and Hispanic New Yorkers resented what they felt were the unit's overly aggressive tactics.

In 1997, in what would turn out to be his most fateful decision as police commissioner, Safir ordered the unit tripled in size to 438 officers. The increase translated into quick results. That year, Street Crime officers seized 1,139 guns, a 59 percent jump over the previous year. Within the unit, some officers felt uneasy about the new recruits, who they felt had been put on the street too quickly. Two years later, those fears would prove to be well founded.

Meanwhile, Safir tried to soften the department's image. But he seemed unable to convince people of his sincerity. He came up with the idea of a "Respect" campaign. He promised increased sensitivity training for officers and formed a civilian Respect Committee to monitor police abuses. He even had the words, "Courtesy, Professionalism and Respect" written on the side of every patrol car.

But credibility problems appeared the very day Safir announced his Respect campaign. His announcement followed a report by the London-based human rights group Amnesty International charging the NYPD with systemic brutality. Some of those claims were distorted. For example, the group cited the fatal police shooting of a black grandmother, Eleanor Bumpurs, in her Bronx apartment during an eviction proceeding but failed to mention that Bumpers had lunged at the officers with a ten-inch kitchen knife.

Nonetheless, Safir denied the obvious connection between Amnesty International's report and the timing of his Respect campaign. He also failed to convince the NYPD's black officers to support it. After a two-hour meeting with top police officials, which Safir attended for only twenty minutes, the Guardians, the department's fraternal group of African American officers, listed its concerns: no input from street-level cops, no definition of what constitutes disrespect, no specified sanctions for noncompliance, and no commitment of staff. Particularly upsetting was that only two of the forty-nine supervisors in the program were black.

Safir further undercut his Respect campaign by the civilians he appointed. One was Dr. Ruth Westheimer, the sex doctor. When asked what advice she had for cops, she said, "I want you to be safe, but I'd rather you wear a vest than a condom."

vi.

After less than a year as first deputy, Tony Simonetti retired. His departure occurred under circumstances as mysterious as any I'd encountered at Police Plaza. While the Mollen Commissions had focused on cops' corruption out in the precincts, here was what appeared to be corruption at the highest levels of the department right at Police Plaza. And it all seemed to be legal.

It began in March 1997 when Jay Creditor, a thirty-six-year-old police officer and PBA delegate, filed for retirement, claiming a line-of-duty injury. If granted, that meant a tax-free disability pension, at three-quarters of his annual salary, each year until he died, amounting to an estimated $1.4 million. But Creditor had a problem. Five days before he was to appear before the city's pension board, he was found guilty in a departmental trial of missing two hundred hours of work over a six-month period. In her decision on March 7, the police department's trials commissioner, Rae Koshetz, wrote that while working at the 110th Precinct in Queens, Creditor had "committed multiple violations . . . by failing to appear, misrepresenting his whereabouts and attending unauthorized therapy for his line-of-duty injury."

She recommended dismissal. "Unless he is fired for this," she wrote, "he will receive a three-quarters disability pension when the Pension Board meets March 12. Not only would it be inappropriate to pay this 36-year-old man without exacting substantial penalty for his illegal behavior, but it would also send the wrong message to other members of the department." Koshetz's decision omitted the obvious: The PBA controlled one-third of the Pension Board's votes.

Then something wild occurred. March 7 was a Friday. At 6:00 P.M., a few hours after Koshetz's decision, Creditor's PBA attorney, Stuart London, received a call from NYPD assistant department advocate Kevin Lubin. Lubin told London the department was willing to make a deal—if Creditor paid a substantial fine for his avoidance of duty. "For $50,000, your client can get a three-quarters pension," London recalled Lubin saying.

"I was shocked. I thought he was kidding. I thought it was a joke," London said. "Something must have happened between the time of Koshetz's decision [earlier that afternoon] and that phone call."

Three days later, on Monday, March 10, Lubin wrote to Simonetti, saying Safir had taken the unusual step of reversing Koshetz's decision that he be dismissed. "The police commissioner reviewed this case and determined that this case be negotiated," his letter read.

That same day, Creditor came up with the $50,000 to pay the fine and was reinstated on the force. He immediately filed for retirement. Two days later, on March 12, he went before the pension board, which, with the PBA's support, granted him his tax-free $1.4 million disability pension.

So what was going on? Had somebody, in city lingo, "called in a contract" for Creditor? Had someone put in the fix? And if so, who?

Making matters more suspicious was that Safir's name could not be found on any document reversing Koshetz's decision. Indeed, it would have been hard for Safir to have signed any document because between March 7 and March 10 he was undergoing double heart bypass surgery at New York University Medical Center. During those four days, Simonetti was running the department.

Those four days were apparently important for Simonetti, because, the next month, he followed Creditor out the door, also retiring with a three-quarters tax-free disability pension, estimated at $120,000 annually. He then joined McAndrews-Forbes, the holding company of Revlon Corporation, doing security work at a six-figure annual salary.

So was the timing of Simonetti's retirement related to Creditor's? Had he been carrying the Creditor contract so that the PBA would vote favorably on *his* disability pension the following month? Despite my repeated questions, neither he nor Safir explained. In fact, Safir gave contradictory answers. At one news conference he said he had made the decision to reverse Koshetz. At another, he said the decision had been Simonetti's.

Because the whole thing smelled, I alerted the Mayor's Committee to Combat Police Corruption. The committee lacked both subpoena power and staff, but it was the only city body that monitored the department. Having ignored the Mollen Commission's recommendation of an outside monitor with subpoena powers, Giuliani had instead formed this toothless committee, headed by a former prosecutor and current corporate lawyer, Richard Davis. Davis at first promised to investigate and said he would obtain the relevant documents. But at his committee's next meeting, he announced he'd changed his mind. He gave no explanation and refused to answer my questions. It looked like another fix was in. Who ordered it remained another NYPD mystery.

vii.

To replace Simonetti, Giuliani pitched his buddy from the Correction Department, Bernie Kerik. Safir objected. Police officials noted it was one of the few times he stood up to the mayor. It was not clear what Safir's objections were. "He just didn't like him," said one of Safir's aides. "The word Howard used to describe him was 'thug.'"

Instead, Safir appointed Patrick E. Kelleher, a short, slight department insider, who had briefly headed both the Detective and Internal Affairs Bureaus under Bratton. When Kelleher was appointed chief of Internal Affairs in 1994, I asked him what his first priority was. He said it was "to protect the good cops." His view was antithetical to that of Guido, the consummate department outsider, who had viewed his job as getting rid of the bad cops.

Nonetheless, Kelleher worked so hard at Internal Affairs, he had to check himself into nearby Beekman Hospital because of exhaustion. I visited him there, planning to write a story. Wearing a hospital gown, he seemed touched by my appearance, believing I had come to see him out of personal concern. I was so moved by what I took to be his naïveté, I never wrote the story.

I think I was predisposed to like Kelleher because his best friend in the department was DCPI's former commanding officer, Captain Tom Fahey. In fact, Kelleher had rescued Fahey from the Intelligence Division, where for the years since the Miller Massacre he'd been hiding out from Giuliani.

Under Mode, Fahey's spot had been filled by Mike Collins, a six-foot five-inch captain I called "Killer," but whose appearance as a bruiser belied his considerable abilities as a schmoozer. Like Fahey, Collins could joke and swap stories with reporters. Like Fahey, he appeared to confide confidential information. Like Fahey, he never divulged a secret the department didn't want him to. His greatest skill, however, was containing the damage Mode caused the department by refusing to return phone calls and losing her temper at one and all. By the time Kelleher was appointed first deputy, it was obvious to everyone at Police Plaza something was wrong at DCPI. Everyone knew what the problem was but no one was prepared to address it. Instead, in the finest NYPD tradition, a solution presented itself that spared an incompetent but well-connected higher-up and punished a competent subordinate. The night after the office Christmas party, which hosts reporters from all over the city and to which Collins had laid out $450 of his own money for food and drink, he was notified he was being transferred. Both Mode and Safir had attended the party but gave no indication then that he was out. Collins was so taken by surprise that when I spoke to him about it few days later, his voice cracked.

To assess these management methods, I called Richard Freedman, chairman of the Department of Management at NYU's Leonard N. Stern School of Business. "Organizational politics at its dirtiest," he said. "The boss has to do something so you find the appropriate victim. . . . It's pure façade." Not for the first time, I asked myself the question: How could anyone take Safir seriously?

When I came up to DCPI the following Monday morning, I received another surprise, but a pleasant one. Who was seated behind Collins's desk but Fahey? His friendship with Kelleher had resuscitated his career. It had taken nearly five years, but he had come full circle. He was now a deputy chief and he was again the commanding officer of DCPI.

Safir had such confidence in Kelleher that, paraphrasing Giuliani, he called Kelleher "the greatest first deputy in the history of the department." I suspected he meant that Kelleher was the most obedient. Years later, in assessing Safir's tenure, Kelleher acknowledged but one misstep: the failure "to get our message out." Translation: Mode had been such a disaster it had been necessary to bring in Fahey. Kelleher also maintained he had been able to voice frank disagreements with Safir. If that were true, I wondered why he had not informed Safir that the way to have gotten his message out was to have dumped Mode, not Collins.

My only concern about Kelleher was that he was too loyal to his friends. Specifically, I wondered about his having protected two cops, a father and son pair, from serious corruption charges. Back in 1993, federal prosecutors had informed the department that Bronx detective John Wrynn had leaked confidential information to the mob, leading to the death of a police informant and endangering the life of an undercover. Yet the department took no action. Four years later, Assistant U.S. Attorney George Stamboulidis wrote to the department, describing "compelling evidence of crimes and administrative violations that justify [Wrynn's] prompt termination." Prosecutors also warned that Wrynn's father, Inspector James Wrynn of the Internal Affairs Bureau, had been caught rifling through internal police documents to leak confidential information to his son about the feds' investigation of him.

The undercover himself had been so concerned he had taken the extraordinary step of writing Safir, providing a detailed description of the case and asking him to personally discipline the Wrynns. Safir never responded. Both Wrynns continued in their jobs. John Wrynn was never charged with a crime. Rather, he was placed on modified assignment and allowed to continue working in the Property Clerk's Office. James Wrynn, his father, remained at IAB.

Why had the department taken no action? One theory was that police officials had been reluctant to act in 1993 while the Mollen Commission was investigating police corruption. Another was that in his position at IAB, James Wrynn had dirt on top police officials. I wondered whether that included Kelleher.

At Safir's next news briefing, I asked Kelleher about his relationship with the Wrynns. He blurted out that years before, James Wrynn had been the department's night duty officer when he, Kelleher, driving to his home upstate, had had a car accident. "As I recall I was unconscious, but there is no indication or no knowledge that he was then present. He was not there," Kelleher said.

"You were unconscious?" I asked.

"Yes, I hit a tree."

I wanted to ask him more about the accident. Had he been driving a department vehicle while off duty? Had he been tested for alcohol? Where upstate did he live? Was it beyond the distance from the city that cops were permitted to live? What had Wrynn said in his report about the incident? Instead, Safir cut off my questions.

Six months later, portions of Stamboulidis's letter were reported in the *Times* by its police bureau chief David Kocieniewski. Only then did the department bring charges—and only against John Wrynn, the son. Instead of firing him, they allowed him to resign. His father, the inspector, was transferred from Internal Affairs but allowed to remain in the department. To me, the Wrynns remained another unsolved NYPD mystery. So did Kelleher's accident.

viii.

Finally, there was Anemone, who as chief of department was in charge of both the uniformed and detective forces but who was proving to be his own worst enemy. Despite attending corporate charm school, Louie soon reverted to being Louie. The Undisputed King of Compstat became so enraged at the responses of two Bronx precinct commanders that he ordered them out of the building, then had them return to another Compstat meeting two days later as a "penalty day." He also feuded with both the chief of detectives, Charlie Reuther, and the chief of patrol, Wilbur Chapman. Early in 1996, Anemone sent Reuther the following memo: "Be prepared prior to each Compstat meeting to become an active and interested participant. Implement and support all policies and decisions as directed. Respond to major crime scenes on a seven day, 24 hour basis. Insure that prisoners are debriefed, accomplices arrested and search warrants and sting operations are increased. Develop progress reports on all unsolved homicide cases and cases where perpetrators are known but not yet apprehended."

Reuther ignored him. Arrest activity and homicide clearance rates were the highest in forty years. Anemone, though, proved relentless. He stalked Reuther for a year before he bagged him and ordered him to join Chief Pineiro—whom Anemone had flopped over his failure to appear at the Pink Floyd concert in the Bronx—at the Criminal Justice Bureau. Shortly afterward, Reuther retired.

Anemone was also after Chapman, the department's highest-ranking black officer. When Anemone transferred two other black chiefs and assigned them to Chapman's office, Louie's enemies at Police Plaza began referring to it as "the Ghetto." So Anemone threw in a white chief he was easing out. I referred to him in "The Confidential" as "the ghetto's token white."

Anemone's feuds were not confined to police officers. In October 1996, a career felon shot and killed Lieutenant Federico Narvaez, who left a wife and six-year-old daughter. At his funeral in Rego Park, Queens, Louie lost it. Not at Narvaez's killer but at fifty-eight-year-old Howard Koeppel, a wealthy Queens car dealer and a Giuliani crony whom Safir appointed a deputy police commissioner after Koeppel donated a Pathfinder vehicle to the department. What had angered Louie was that at the funeral Koeppel violated the police department protocol. He made the mistake of sitting in the first pew, reserved for elected officials and police brass—in this case, Giuliani, Safir, Simonetti, and Anemone. "This guy," Anemone explained years later, "'invaded' the funeral ceremony, a solemn religious occasion, by pushing his way through police officers posted at the church, based on his friendship with Rudy and Howard. Then he invites himself to a front-row seat, where he now begins to flamboyantly preen, front and back, in what I believed to be an obviously disrespectful display of showcasing himself."

After the service, Anemone let Koeppel have it so harshly that Koeppel burst into tears. "I can't repeat what he said," cried Koeppel. "I couldn't repeat those words. He said he would knock my . . . head off. He was like a mad dog."

Said Anemone: "I was wrong for not controlling my anger, and for cursing in church, for the first and only time in my life."

Koeppel was so afraid of Anemone he said he considered filing an order of protection. He wondered out loud if Anemone had attacked him because he was Jewish, a claim denied even by Anemone's enemies. As one of them put it, "Louie's an equal opportunity abuser. He's equally unpleasant to everyone." While Giuliani called the incident "much ado about nothing," Koeppel complained to Safir. He reported that Safir had termed Anemone's conduct "inexcusable."

Equally damaging for Anemone was his relationship with police officer Frank Livoti. In December 1994, Livoti, a PBA delegate in the 46th Precinct in the Bronx, had provoked a confrontation with Anthony Baez, a twenty-eight-year-old asthmatic who was playing touch football with his brothers outside their home. Livoti then used a department-banned choke hold to subdue Baez, which purportedly led to his death.

Livoti had a history of trouble. At the time of the Baez incident, he was on disciplinary probation with a dozen civilian complaints against him, all but one for using excessive force. In 1991 he had slugged a lieutenant in his precinct. Anemone interceded, overruling the precinct commander's request to transfer Livoti, insisting that the commanding officer of the precinct handle the issue, rather than sending the problem to another precinct. The Baez family attorney, Sue Karten, would later say she held Anemone responsible for Baez's death. "If he had removed Livoti in 1991 it never would have happened."

After Baez's death, Borough President Fernando Ferrer asked Safir to appear at a public hearing in the Bronx. Safir demurred, instead sending Anemone. "I did not shirk my duty," Anemone said. "I went and took a hit for the team." He did so by defending Livoti. "The mere fact that eleven complaints were lodged against this officer," Anemone told the hearing, "over a career that extended probably eleven or twelve years or more in the police department with a distinguished career of service to the community, we are not going to prejudge him. This is an officer that has been very active in solving community problems, doing the kind of work that the citizenry of the city and certainly this country are looking for."

Needless to say, Anemone's remarks did not make him any new friends in the Bronx. Yet again, when it came to the police department, things are not always what they seem. There was another side to Anemone that the public never saw. I only happened to catch a glimpse of it after his retirement when William Morange was appointed chief of patrol. Before his appointment, Morange had commanded the 28th Precinct in Harlem. He had been so well regarded there he was known affectionately as "The White Prince of Harlem." At his swearing-in ceremony at Police Plaza, the first person I saw rush up to the podium to congratulate him was Father Lawrence Lucas, a Roman Catholic priest I had met in the Bronx twelve years before at the trial of Larry Davis. Davis, who had shot six cops, had become a folk hero in the Bronx and Lucas had brought a class of students to observe the trial as an antipolice civics lesson. Entering the courtroom, he had strode over to Davis's attorney, William Kunstler, and given him a bear hug of support.

Seeing Lucas's unconcealed affection for Morange made me question some of my assumptions about the police and the city's minority communities. Relations between them are more nuanced and complex than the media—myself included—portray them. It turned out that another chief whom Lucas said he respected was Anemone, who years before had commanded Harlem's 32nd Precinct. When I asked Anemone about this, he said that while Lucas "distrusted the police, underneath it, he felt we were both men of good will" and had accepted Anemone's offer to speak at his precinct.

"And he wasn't the only local official we met with," Anemone continued. He'd also met with Calvin Butts, the outspoken minister of the Abyssinian Baptist Church; Virginia Fields, then the Manhattan borough president; and Assemblyman Keith Wright, whose father, Justice Bruce Wright, had allowed so many suspects released without bail that cops gave him the sobriquet "Turn 'Em Loose Bruce."

"In the police department," said Anemone, "you learn how to work with everyone. I'm amazed you guys are shocked by this."

I was shocked. Not about what Anemone thought of the media shock but how someone sensitive to the feelings of so many minority officials could have appeared at a Bronx public meeting after Baez's death and praised Livoti as Anemone had.

In the fall of 1996, Livoti was acquitted by a Bronx judge of killing Baez. The PBA leadership attended his trial. Its president, Phil Caruso, hugged and kissed him. First Vice President Matarazzo called him "an adopted son." Two years later, Livoti was convicted in federal court of violating Baez's rights and sentenced to seven years in prison. While awaiting trial, Safir had him tried at Police Plaza on departmental charges. He was found guilty. At a news conference, Anemone was made to stand at Safir's side as the police commissioner announced Livoti's dismissal from the department.

For Louie, it was downhill from there. When his executive officer was promoted to chief of Bronx detectives, Anemone was unable to select his replacement. Safir and Kelleher did it for him. Perhaps, in light of Anemone's having transferred the two black chiefs to "the ghetto," they selected a black officer, James Lawrence.

In June 1999, a Brooklyn Law School students' association planned to honor Anemone and other law enforcement lights, including the head of the FBI's New York City office and former police commissioner Ward, a Brooklyn Law School graduate. When Safir, a Brooklyn Law School nongraduate, learned of this, he tried to upstage Louie. He contacted the association's president and asked to be honored as well. Its president named him man of the year.

"It was all about penis envy," said Anemone. "Almost from day one I never met a more insecure guy. He felt threatened by me, and all I wanted was to do my job. He surrounded himself with sycophants, as did Rudy, and had not a clue about true and loyal service to the city. Is it any surprise then that he campaigned and twisted arms for the Brooklyn Law School award?"

Anemone did not attend the law school ceremony. The next day, June 10, 1999, he announced his retirement. At his farewell news conference, he gave no explanation for his departure. He said only that he was burned out after thirty-two years. In a farewell article, *The New York Times* described him as "an architect" of the department's "successful but often criticized crime-fighting tactics," and "the driving force behind Compstat, feared for his merciless questionings of precinct commanders and his intolerance of failure."

His dream of becoming the first Italian American police commissioner was gone. Some said he had expected Giuliani to intercede for him, even to ask him to reconsider and stay. Giuliani did not. At his farewell dinner at the Marriott Marquis Hotel, Anemone spoke of his joys and sorrows as a top NYPD commander: his leading a rescue mission that landed helicopters atop the roof of the World Trade Center amid the swirling snow and smoke from the terrorist bomb in 1993; his ordering cops from the emergency rooms of Columbia Presbyterian and St. Barnabas Hospitals to find the killers of both Street Crime cop Kevin Gillespie and another dying police officer. His voice thick with emotion, he concluded, "They [police officers] ask for the benefit of the doubt when acting in the line of duty. Mistakes, honest mistakes will always be made in this business." He could well have been speaking of himself.

Anemone had asked John Miller to serve as his master of ceremonies. Miller advised him to make sure that no one objected. Giuliani was said to feel "uncomfortable" with Miller, who was to introduce the mayor, so Miller stepped aside.

In the end Giuliani didn't show up. Anemone was no longer of use to him. The mayor had cast his lot with Safir. For that he would pay a price.

SEVEN

The Tragedies of Abner Louima

and Amadou Diallo

i.

The anonymous thirty-second message on columnist Mike McAlary's voice mail at the *Daily News* described an assault so shocking it was hard to believe. "Mike McAlary, Mike McAlary, you don't know me but I'm calling because in the Seven-O precinct in Brooklyn on August the 9th at about 0400 hours, they, the cops, there sodomized a prisoner. They took a nightstick and shoved it up his behind and up into his bladder. The patient is currently at Coney Island Hospital. His name, his last name, is L-O-U-I-M-A.

"Now they're trying to cover it up because it was two white officers, and they did this to a black guy that they had locked up for disorderly conduct. And now they're charging him with assault in the second. All this information can be verified if you call Coney Island Hospital or the Seven-O Precinct. I will not call you again."

The Mike McAlary who received this message at 7:55 P.M. Monday, August 11, 1997, was no longer the tough guy of the tabloids nor the heir apparent to Jimmy Breslin. His Safir-Timoney "lightweight" column was barely a year old, but it felt like a lifetime for a man who could no longer count on a future. The first blow was professional, the libel case filed over his flawed coverage of the Prospect Park rape case. As the magazine *Vanity Fair* headlined an article by longtime investigative reporter M. A. Farber in October 1995, McAlary had "earned himself a $12 million lawsuit with his exclusive 'scoop' that a 27-year-old black lesbian had faked her own rape." Although the trial did not hold McAlary liable for damages, it savaged his reputation. Twenty-five *Daily News* staffers signed a petition calling his column on the rape a "disgrace." Farber's article quoted a law enforcement source on McAlary saying, "I wouldn't trust him with my oldest pair of jockey shorts."

The pressure from the libel suit had been so draining that McAlary ignored the warning signs of another problem, this one physical. He didn't think anything was wrong when he felt weak and tired. But he was in terrible danger, in a fight for his life. In late 1996, doctors found a cancerous tumor growing in his colon. He was thirty-eight-years old.

He kept his cancer a secret and sought to slip away from the rigors of daily journalism to concentrate on his fiction. He had recently completed a first novel, as well as a major magazine piece, optioned for a movie. At 10:00 A.M. Tuesday, August 12, the morning after he received that voice-mail call, McAlary's oncologist on the Upper East Side was giving him a cocktail of 5-FU and leucovorin, anticancer drugs that kept him alive. But the reprieve was temporary, like being on death row, as he wrote in "The Last Cop Story" in *Esquire* magazine in December 1997. Despite his troubles, he couldn't get that phone message out of his mind. He noted that the caller had used police jargon. The "Seven-O" for Brooklyn's 70th Precinct, and the military-like time of "0400 hours," 4:00 A.M. It sounded as though the anonymous voice belonged to a cop.

Before leaving for the doctor that morning, he had played the anonymous phone message for his wife, Alice. She urged him to investigate. "You have to do it," she said. "If this happened and you ignored this tip, you will never be able to look at yourself again." Battered and weak, McAlary was not yet done. He put his pain behind him and from his doctor's office raced out to Coney Island Hospital.

ii.

The patient he found was a "scrawny, even delicate" thirty-year-old security guard with a thin goatee and a mustache. Wincing from pain, an IV in one arm, a plastic tube in his abdomen, Abner Louima was handcuffed to his hospital bed. Police were treating him like a criminal. McAlary could see Louima's urine running red down one of the tubes, flooding into a plastic bag that hung at the foot of the bed. The cops' savagery had punctured his small intestine and bladder and perforated his colon. "Thank you for coming, Mac-Cleary," Louima whispered.

Louima, a Haitian immigrant, described himself as an innocent bystander who never should have been arrested. At 4:00 A.M. the previous Saturday, he had been in a rowdy crowd that had spilled out of the Club Rendezvous, a Haitian nightspot in Brooklyn. Two women began fighting on the street. In the confusion, Louima argued with a burly, dark-haired officer who had run over to stop the melee. Louima's cousin coldcocked the officer, knocking him to the ground. But the officer arrested Louima, blaming him for the punch, the first of many horrible mistakes that night. The officer handcuffed Louima and threw him into the backseat of an unmarked patrol car driven by another officer. Louima's dark night had begun.

As they drove to the 70th Precinct, they made two stops, Louima said, meeting with officers in another patrol car. "They kicked and beat me with their radios," Louima told McAlary. "They were yelling, 'You people can't even talk English. I am going to teach you to respect a cop.'"

At the station house, the "lesson" continued as the patrol car driver removed Louima's belt, causing his trousers to slip down, then paraded him, in his underwear, past the front desk. He couldn't hold them up because his hands were cuffed behind him. "My pants were down at my ankles, in full view of the other cops," Louima said.

Louima said the driver led him, rear-cuffed and in his underwear, down a hallway in the back of the precinct, past a room of holding cells, to the bathroom. Inside, the burly, dark-haired officer was waiting for him. Louima said the cop pulled down his underpants. When Louima cried out, he said the officer he described as "the driver" put his foot over Louima's mouth and pulled him up by the handcuffs. Then the burly dark-haired officer shoved a long wooden stick, like the handle of a bathroom plunger, up his rectum. "You niggers have to learn to respect police officers," he said to Louima. "If you yell or make any noise, I will kill you.'"

But the officer was not finished. Louima said his tormentor pulled out the stick and "shoved it in my mouth, broke my teeth and said, 'That's your shit, nigger.'" The officer then dumped him, moaning and bleeding, into a holding cell. For the next two hours, no one came to help him. "Later, when they called the ambulance," Louima said, "the cop told me, 'If you ever tell anyone . . . I will kill you and your family.'"

McAlary was skeptical of Louima's story. In all his police reporting, he had never seen, heard, or imagined an evil like this. Yet the details Louima described matched his internal injuries. Back at the *News*, McAlary's editors were equally skeptical of McAlary. It wasn't merely that he was relying on a single named source. Their doubt stemmed from his libel suit from the Prospect Park rape case. His editors wanted confirmation and turned to its police bureau chief John Marzulli down at the Shack. Marzulli confirmed that not only had an internal investigation begun into Louima's allegations incident but that people in Internal Affairs believed there was substance to them. Only then did the *News* go with the story, alerting the public to one of the worst brutality scandal in the NYPD's history.

"Tortured by Cops," the *News* announced on the next day's front page, with a picture of the frail Louima in his hospital bed. "Security Guard Tells McAlary." For days, the headlines captured the city's rage and the NYPD's widening investigation: "SHAME. Cops Charged in Torture, Beating at 70th Precinct. Two Sergeants Eyed as Probe Widens." "Heads Roll: Top Brass, 10 Cops Bounced as NYPD Vows to Clean House." In his first-day column, McAlary called Louima's ordeal "a story to stop the city . . . a tale straight from the police dungeon . . . crudely medieval." And so it was. Even the most jaded officers could not believe it. The first comments from One Police Plaza and from the PBA reflected their disbelief. The assault, the sodomy, this outrageous abuse of police power, never happened, both department and union officials initially told reporters. McAlary and Marzulli knew better.

It *had* happened. And it was worse than even Louima realized. Although twenty officers had been at the precinct when Louima was sodomized and a roomful of officers had seen him rear-cuffed, his pants down around his ankles, not one had tried to protect him. Granted, officers might not have been aware of the torture behind a closed bathroom door. Yet no one questioned why Louima became a bloody, moaning pulp in the holding cell. Not a single officer that night reported anything unusual.

"Why did no one stop this? Where were the superior officers?" asked Louima's attorney. The answer was that on that late Friday–early Saturday morning tour, there were no superior officers at the 70th Precinct. Louima's assault had happened on the midnight, the graveyard shift, when bosses are scarce and, as the Dirty Thirty scandal showed, crime and mischief can flourish. The Mollen Commission had warned of the perils of placing young, thirty-something sergeants in charge of precincts on those late-night tours, especially on weekends. But Giuliani had rejected all Mollen's recommendations.

On the night of Louima's attack, there was no captain or even a lieutenant at the precinct. The highest-ranking officer had been a desk sergeant, who in violation of the patrol guide, never inspected the holding cell where Louima lay, moaning and bleeding, for two hours before someone finally called an ambulance at 6:00 A.M. Leaving his shift, this sergeant reported nothing unusual.

Nor did Louima's suffering register with the first day-shift boss, the executive officer, Captain William Walsh, who arrived at the station house at 6:20 A.M. Saturday. The precinct's daily log showed that the captain had learned of the trouble at the Club Rendezvous. An entry noted that he had called the club's owner at home at 7:15 A.M. to say the police were issuing a disorderly establishment ticket. That was the extent of the problem as far as the captain was concerned. This bureaucratic step was Walsh's only known action regarding Louima. Yet how could Walsh not have known Louima had been injured? When he arrived for the day shift, an ambulance team of paramedics was waiting at the precinct for the required police escort to take the "prisoner" to the hospital.

The paramedics had to wait nearly an hour and a half until two day-shift cops could accompany them. Arriving at the hospital in the ambulance, the pair of cops told the nurses a lie: They blamed Louima's injuries on homosexual sex inside the Club Rendezvous's bathroom hours before. The cover-up had begun.

It would continue through three trials over the next five years. Once again, the Patrolmen's Benevolent Association, the police union, would play a sinister role. The day McAlary's story broke, a PBA lawyer, a PBA trustee, and a PBA delegate who was the brother of the dark, burly officer at the center of the scandal met in the 70th Precinct basement with the four cops subsequently charged. One of those four was himself a union delegate. Depending on whose account you accepted, the four cops were told either to stonewall or to get their stories straight. Either way, this basement meeting bordered on obstruction of justice.

Three of them would be convicted of precisely that. The blue wall of silence may have fallen in the Dirty Thirty scandal, where the PBA had had little official involvement. It remained firm in the 70th Precinct in Brooklyn.

The sodomizing of Abner Louima would become a national symbol of racism, police brutality, and cover-up. The Rodney King beating in Los Angeles six years before paled in comparison. Unlike the case of the adrenaline-pumped cops who beat King after a high-speed chase, Louima's sodomizing had been deliberate, premeditated, and sadistic. His story reverberated across the city and beyond, sparking marches, candlelight parades, and midnight vigils. Four thousand protestors massed outside the 70th Precinct station house, shouting insults at officers. Fifteen thousand, many waving toilet plungers, marched miles from the heart of Brooklyn over the Brooklyn Bridge to City Hall. The *Times* called the attack "the most politically explosive in the city's history." Haiti's ambassador to the United Nations condemned it. Editorials and television reports echoed the revulsion from across the country.

Federal prosecutors threatened an investigation into whether Louima's attack reflected a systemic pattern of brutality. If proved, that meant the federal government would monitor the NYPD, robbing Giuliani of power and control. "Among the most disturbing aspects," said U.S. Attorney Zachary Carter of the Eastern District, "is that one or more officers are alleged to have committed an act of almost incomprehensible depravity within the police precinct and with the apparent expectation that they would get away with it."

Dennis Walcott, president of the New York Urban League and cochairman of Safir's Respect Committee, said, "This case reinforces all the stereotypes that people have about police." Referring to Giuliani, he added, "Whether he agrees with it or not, he knows there is a major difference in this city as to how the police department is viewed." He meant there was a different view of police held by whites and blacks.

For Giuliani, the timing spelled political disaster as it hit three months before the 1997 mayoral election. Louima himself injected politics into his ordeal, claiming that his police tormentors had taunted him by saying, "This is Giuliani time; it's not Dinkins time." The implication was that the mayor approved torture. Interviewed on the television program *Nightline*, McAlary denied Giuliani was a bigot. "But does he enable cops to feel like they can go further than their bosses would allow them to? I believe yes."

A *Times* story chided the mayor more diplomatically. "No one has suggested Mr. Giuliani has deliberately encouraged officers to act brutally. But Mr. Giuliani's famously bellicose public posture and close identification with the police has, many critics charge, fostered an atmosphere subject to easy misinterpretation by the worst elements of the Police Department." Both the *Times* and McAlary, I felt, were correct. But both missed the larger point. I agreed with McAlary that Giuliani was no bigot. I agreed with the *Times* that he did not deliberately encourage cops to break the law by behaving brutally. But their suggestion that Giuliani, as the *Times* put it, had "fostered an atmosphere subject to easy misinterpretation" was misplaced. Rather, it was the culture of the police department that had encouraged the cops to believe that their actions would be protected by their fellow cops: their belief in the blue wall of silence.

Exploiting the scandal, Al Sharpton—whom Giuliani had ignored since the Harlem mosque standoff his first week in office—made police brutality the centerpiece of his mayoral campaign. He blasted Giuliani's defense of cops accused of past misconduct as "a signal to people in the police force that are abusive that they will be defended and they do not have to act with caution." He and former mayor Dinkins visited Louima in the hospital. Sharpton then marched with Louima's family to City Hall, proclaiming that public outrage would win him the September Democratic primary. He was successful enough to force a runoff with front-runner Ruth Messinger.

Giuliani moved quickly to contain the damage. At a City Hall news conference, flanked by Safir and the head of the Internal Affairs Bureau, he called the accusations "shocking" and vowed that "every effort will be made to investigate these allegations as quickly and thoroughly as possible." The charges, if substantiated, he continued, "should result in the severest penalties, including substantial terms of imprisonment." He and Safir visited Louima in the hospital. Meeting with Haitian leaders, Giuliani announced the establishment of a twenty-nine-man task force at a cost of $1.5 million to ease police-community tensions. He also altered his policy of extending the benefit of the doubt to accused cops. In the Louima attack, he offered his strongest public condemnation of police officers. "I would like an explanation why people sat around while [Louima] was suffering and were not able to figure out how to get him to the hospital." As for Louima's "It's Giuliani time" quote, the mayor dismissed it, saying, "The remark is as perverted as the alleged act." Indeed, Louima later admitted he had made it up.

Safir, too, acted swiftly, punishing and dismissing the entire leadership of the 70th Precinct. He transferred the commanding officer, on vacation at the time of the attack; docked the pay of the desk sergeant; and restricted the do-nothing Captain Walsh to modified duty. He placed nine other officers on desk duty. But, typically, he went too far. He transferred into the precinct twenty-four black cops, who filed a discrimination suit, maintaining that race was the reason for their assignments. At trial, they were each awarded $50,000.

Prosecutors also moved quickly. The afternoon McAlary's first story appeared, they charged police officer Justin Volpe as the cop who had sodomized Louima. Within days, they charged officer Charles Schwarz as "the second man" inside the bathroom who had held Louima down. Volpe and Schwarz, together with their respective partners, Thomas Bruder and Thomas Wiese, were also charged with having beaten Louima on the ride to the station house. Prosecutors charged their patrol sergeant, Michael Bellomo, of covering up those attacks.

Yet again, when it comes to the NYPD, things are not always what they seem. Volpe, the attacker, defied stereotyping. His background seemed worlds from barbarism. He was a twenty-five-year-old college graduate, whose grandfather had been, of all things, a banker. His father, Robert Volpe, was an ex-detective, known as the "art cop"—an expert in fine art who traveled across the country exposing forgeries. His mother was a schoolteacher. Volpe himself lived at home with his parents. This young man, accused of the most heinous act of brutality and racism, was dating a black woman, a civilian employee at the precinct, who said they were planning to marry. The only red flag, it turned out, was that he was a steroid user.

Robert Volpe hired the wily criminal attorney Marvyn Kornberg to represent his son. From his office across from the Queens County criminal courthouse, the sharp-tongued Kornberg personified the brassy patter of city life among club-house pols, union big shots, mobsters, detectives, and reporters, whose stories were memorialized by Jimmy Breslin as New York lore. Kornberg had reveled in the tabloid headlines for more than a decade. He had represented one of the black victims of the infamous 1985 stun-gun case in the 106th Precinct, giving Breslin the exclusive, which ran on the front page of the *Daily News*. The following year, Breslin won a long overdue Pulitzer Prize. A decade later, the *News* named Kornberg among the city's ten best criminal lawyers. On his office wall, he kept a laminated copy of that article with a sign that read, "Kornberg's Rule of Law: Presumption of Innocence Commences with Payment of Retainer."

Like the best criminal attorneys, Kornberg had no ideology. To him, defending cops was no different from defending civilians who sued cops. By the time of the Louima attack, his reputation was that of the city's go-to guy for cops in the deepest trouble, as Volpe surely was. As Kornberg said to McAlary when he took the case, "My bank just presumed Volpe innocent."

Hoping to humanize Volpe, Kornberg allowed McAlary to interview him, making sure Volpe brought his black girlfriend. Volpe himself was still in cover-up mode. "It didn't happen the way they are saying," he told McAlary. "It wasn't me. If it happened, it wasn't me. It happened before. A lot of stuff is going to come out about that club. There may have been a fight in that bathroom."

Meanwhile Schwarz's partner Wiese, who was a union delegate, added more confusion. He told the authorities that he—not Schwarz—had been the second man inside the bathroom. In Wiese's telling, he had been sitting outside, playing with the precinct's stray dog, when he heard scuffling and the sound of a body hitting the bathroom floor. He said he entered to find Volpe bent over Louima, brandishing a stick covered with excrement. Conveniently, Wiese claimed to have entered the bathroom *after* Volpe's attack, sparing him from complicity.

But Wiese, like all the others, did not report the incident at the time. So what did his account mean? Prosecutors dismissed it, maintaining he was covering for Schwarz. Yet I came to wonder whether prosecutors had rejected it too quickly. For whatever reason, Wiese was placing himself in that bathroom, implicating himself when he had no reason to—unless he had something to hide. I wondered whether his sitting outside the bathroom with the dog meant that he had served as a lookout for Volpe. I also wondered whether by entering the bathroom he had interrupted Volpe's attack. If he had indeed entered the bathroom, that meant that he, not Schwarz, had been the "second man."

Louima had identified the second attacker only as "the driver" of the patrol car that took him to the station house. He had been unable to identify Schwarz either from a photo array or in person. Could Louima have mistaken him for Wiese? The irony was that even though an officer had breached the blue wall by coming forward, no one believed him.

iii.

The trial in March 1999, nearly two years after the attack, began with Kornberg's flair for the outrageous. Continuing the lie spread on the first day at Coney Island Hospital, he suggested, falsely, that Louima's internal injuries had been caused not by his client, Volpe, but by rough homosexual sex at the Club Rendezvous. As Kornberg delicately put it, Louima's injuries were "not consistent with a nonconsensual insertion of an object into his rectum."

The "gay defense," as I termed it, placed Kornberg again in the media spotlight, which he loved. His defense also brought him torrents of criticism, which he also seemed to enjoy. Other criminal lawyers derided his methods. Editorial writers questioned his ethics. A longtime defender of cops blasted his "shameful gutter tactic." No less than Sharpton—ordered to pay $65,000 for falsely accusing an upstate prosecutor of raping Tawana Brawley—called Kornberg's homosexual allegations "beyond the realm of any decency."

Safir, meanwhile, in perhaps his finest moment, ordered hundreds of Internal Affairs detectives to investigate the Louima case. As the Mollen Commission had noted, under the glare of the media spotlight, the NYPD can perform very effectively. Within days, they came up with four 70th Precinct officers whose stories would shatter at least a section of the blue wall. Their star witness was Eric Turetzky, who had responded with Volpe to the fight outside the Club Rendezvous. No angel, Turetzky had crudely told a pregnant woman that if she did not move he would smack her in the stomach. Whatever his motives, Turetzky agreed to testify against Volpe. As the first officer to breach the blue wall, he was labeled a hero by Safir and the media. Like Serpico three decades before, he received twenty-four-hour police protection. His coming forward even prompted Serpico to write to the *Times*: "One of the most telling developments in the recent calamity is that Eric Turetzky, the police officer credited with toppling the 'blue wall of silence' by stepping forward to identify the precinct's rogue officers, now finds himself in need of police protection—from other police."

Turetzky did not disappoint. He testified that back at the precinct, he had seen Schwarz lead Louima, rear-cuffed, his trousers around his knees, from the front desk toward the bathroom. He acknowledged he hadn't seen Schwarz enter the bathroom. But fifteen minutes later, he saw Volpe escorting Louima, still rear-cuffed, trousers still down, to a holding cell. "He was holding Mr. Louima in his left hand, and in his right hand was a stick," Turetzky testified. "His uniform was a little bit messed up. . . . When he turned to place Mr. Louima in his cell, I observed he was not wearing his nameplate or his badge. . . . He was swinging the stick around like a sword and hitting it against the wall of the arrest processing room."

IAB came up with three other police witnesses. Each proved damning to Volpe. Sergeant Kenneth Wernick testified Volpe had boasted about torturing a prisoner with a stick. "I broke a man down," Wernick said Volpe had bragged. Officer Mark Schofield testified he had loaned Volpe a pair of gloves just before the attack and that Volpe had returned them covered with blood. Officer Michael Schoer said Volpe had taunted him by waving the end of the excrement-covered stick in his face. As Schoer left the witness stand, he stood and for a moment stared at Volpe with a look of disgust.

Kornberg never cross-examined them. He had, in effect, thrown in the towel. In the midst of the trial, he announced Volpe was dropping his defense and would plead guilty. He was sentenced to thirty years in prison.

But it wasn't over. In fact, the case became more confusing than ever. The confusion focused on Schwarz and his role as "the second man" and was abetted by a chain of decisions by the trial judge, the chief prosecutor, and Schwarz's attorney. In pleading guilty, Volpe maintained to Kornberg that Wiese, not Schwarz, had been the second man in the bathroom. Or as Kornberg put it in his best Queens Boulevard patois to Schwarz's PBA attorney, Stephen Worth, the day before Volpe took his formal plea, "My guy can take your guy out of the bathroom."

In a variation of Wiese's account, Volpe told Kornberg that while Wiese had not participated, he had seen everything that happened and done nothing to stop it. But the jury never heard Volpe identify Wiese as the second man. Federal prosecutors objected to Volpe's naming him because it was at odds with their case against Schwarz. Instead, prosecutors claimed that Volpe, like Wiese, was lying to cover up for Schwarz.

The patrician, eighty-year-old federal trial judge Eugene Nickerson—a descendant of President John Adams—went along with the prosecutors. Nickerson ruled that Volpe had to structure his plea to avoid identifying the second man by name. Volpe was permitted to say only, "There was another officer in the bathroom with me. That police officer saw what was going on, did nothing to stop it. It was understood from the circumstances that that police officer would do nothing to stop me or to report it to anyone."

Finally, in the most bizarre decision of all, Worth chose not to call Volpe as a defense witness for Schwarz—or even to interview him. It was, as Kornberg put it, "a colossal blunder." Worth, I knew, distrusted Kornberg. The year before, the two had bid for the PBA's annual $10 million retainer after the union's former law firm had been convicted of bribery and extortion. Although Kornberg maintained his bid had been lower, Worth won the contract.

In refusing to call Volpe, Worth maintained that Volpe was radioactive, that no jury would believe him. "Justin Volpe, the man who has admitted to torturing another individual?" Worth scoffed. On the other hand, Volpe's testimony seemed crucial in clearing Schwarz. Louima had not been unable to identify him. He could say only that the second man inside the bathroom had been "the driver" of the patrol car that had taken him to the precinct. Turetzky testified only that he had seen Schwarz leading Louima *toward* the bathroom, not entering it. How could Worth have not called Volpe? I asked myself.

Instead, in his defense of Schwarz, Worth claimed that Volpe had acted alone, that Louima had fabricated the second man to "preserve his manhood" because he hadn't fought back. There was nothing to back up this claim, and his defense failed. Schwarz was convicted as the second man. Hearing the jury's verdict, he looked up in disbelief. It was, I felt, the spontaneous reaction of an innocent man—at least to his having been "the second man." He was sentenced to sixteen years in prison. Volpe's partner Bruder and Wiese were both acquitted of participating in the assault of Louima while driving him to the precinct, as was Sergeant Bellomo.

By the time the trials ended, I felt I knew less about what had actually happened inside that bathroom than I had before the trials started. Wiese's account was confusing enough. Volpe's, which to some extent matched Wiese's, made it even more so. I was still uncertain about Schwarz. If he wasn't the second man, I asked myself, why had he denied leading Louima toward the bathroom when others had seen him do it? Perhaps he knew Volpe was going to tune Louima up, as they called it in the department, but had no idea Volpe would go as far as he did. Maybe *he*, not Wiese had been the lookout. The breach of the blue wall had only confused me more.

My confusion grew with time. In February 2002, a federal appeals court overturned Schwarz's conviction. The judges appeared to share my doubts. Because of Worth's inept defense, they ordered a new trial. "Schwarz had an obvious strategic advantage in implicating another officer in the bathroom assault," the judges wrote. "Worth could have relied on Volpe's potential testimony, Louima's inability to identify Schwarz . . . and Wiese's own statement that he had been the officer who escorted Louima to the restroom to argue with considerate force that the second officer was Wiese." Instead, the judges said, Worth "advanced the implausible and factually unsupported theory that Volpe acted alone," adding that he "did so in a manner that sought to avoid implicating Wiese."

But the judges concluded with something I had missed. They stated that Worth had a professional conflict of interest because of his representation of the PBA. "We are convinced," they wrote, "that no effective conflict-free defense attorney would have acted as Worth did, and thus, only Worth's conflict could explain his actions." Besides representing Schwarz, the judges pointed out that Worth, with his $10 million annual PBA retainer, was also representing the union. With Wiese as a delegate, it was facing a multimillion-dollar civil suit that Louima had filed. "As a result," the judges wrote, "Worth faced an actual conflict between his representation of Schwarz, on the one hand, and both his professional obligation to the PBA and his self-interest, on the other." Casting Volpe as an aberrant officer, they said, "would have been consistent with any defense advanced in the civil case. Implicating a second officer—especially a union delegate—would have added fuel to the suit that a PBA conspiracy or cover-up existed."

Yet I wasn't certain the judges had gotten it right either. As I read their decision overturning Schwarz's conviction, I found myself thinking of something else. The judges had ridiculed Worth for claiming there had been no second officer and saying Louima had manufactured him out of masculine pride. But I wondered whether in his terrified state Louima may have believed a second officer was helping Volpe when in fact Wiese had stood by and done nothing to stop him. Perhaps Wiese had even tried to help Louima, as Wiese claimed, and Louima had misinterpreted his actions. Maybe Worth had got it half right.

Louima ultimately became a wealthy man. Both the city and the PBA settled his civil suit for $8.75 million. The city's share, $7.125 million, was the largest amount ever paid in a police brutality suit anywhere. The PBA paid $1.625 million, the first time a police union had paid off on a police abuse claim. Still, the settlement did not answer the question about Schwarz, who on the eve of yet another trial pleaded guilty to perjury for stating he had not led Louima toward the bathroom. He continued to deny he was the second man.

So what did the Louima case mean? Giuliani and Safir had defused its worst aspects by aggressively pursuing Volpe. The idea of a federal monitor overseeing the police died. Sharpton lost the Democratic primary and Giuliani won re-election. Giuliani and Safir appeared to have dodged a bullet. They would not be as lucky the next time.

For the PBA the repercussions were all negative. IAB's former head John Guido was so outraged that he called in from retirement to insist the union had to change the way it did business. "The entire NYPD culture has to change," he said. "The PBA has got to come out and say, 'Brutal cops are hurting us.'" Guido may have been correct but the PBA made no such acknowledgment.

As for the cops, their loyalty to each other had prevented them from doing their duty to report Volpe's attack. "Here there was one bad guy, Volpe," said a lawyer involved in the case. "The others all got caught up in it and so did the union. Had the others not protected him, they would have been spared."

Then without realizing it, the lawyer hit on the nub of the problem. "I am so impressed by what these people do for society for such little money," the lawyer added. "But as much as I love and respect them, I know they will never fully trust me. To them I will always remain an outsider."

Today, more than a decade after Volpe sodomized Louima, no one can say with certainty that there was a second man in the bathroom with them. No one can say with certainty that he was Chuck Schwarz. No one knows whether Volpe sought to protect Schwarz in his guilty plea by fingering Wiese. No one knows whether Wiese sought to protect Schwarz with his story of entering the bathroom. For that matter, no one knows whether Schwarz himself pleaded guilty to perjury to protect his partner Wiese.

iv.

Finally, there was McAlary. His bringing this tragic story of police brutality to public light would, a year after that anonymous phone call, win him the Pulitzer Prize. As he and his wife, Alice, walked into the *Daily News* newsroom to accept his colleagues' congratulations, she began to cry. So did others. They knew what lay ahead.

That December, McAlary was admitted to Columbia Presbyterian Hospital. One of his first visitors was Timoney. Although McAlary's "lightweight" column had cost Timoney his job and nearly part of his pension, Timoney had never deserted him. At Bratton's farewell dinner two years before, speaker after speaker had raked McAlary for putting Timoney in harm's way. Timoney defended him, saying he had specifically told McAlary to print his quotes. Over the next two years, he would draw even closer to McAlary, even as McAlary would hurt him again.

The novel McAlary had completed was called *Sore Loser*. Its hero was a New York City police inspector whose teenage daughter is hooked on heroin. At the time, McAlary knew about Timoney's daughter. It was a secret her father had kept from the public — until McAlary's novel revealed it.

Again, Timoney forgave him although his friends didn't. One Saturday in December, he drove up from Philadelphia, picked up Maple and visited McAlary in the hospital. He was already fading. Growing up in Ireland, Timoney recalled having seen sick people with "dead eyes." He said to Maple, "He won't last till Christmas."

The week before Christmas, I visited McAlary in the hospital. He was asleep, full of tubes and doped up on morphine. His parents had driven down from New Hampshire and were at his side. They woke him, and though he could barely speak, he began to praise "The Confidential" to them. "This is the best police reporter in the city," he said of me. "No, Mac," I interrupted. "You are." I reminded him that when the column had debuted four years before, he had been the first person to call and offer congratulations, and that he had broken more police stories than any other columnist and reporter combined.

He died on Christmas day. That morning in Philadelphia, Timoney did a series of early morning roll calls, then headed to New York to join his family. While on the Jersey Turnpike, his phone rang. It was McAlary's closest newspaper friend, Jim Dwyer, telling him that McAlary had passed on. He *had* lasted till Christmas. Timoney thought, The son of a bitch made a liar out of me.

Hundreds of people attended McAlary's funeral near his home on Long Island, including Timoney, Ray Kelly, and Andrew Cuomo, the former governor's son, with his then wife Kerry Kennedy, Robert Kennedy's daughter, the two of them holding their babies. There was also a slim black man who sat in the rear of the church and kept to himself. It was Abner Louima.

v.

On the night of Feburary 4, 1999, on the eve of Louima's trial, four cops from the Street Crime Unit were riding in plainclothes in an unmarked patrol car in the South Bronx. The senior man, Sean Carroll, had been in the unit just over two years; the three others, only three months. They had no supervisor. Until that night, they had never worked together. Nor had they ever been in the neighborhood they were patrolling.

As they rolled past a small apartment building at 1157 Wheeler Avenue, Carroll, in the passenger seat, noticed a slim black man over his right shoulder. The black man was standing inside the building's vestibule, peeking in and out. Carroll ordered the driver, Officer Kenneth Boss, to back up the car. Carroll got out and walked toward the apartment building. Officer Edward McMellon, seated in the backseat, followed. Boss and the fourth cop, Richard Murphy, also got out, staying a few paces behind. Approaching the black man, Carroll asked for identification. The black man didn't appear to respond. Instead, he retreated deeper into the vestibule, reached into his back pants pocket, then turned quickly back to Carroll. This second turn doomed him.

"He's got a gun. He's got a gun," Carroll shouted and began to fire. Retreating, Carroll fired sixteen rounds. McMellon, also retreating, slipped and fell but got off sixteen rounds. Seeing him fall, Boss and Murphy thought he had been hit. Boss fired five times; Murphy, four. In all, they fired a total of forty-one shots. Nineteen struck the black man. Approaching him as he lay dying inside the vestibule, a stunned Carroll realized that the gun he thought he saw was the black man's wallet, which lay on the ground beside him. Carroll fell to his knees and began to sob.

He lifted the black man's shirt to try and resuscitate him. Then he saw the two bullet wounds in his stomach. He stopped, took the man's hands in his, then began rubbing the black man's face. "Keep breathing," he whispered. "Please don't die. Please please don't die."

The fatal shooting of twenty-three-year-old Amadou Diallo, an unarmed immigrant from the West African country of Guinea, would become the defining moment of Safir's tenure as police commissioner. Unlike Volpe's aberrant sodomizing of Louima, Diallo's death was a direct result of police policy—specifically, Safir's expansion of the Street Crime Unit. So anxious was Safir to expand the unit that commanders had ignored the guidelines set by its commander, Richard Savage, that recruits have no prior civilian complaints or prior shooting incidents. Three of the officers in the Diallo shooting had civilian complaints. Three had previously fired their weapons.

As for that sixth sense that its commander had boasted the best Street Crime officers possessed, Carroll, the lead officer, had completely misread the situation. Every assumption Carroll made about Diallo proved false. It apparently never occurred to him that Diallo might live in the building in which Carroll spotted him or that he might not understand colloquial English. It never occurred to Carroll that although he and McMellon wore police shields around their necks, their appearing in plainclothes might have frightened Diallo into silence. Or that the reason he had reached into his pocket to remove his wallet might have been due to his immigrant's understanding that the authorities wanted to see his papers. Once again, the department's treatment of a man with black skin had tragic, and cataclysmic, consequences.

As in the Louima case, the first reaction out of Police Plaza was denial. Not that the event hadn't occurred. No one disputed that the police had fired forty-one shots, nineteen of which had struck Diallo, in what the police term "contagious shooting." Rather, it was that the shooting couldn't have happened the way it appeared to have. Cops don't shoot down unarmed civilians without a reason. There had to be an explanation. The first anonymous comments out of Police Plaza and the PBA reflected this. But in their haste to justify the shooting, they got it all wrong.

First, they said Carroll might have been suspicious because Diallo was making "furtive gestures," as though serving as a lookout for a push-in robbery team, so-called for pushing in apartment doors. The problem was that no one had reported any push-in robberies in the neighborhood. Next, they said Diallo "remarkably" resembled a rapist the police were searching for. How Carroll could have spotted a resemblance yards away in the darkness remained a mystery. Finally, there was the illegal immigrant theory. If Diallo were here illegally, that might explain his refusal to identify himself. Police subsequently ransacked Diallo's apartment in an attempt to find a hint of criminal activity. There was none. A street peddler, he had never been arrested. He was, in fact, here legally, although the story he had given U.S. immigration officials—that his parents were dead and that he needed political asylum—was untrue. Until his death, the last day of his life had been like any other for him. He had worked ten to twelve hours peddling videotapes in Lower Manhattan. He had taken the subway home around midnight, then stepped outside into a chilly February night, Most important and inescapable, he was unarmed. There was no gun.

Article 35 of the New York State penal code spells out the circumstances when a police officer may justifiably use deadly physical force if he reasonably feels his life or that of his partner is threatened. What this means is that even in a worst-case scenario, as the Diallo shooting was, if an officer makes a reasonable mistake, no matter how deadly the consequence, his actions are not considered criminal. There is also an unwritten contract between police and society that anyone familiar with our criminal justice system realizes; it is not law, but it has been custom and practice everywhere in the United States. It goes something like this: Because police officers put their lives on the line to protect its citizens, those citizens will give its police officers every benefit of the doubt. Unlike Volpe's sodomizing of Louima, which was deliberate, premeditated, evil, and unjustifiable on any grounds, Diallo's shooting, so the argument went, was a tragedy, not a crime.

There is another unwritten fact of American life. There exists a racial divide between white and black Americans in their perceptions of the police. By and large, white Americans trust the police. By and large, black Americans do not. The nation came face-to-face with this in the O. J. Simpson case. Virtually all white Americans believed Simpson got away with murdering his white wife, Nicole. Virtually all black Americans cheered when he was found not guilty, feeling that he bested a racist system. Furthermore, the prosecutors—a white woman and a black male—misjudged the middle-class, black women jurors they selected. They thought middle-class black women would feel the same sympathy that white women felt toward Nicole and the same revulsion white women felt toward O.J. Instead, the black women jurors sympathized with O.J. and reviled Nicole.

In New York City, the racial divide was on view in a series of police-related shootings a generation before. In the early 1970s there had been the Black Liberation Army killings of police officers. In 1972 there had been the fatal Harlem mosque shooting of police officer Philip Cardillo (for which no one was convicted). A year later, Thomas Shea, a white police officer, shot and killed Clifford Glover, a ten-year-old black boy, who was fleeing across a vacant lot with his grandfather, whom Shea was pursuing. At his trial, Shea testified he had fired at the ten-year-old in self-defense. "The boy made a reaching motion and I saw what I believed was a revolver." No revolver was found. A jury of eleven white men and a black woman found Shea not guilty.

Three years later, on November 25, 1976, Robert Torsney, a white police officer, was patrolling the day before Thanksgiving when he stopped Randolph Evans, a fifteen-year-old black teenager. For no apparent reason, Torsney put his gun to Evans's head and shot him dead. At his trial, Torsney testified he had fired after he saw Evans "pull out a silver object which looked like the barrel of a gun." No gun was found. An all-white jury found Torsney not guilty.

A decade later, with increasing numbers of blacks on juries, the dynamic had shifted. Many blacks appeared to be not only antipolice but antiwhite. Nowhere was this more apparent than in the Bronx, with its large black population, where police referred pejoratively to "Bronx juries." In 1988—two years after Larry Davis shot six white cops in his sister's Bronx apartment—he went on trial. A jury of ten blacks and two Hispanics found him not guilty, accepting his assertion that he had fired in self-defense. The jury also acquitted him of six counts of aggravated assault. He was convicted only of the least serious crime, possession of a weapon.

The year before that shooting, a black police officer, Marvin Yearwood, had gone on trial for fatally shooting an unarmed white teenager, Paul Fava. "It was as bad a shooting as I've seen," said Yearwood's attorney Bruce Smirti. "The kid was standing on an elevated subway platform. Yearwood was questioning him, gun cocked against the kid's head, when it accidentally discharged. You could see the muzzle imprint on the skin of his temple." A Bronx jury acquitted Yearwood.

To combat what they viewed as reverse prejudice, attorneys for indicted police officers devised a new tactic. White officers accused of killing blacks began waiving their right to a jury trial, opting instead to have a judge preside over their cases. Usually, that judge was an older white man, specifically selected as close to retirement age so that he could ignore political pressure. That, at least, was the stated reason.

In 1987, police officer Stephen Sullivan went on trial for fatally shooting Eleanor Bumpurs. Sullivan waived his right to a jury and was tried in State Supreme Court by Justice Fred Eggert. Eggert acquitted him, then retired. In 1996 when Frank Livoti went on trial for killing Anthony Baez, he, too, waived a jury trial. He was tried by a white judge, Gerald Sheindlin. Sheindlin acquitted him. In 1998, Michael Meyer, a white, off-duty police officer, shot Antoine Reid, an unarmed squeegee man, and was charged with attempted murder. Another white judge, John P. Collins, acquitted him.

But the Diallo shooting was different. It resonated among New Yorkers, black and white, in ways the city had never seen before. First, there was the starkness of his death. Four police officers had killed an unarmed civilian. They had fired forty-one shots at someone having no criminal record, who was standing by himself, minding his business. For reasons they could not explain, the cops had believed he might have committed a crime. They had believed he had a gun. The sole explanation for these misjudgments was that the man was black.

Then there were Giuliani and Safir. There was Giuliani's bellicose public posture and identification with the police and his single-minded determination to reduce crime at the expense of all else. And there was Safir being Safir. Because the shooting had resulted from official police policy—Safir's expansion of the Street Crime Unit—Safir defended the officers. Giuliani defended Safir. The two became hostage to their own failed policies.

Failing to recognize the shooting's import, Safir went off to California with his wife the following weekend to attend a weeklong police chiefs' conference. The department made no announcement of his whereabouts. I got a tip that he was in Los Angeles playing golf with other chiefs. Newsday sent a photographer. After the story appeared, Giuliani had him cut his trip short and return to New York.

The following month, Safir made another stealth trip to California—this one to attend the Oscars. The Sunday night of the Academy Awards, he was spotted on national television in a tuxedo, standing next to the actress Helen Hunt. To attend the ceremony, he had canceled his Monday morning's appearance before the City Council to testify about the Diallo shooting. Mode had given as the reason for his cancellation a "scheduling conflict," citing unspecified "important meetings."

After reports of his Oscar appearance played on the Sunday night news,

Giuliani ordered him to return on the red-eye so that he could appear the next morning before the council.

It grew worse. When reporters examined the circumstances of his trip, they discovered Safir had been flown to California on a Revlon corporate jet and spent two nights at a four-star Beverly Hills hotel—paid for by Revlon's CEO. When the Conflict of Interest Board hesitated to discipline Safir, I provided weekly updates in "The Confidential," describing what I termed the city's "four-corner stall." More than a year later, Safir repaid Revlon's CEO, George Fellows, $7,100 for the cost of his Oscar excursion.

Meanwhile, the Diallo crisis was building. *The New Yorker* ran a provocative cover cartoon of cops at a shooting gallery firing forty-one shots. Bruce Springsteen wrote a song, "American Skin," which mentioned the words "forty-one shots" nine times and which, a year later, he sang at Madison Square Garden. Even the *New York Post*, the unofficial mouthpiece for Giuliani and the police department, ran front-page headlines: "In Cold Blood," "Justice Must Be Done," and "We Are All Crying."

Diallo's mother Katiadou arrived from Guinea and announced she was seeking justice for her son. She took up temporary residence and wrote a book, *My Heart Will Cross This Ocean*, with the subtitle, *My Story: My Son Amadou*. The city subsequently awarded her $3 million.

At the same time, monthlong daily protests began outside Police Plaza. Partly this was political payback from Sharpton, who was expert in exploiting a racial wound and turning it into theater. The demonstrations quickly assumed the stature of civil rights protests. Black political leaders from former mayor Dinkins to Congressman Charles Rangel to Jesse Jackson appeared. The protests were meticulously orchestrated. After marching outside on the plaza, small groups attempted to enter headquarters, disregarded orders to halt, and got themselves arrested. As Rangel's chief of staff James Capel said of the congressman's planned arrest, "Unless there's snow or rain that will give him pneumonia, he is likely to commit some acts of civil disobedience."

Yet the demonstrations were more than grandstanding. They reflected the anguish of most black New Yorkers. The NYPD's former deputy commissioner for community affairs Wilhemina Holiday spoke for many when she said, "This could have happened to any one of us. It's a sad state of affairs when police officers believe all blacks and Hispanics are criminals." Although Ben Ward, the city's first black police commissioner, didn't appear, Holiday announced he supported the protestors. At the fiftieth anniversary dance of the Guardians Association, Ward told black police officers he wanted to see the four cops suspended. He also blasted the Bronx district attorney, Robert Johnson, "for taking too damn long" in his grand jury investigation.

The Diallo shooting also prompted shocks of recognition by two prominent black New Yorkers. According to the *Times*, Deputy Mayor Rudy Washington, the highest-ranking black in Giuliani's administration, told the mayor that white officers had harassed him more than once, presumably because of his race. One incident, which occurred near his home in southeast Queens, had brought his wife to tears.

Former chief of department David Scott told of an incident some years before in which he had transferred the white precinct commander and white desk officer of the 103rd Precinct in Queens after they treated him disrespectfully. Scott had appeared at the precinct in civilian clothes. When he related this at a dinner dance of black law enforcement officials, he received a standing ovation. That incident, he later pointed out, had not occurred under Giuliani but during the Dinkins administration.

The black weekly, the *Amsterdam News*, then reported that Scott more recently had been stopped near his home in Queens by a white cop who called him "Homey." Scott denied that anecdote. "It never happened to me," he said. "The *Amsterdam News* printed it, but it was folklore, not fact."

Safir, meanwhile, seemed desperate to be photographed with virtually any black group or leader, even expressing the possibility of meeting with Sharpton. Such a meeting was, of course, anathema to Giuliani and never occurred. Instead, Safir found an obscure African, Sidiqui Wei, a native of Sierra Leone who headed a Brooklyn group called the African United Congress. Wei said he viewed himself as a bridge between the city's American and African blacks, who were said to number about two hundred thousand in New York. He said he had attended Diallo's funeral and heard Sharpton refer to him as "Brother Sidiqui." Rangel, however, called Wei a "fraud," apparently because he was not an African American in the conventional sense.

Safir belatedly attempted to soften the image of the Street Crime Unit. But a well-publicized "cultural diversity" class at the Police Academy auditorium ended in chaos. About 150 cops attended the all-day session, run by a black sergeant and featuring role-playing and lectures on stereotyping and civilian straight talk. The meeting became so fractious that one of the unit's few black officers got into a confrontation with the sergeant, accusing the sergeant of having called him an Uncle Tom. At the next session, a white PBA trustee acted as mediator.

With no explanation, Safir then announced he was placing the entire Street Crime Unit in uniform; he promoted all its officers to detective specialist, then transferred its last commander, Bruce Smolka. While the media wrote that Safir was "overhauling" and "reforming" the unit, he had, in effect, ended it. Apparently without realizing it, he had re-created the defunct and discredited Tactical Patrol Force, which two decades before, also free of precinct supervision, had roamed the city in uniform as the Street Crime Unit did in plainclothes. In one of his first acts as commissioner in the 1980s, Ward had abolished it, citing its poor image in minority communities.

The Street Crime officers understood what Safir's move to uniform meant. From atop their Randalls Island headquarters building, they flew a white flag of surrender.

In April 1999, the four Diallo cops were indicted. Bronx District Attorney Johnson was then New York State's only black district attorney and a cautious supporter of the police. "In every corner of this county, [black] people are concerned about public safety and are not anti-police," he explained. But, he added, "There is a small percentage of the police who use excessive force or disrespect the community."

It was Johnson who pursued Larry Davis after his two predecessors—both white men—had failed to convict him for shooting the six cops. When he was at last convicted in 1991 of killing a drug dealer, Johnson said the guilty verdict "means that a very dangerous individual is going to be made to pay for his wanton acts. . . . The people intend to seek the maximum sentence." And Davis had gotten the max: twenty-five years to life.

Despite his pursuit of Davis, Johnson was perceived in certain law enforcement circles as "anticop" because he opposed the death penalty. Anti-Johnson feeling crescendoed after the death of the Street Crime cop Kevin Gillespie, killed in the Bronx in 1996. The department took it hard. A former marine with a young family, he had been rushed to St. Barnabas Hospital, where the hallways and emergency room were filled with crying cops. Anemone had been there. "I spoke to the [cops] from the heart," he said, "and told them they were needed on the streets to capture Kevin's killers. They responded and did just that."

Because of Johnson's opposition to the death penalty, Governor George Pataki took the extraordinary step of removing the Gillespie case from his jurisdiction. Instead, he appointed a special prosecutor to try it. He never had the chance. While awaiting trial, the alleged killer hanged himself in prison.

In the same *New York Times* interview in which he called Bratton "some airport cop from Boston," Safir added that he had "no respect" for Johnson. "None whatsoever." He later claimed he was misquoted.

Many expected Johnson to present to the Diallo grand jury evidence that would end with the four officers being charged with the lowest counts: either reckless endangerment or criminally negligent homicide. Johnson did that. But he also presented evidence of the highest count—second degree, or intentional, murder. The PBA and the rest of the city's criminal justice establishment were quick to claim he had overcharged the cops, that indicting them for intentional murder meant they had deliberately set out to kill Diallo. Johnson maintained he had no choice: The cops had refused to testify before the grand jury to explain their actions, and that left him with four officers having fired forty-one bullets, nineteen of which had struck an unarmed man, with no justification at all. "Without somebody saying what had happened, there was no basis for making any other judgment," he said. Few in the police department accepted his explanation.

Matters grew worse for the cops with the selection of the trial judge later that year. This time, the case was not given to an older white man. It was assigned, supposedly at random, to Justice Patricia Anne Williams, one of the Bronx's few female black judges. Williams's educational credentials were blue-chip. A graduate of Cornell, Columbia, and Yale Law School, she had served as an assistant U.S. attorney under Giuliani and had been an associate at the white-shoe firm of Wilekie, Farr and Gallagher. But she carried baggage. Assistant district attorneys in Manhattan, where she had first been assigned, had complained about her. Some said she was too dismissive of police testimony. After she was transferred to the Bronx, Johnson's office made similar complaints. When she came up for reappointment at the end of 1999, Johnson sent a letter to the mayor's reappointment committee. "There was more than one decision she made we took exception to," he said.

As his attorney, Sean Carroll hired Marvyn Kornberg. But his handling of the Louima case dogged him. Carroll picked up on tensions between him and Worth, whose PBA funds were bankrolling the cops' defense; he dropped Kornberg and hired Burton Roberts and John Patten. The low-keyed Patten had won acquittal for Sergeant Michael Bellomo in the Louima case. The seventy-six-year-old Roberts had recently retired as the supervising justice of the Bronx. Before that, he had served for a decade as Bronx district attorney. Flamboyant, boastful, and combative (he once threatened to punch me out because he objected to something I had written about him and Bronx Democratic chairman George Friedman had to intercede), Roberts's selection, nonetheless, proved to be a prophetically wise decision.

As the chief administrative judge for the criminal term, Roberts had supervised Williams. But that was then. Appearing before her in the Diallo case in the fall of 1999, he began to argue a point of law when she interrupted and dismissed his argument. Everyone present realized the four cops were in trouble.

Which was worse? A Bronx jury or a judge distrustful of cops? As one of their lawyers put it, "We were horrified by the thought of a jury trial. For the jurors, the issue was not the cops' guilt or innocence but how long a jail term they would receive. But if we waived a jury trial, we were scared to death to have it before Justice Williams. We were convinced she would convict Carroll and McMellon, the first two cops who had fired at Diallo. Not for intentional murder and maybe not for manslaughter but of something."

Another lawyer in the case put it this way: "Bronx juries don't trust cops, period, and could have convicted all four of murder. As much as she [Williams] may have distrusted cops, she was intelligent enough that she might draw a distinction between Caroll and McMellon and the two cops behind them, who fired to protect them."

To Roberts, there was but one way out. The trial had to be moved. The Rodney King beating in California served as something of a precedent. Because of publicity, it had been moved from Los Angeles, where the shooting had occurred, to surrounding Simi Valley, a blue-collar suburb. There the officers were all acquitted (although they were subsequently convicted in federal court).

Roberts decided to commission a poll of Bronx residents to show the cops could not get a fair trial there. The cost was $20,000, but Worth, who controlled the funding, refused to pay. Roberts went ahead anyway, pressing the change-of-venue motion and raising the money for the poll on his own from a wealthy friend who was never publicly identified. Roberts's instincts appeared correct. The poll found that 81 percent of Bronx residents found no justification for the Diallo shooting. Roberts's former law clerk, Bennett Epstein, then drew up the change-of-venue motion before the Appellate Division of the First Department. Besides the poll results, the motion focused on the pretrial publicity, including the daily demonstrations outside Police Plaza and *The New Yorker*'s provocative cover cartoon of the cops firing forty-one shots at a shooting gallery. In late December, before the cops formally decided whether to waive a jury trial, a five-judge panel of the Appellate Division voted to move the trial from the Bronx.

"I thought it was a mistake. It was a relatively junior panel of judges," Johnson said, "and their decision short-circuited the court's own process. There was no effort to even try and screen an impartial panel. I know that the judge, the defense, and I were preparing to do that. It would have required some work and effort but it could have been done."

And there was something else. Had the cops waived their right to a jury, as expected, and gone before Justice Williams, the poll and the pretrial publicity issue would have been irrelevant. By moving the trial from the Bronx, the Appellate Division implied that not only could a black jury not preside fairly but neither could a black district attorney or a black judge. To put it another way, was moving the trial out of the Bronx a safeguard for the cops or a legal loophole?

Instead of moving the trial to the Bronx's nearby Westchester suburb, the panel voted to move it to Albany County, 120 miles away. Their stated but nonsensical reason was that Albany's racial makeup more closely resembled the Bronx's. Safely out of the Bronx, the cops opted for a jury trial. The state's chief administrative judge, Jonathan Lippman, handpicked Justice Joseph Teresi to preside. Although part of the purpose of moving the trial to Albany was to get away from the New York press coverage, one of Teresi's first actions was to grant a broadcast motion for live coverage so that the case could be seen and heard in the Bronx. He also insisted that a significant number of African Americans be selected on the jury.

"He was a man of great determination but not a man who carefully followed the letter of the law," said Eve Burton, then the counsel for the *Daily News*. In violation of the law, he sealed documents introduced as evidence, including three of the cops' prior shootings. As Burton put it, Teresi "sealed every crucial document and denied a dozen motions made by the press to review information after it was shown to the jury." She filed suit in the Third Department on behalf of the New York City media but the case just sat. "For the first time that I can remember in all my years of practicing law, the judiciary by taking no action allowed critical public documents to remain sealed until the entire case was finished."

The trial began and ended in February 2000. With no civilian witnesses to refute them, the four cops were their own defense witnesses. Prosecutors presented scant evidence to discredit their accounts. A not-guilty verdict seemed a foregone conclusion. As the verdict was rendered, Teresi again acted summarily. He summoned the state court's spokesman David Bookstaver to his chambers. Though Teresi said nothing in explanation to Bookstaver, he apparently feared Bookstaver would prematurely alert the media to the jury's decision. For the next thirty minutes, Teresi ordered two sheriff's deputies to hold the director of the state's Office of Court Administration Communications captive in his chambers. When Bookstaver tried to leave, the deputies stopped him. When he attempted to telephone for help, one of them took his cell phone. Although Bookstaver represented the highest level of the court system, and although he brought Teresi's detaining of him to the attention of the highest levels of the state judiciary, no action was taken against Teresi.

The night of the four cops' acquittal, Teresi turned up at their celebratory party at the bed-and-breakfast where three of them were staying. "I remember the doorbell rang," said one of the participants. "It was Judge Teresi. He stopped by, unannounced, to wish the cops the best."

Safir, meanwhile, remained blind to the end. In his book *Security*, published in 2003, three years after he left office, he would say of the Street Crime Unit's formal disbanding the year before: "It cannot be a coincidence that in the first four months of 2002, there has been a 22 percent surge in shootings and without SCU policing the streets, we have seen more guns on the streets being used in target-of-opportunity shootings and innocent bystanders, even children are once again being caught in the cross-fire."

He made no mention of the Diallo shooting, and did not acknowledge his role in causing it by having too quickly expanded the Street Crime Unit. There was no understanding of how the shooting tarnished Giuliani's legacy—even his enemies had had to acknowledge his success in dramatically lowering the city's crime rate.

Giuliani was equally blind but in a different way. Although he had called Safir "the greatest police commissioner in the city's history," he would ignore Safir's recommendation for his successor when he retired in August 2000. Instead, Giuliani would choose his friend Bernard Kerik, who would further damage Giuliani's reputation.

EIGHT

How Well Do You Know Bernie Kerik?

i.

My publisher, Judith Regan, called me in the fall of 2002 at my office in the Shack at Police Plaza. We had a bizarre and uncomfortable conversation, unlike any we'd had before. Just two months earlier, she had agreed to publish my book about the 1975 murder of a Connecticut teenager, Martha Moxley, and the twenty-seven-year struggle to convict a Kennedy cousin, Michael Skakel, of killing her. I was thrilled to have her behind me because she was a marketing genius. Shrewd and self-assured, she seemed always ahead of events, fashioning bestsellers from scores of newsmakers, whether General Tommy Franks of the Iraq war or baseball's Jose Canseco. Her success sparked envy in publishing circles as did her nonbookish looks. In short, she was a knockout.

True, she may not have been as sweet as she looked. I had heard stories of a troubled personal life, including a very public divorce that the *Daily News* had chronicled for a decade. But she loved her authors. My dealings with her had been smooth and soft.

She sounded no different on the phone from the few times I had met with her: direct, businesslike, and in control—or so it initially appeared. I had assumed she was calling to discuss my book. Instead, she blurted out, "How well do you know Bernie Kerik?"

Kerik, Safir's successor, had served sixteen months as police commissioner, leaving at the end of 2001, when Giuliani's term as mayor expired. Judith knew him better than I, better than most people, for that matter. He, too, was one of her authors, and she had worked magic on his autobiography, *The Lost Son*. She had turned the story of his hardscrabble past into a bestseller. The title came from Kerik's claim that his mother had abandoned him as a baby and ended up a prostitute—murdered by a pimp—and that he had spent his life searching for her. In Judith's dexterous hands, his lifelong search for his mother became a tale of overcoming hardship. As she gushed in her publicity blurb, "When Bernie Kerik walked into my office and told his story, my life was transformed." His, she wrote, "is a uniquely American tale that barrels from the sagging row houses of Paterson, New Jersey, to the cocaine fields of Colombia, from the razor wire on Rikers Island to the heights of power as New York City's 40th police commissioner."

Such exuberance all but confirmed to me the rumors at Police Plaza: The two were having an affair. Regan had fallen for the tough-guy police commissioner who had guided the city through 9/11. They were known to work out together mornings at the New York Sports Club in Rockefeller Center. Kerik was said to have spent nights at her Central Park West apartment with his detective detail camped outside in their cars. I even wondered—although Judith denied it—whether Kerik had influenced her decision to publish my book.

To answer Judith's abrupt question about him, I began blathering into the phone, saying he had been a refreshing change from Safir. She cut me off. In the direct, businesslike tone with which she had begun the conversation, she said, "Do you know about his girlfriends?"

His girlfriends? Judith was his girlfriend. As I listened in astonishment, she revealed she'd recently broken off their affair because Kerik had reneged on his promise to leave his wife. "Do you know we even went to look at apartments together? He literally used to cry in my arms about how guilty he felt. It was all an act. It was all calculated so that I would help him sell his book and get it onto the bestseller list."

As if her love triangle weren't dramatic enough, Judith's next allegation left me fumbling for words. "He has been threatening me and he is stalking me as well as my two children," she said. "When I told him I didn't want to see him again, he refused to accept it. He refused to stop calling me. He began following me and my children. Once he told me exactly where my son—a student at MIT—was on I-95 as he drove back to school."

I found myself hanging on to her words, on every incredible detail she was relating. Judith was saying that the man who had been the city's top law enforcement official was not only unstable but had been on the cusp of breaking the law. My first instinct was denial. Her portrait of a jealous maniac was not the Kerik I knew. Unlike Safir and other out-of-control egos around Police Plaza, Kerik seemed not to have lost his humility. In fact, he radiated a childlike innocence.

I wondered whether Judith had concocted her scenario because Kerik had chosen to return to his wife. Could blackening his name be her revenge? Whatever was happening, the last thing I wanted was to be a part of their personal soap opera.

She then swore me to secrecy, afraid that Kerik would retaliate. "He's cunning and charming and manipulative and he will stop at nothing. I think he's even capable of murder."

I was now shocked into silence. Despite my doubts, I was concerned for her.

Finally, I said, "Judith, if you make a written complaint, I will write the story." She never did. Yet, as usual, her insights were ahead of everyone else's. Two years after her phone call to me, the dark side of Kerik that she had been the first to see would be revealed to the world in living color.

ii.

In 2000 when he retired, Safir recommended as his successor the popular Joe Dunne, a thirty-one-year veteran, who had replaced Anemone as chief of department the year before. At Dunne's swearing-in, the overflow crowd at Police Plaza had given him a standing ovation, the applause especially heartfelt from black officers and civilians from the Brooklyn precincts he had commanded. With Safir's retirement, Dunne seemed the obvious candidate to bridge the city's racial divides that had widened with the Louima and Diallo tragedies. Six-feet three-inches tall, with a shock of black hair, Dunne even looked like a police commissioner. For once, it seemed Safir had gotten it right.

Instead, Giuliani waited until Safir had literally walked out of Police Plaza for the last time before announcing Kerik's appointment. It was easy to see why.

Kerik's appointment made no sense. He had been in the NYPD but eight years, rising only to the rank of third-grade detective. He lacked a college degree, a requirement created by Ben Ward for the top brass above the rank of lieutenant. Kerik's sole qualification was his closeness to Giuliani. He had served as Giuliani's driver and bodyguard during the 1993 mayoral campaign. Like Lategano, he had ingratiated himself with Giuliani into his top tier of advisers. Giuliani's election had led to his swift rise, from city hall security chief to number two in the Department of Correction to the head of all city prisons in 1999.

In his bestselling book *Leadership*, published in 2002 as he prepared to run for president, Giuliani explained why he had selected Kerik to become police commissioner. "The reasons boil down to factors of chemistry and feel. Also I saw the years that Bernie spent away from the NYPD as an advantage. . . . It helps to have someone who feels that their loyalty is not just to the department but also to the mayor and citizens of New York." He added, "I thought Bernie stood a better chance of connecting with the police officers, having been a detective in the field and not part of the brass at headquarters." For such nonsense, Giuliani would pay dearly.

Giuliani appeared to have learned something from having antagonized Timoney. Before announcing Kerik, he praised Dunne as a "warm, healing presence" and "a cop's cop" who had "served in some of the city's most challenging precincts and was universally respected and liked." He then was able to persuade Dunne to stay on as first deputy.

"I'd be lying if I said I wasn't disappointed," Dunne said. "But I'm a cop. I would have stayed on if they made me dogcatcher."

Kerik, meanwhile, would prove a more complex figure than anyone could have imagined. In his autobiography, published at the end of his term as police commissioner, he would describe his father as an alcoholic who raised his family in a dreary section of Paterson, New Jersey, in circumstances a notch below the working-class status of most police officers. He'd dropped out of high school, but a fascination with the martial arts derailed his route to juvenile delinquency. He excelled, earning a third-degree black belt in tae kwon do, a Korean form of kickboxing. At nineteen, he enlisted in the army and served three years in Korea. There he trained canines, competed in tae kwon do tournaments, and fathered a daughter out of wedlock. He subsequently worked for three years as a contract military civilian in Saudi Arabia as a hospital security chief, although he would embellish this and claim he had worked for a Saudi prince. Returning to New Jersey in 1984, he joined the Passaic County Sheriff's Department, becoming warden of the Passaic County Jail at a salary of $50,000. When he left a year later to become a New York City police officer, he had to take a $30,000 pay cut, a financial sacrifice that nearly ruined him. He had a baby son, had recently separated from his first wife, run up debts of $20,000, and eventually declared bankruptcy. Money and debt would loom large in his life.

Kerik also spun a tale about how he nearly missed becoming a New York cop. While overseas, he claimed the NYPD had refused to mail him an application, so Kerik said he wrote to Mayor Koch, who personally intervened and ensured the application was sent to Saudi Arabia. Koch, however, didn't remember doing this, and was surprised when, in August 2000, he received an invitation to Kerik's swearing-in ceremony. "I didn't know why I was invited," Koch said. "I didn't know him. When I asked, Kerik said I was responsible for his selection as police commissioner."

Koch attended the ceremony, which, like Safir's, was held outdoors, in front of City Hall, with Denny Young again as master of ceremonies. (This time, he remembered to introduce the police commissioner.) At Kerik's side was his Syrian-born wife, Hala, their newborn daughter, Celine, and Kerik's son, Joe, from his prior marriage. It was a hot day with a strong summer sun, and Koch took out a clean handkerchief and gave it to Hala to cover Celine's head. Later, Kerik told Koch they had kept his handkerchief as a souvenir.

Kerik's lack of formal qualifications notwithstanding, One Police Plaza did not crumble in the sixteen months he served as commissioner. Like Safir, he left the Bratton-era reforms in place and crime continued to fall. He also went out of his way to ease the tensions Safir had created. He courted the department's black and Hispanic officer groups as well as black and Hispanic citizens. With his shaved head, massive shoulders, and impeccably tailored suits, he looked like a high-class bodyguard and radiated confidence and goodwill.

At Police Plaza, Kerik paroled the department's highest-ranking Hispanic chief, Rafael Pineiro, from the Criminal Justice Bureau, to which Anemone had sentenced him four years before. He also ended the house arrest of a white chief, Mike Scagnelli, who had spent the past year hiding out in the chief of detectives' office. Following Scagnelli's dustup with the head of the mayor's security detail, Safir had stripped him of his command.

Kerik even made overtures to reporters. Not only did he return phone calls, sometimes he initiated them. While Dunne was still in contention for police commissioner, Kerik called me to introduce himself and made a point of mentioning "The Confidential." He snickered as he said it, which I took as an acknowledgment that he was in synch with the column's tone. Later, as I came to know him, I realized he had been trying to charm me. Even when I later poked fun at him in "The Confidential"—for ordering thirty plaster of paris busts of himself or for addressing a group at the Harvard Club on foreign policy—he never became angry. Instead he curried sympathy, saying in a hurt tone, "Lenny, why do you always mock me?"

And whose star rose with Kerik but that of DCPI chief Tom Fahey. It turned out Fahey had been Kerik's captain when the future police commissioner was a rookie in Midtown South Precinct. Now a deputy chief, Fahey was one of the few chiefs—perhaps the only chief—Kerik knew and trusted. For the next sixteen months, running DCPI and then Manhattan detectives, Fahey would wield as much influence as any chief in the police department. (At one point Kerik even pushed to appoint Fahey chief of detectives, but Giuliani wouldn't go along.) It was quite a turnabout for someone the mayor had left for dead five years before.

As his chief of staff, Kerik appointed a crony from Correction, John Picciano, known as "Pitch." Kerik considered Pitch his "fixer"—his go-to guy to work the system and get things done. When Pitch had tried to work the system at Correction, he nearly ended up in handcuffs. He joined with the El-Beys, a group of largely African American correction officers who avoided paying income tax by claiming no fewer than ninety-nine exemptions on their W-2 forms, a stunt that got most of them indicted or fired. In giving them the boot, Kerik, then correction commissioner, said, "By submitting false tax documentation in an attempt to evade their tax responsibilities, they have dishonored their sworn oath to uphold the law and discredited themselves." Pitch was somehow able to avoid indictment, together with Correction Officer Jeanette Pineiro, who happened to be Kerik's girlfriend.

As police commissioner, Kerik tapped Pitch for a large project: the renovation of Police Plaza and the many city buildings that housed police precincts. Kerik had fired Deputy Commissioner for Management and Budget Joe

Wuensch over this issue, then let his fixer loose. Pitch's plans proved a joke, and a waste of money. He paid $200,000 for four high-tech security doors, which proved to be too heavy and too big for the headquarters on Centre Street.

Like Kerik, Pitch had a disjointed personal life. Married, with five children, he, too, had a girlfriend in the Correction Department. According to a criminal complaint she filed with Queens police in August 1998, after they had argued all day by phone, Pitch allegedly stormed over, climbed a balcony to enter her apartment, pulled her hair, pushed her to the floor, and took out his gun and threatened to shoot her. When the girlfriend refused to press charges, cops from the 104th Precinct merely notified the Correction Department, which temporarily removed his guns.

When I learned of the story and questioned Pitch, he denied pulling a gun and said that his girlfriend had retracted her complaint. So I didn't write about the incident, telling myself the story was two years old and of marginal news value since the incident had occurred while Pitch was at Correction, not at the NYPD. A few months later, I bumped into him at the PBA's Widows and Orphans Christmas party at the South Street Seaport. As I waited for the elevator, the doors opened, and there he stood with his family. In the few seconds before the doors shut, he quickly introduced me to his wife. As the doors closed, he and I stared at each other for a moment in silent male understanding.

Of course, I should have written the story, for it revealed the character of a man at the highest level of the police department. The story did get published in 2002, after Kerik had left the department, by the *Daily News*'s John Marzulli. He had also learned that Kerik, then first deputy commissioner at Correction, had protected Pitch by directing subordinates to cover up the incident. In retrospect, I blame my failure to have reported it on the access Kerik and Pitch were granting me, more than I'd ever had in the NYPD. Kerik's charm was paying off. And I wasn't the only one taken in. Democratic mayoral candidate Fernando Ferrer, a Giuliani critic, actually praised Kerik for his personnel choices. "What captured my attention," said Ferrer, "was that he understood the problem he was inheriting. He took bold steps to address them, reaching out to churches and community groups. Something I did not expect was his top command, putting very credible people in there."

iii.

At the age of forty-eight, Jack Maple was dying. The parallels with McAlary were eerie. Like McAlary, the cause was colon cancer. Like Mac, Jack had been too busy to heed the warning signs. He was flying all over the country, remaking himself into a consultant for troubled police departments. After leaving the police department with Bratton in 1996, he gave himself some downtime by spending that spring and summer on a thirty-one-foot whaler named for his wife-to-be, Transit Police lieutenant Brigid O'Connor, while dreaming up new schemes — in particular, a cable station devoted to crime, or, as Maple put it, a continuously running, twenty-four-hour, CNN-like "Perp Channel." He even joked of hitting up the Police Foundation for start-up money.

Reality called and he went into business with Bratton's media consultant, John Linder. Their first job was a challenge: New Orleans, where a group of wealthy citizens had paid Linder $140,000 for Maple to devise a Compstat program for its foundering police department. That department's problems were beyond even Maple's capacity. When he arrived, two cops were on death row for murder.

While Maple couldn't fix that police department, he did have success elsewhere. He became such a hit that his autobiography, *The Crime Fighter*, inspired *The District*, a TV series in which the hero, played by Craig T. Nelson, wore two-tone shoes and was named Jackie. *The Crime Fighter* featured Maple on the cover in sunglasses, a bow tie, and a Homburg. It was his personal primer on how he, Bratton, Timoney, and Anemone had turned around the NYPD. Bratton was General George Marshall; Timoney, Eisenhower; and Anemone, Patton. Maple dubbed himself "Deputy Commissioner of the World." Nobody ever said these guys lacked egos.

By the time Maple fell ill, New York had acknowledged him as the architect of its dramatic drop in crime. Knowing the end was near, he tried to get his life in order. He married Brigid in a rooftop ceremony at his apartment building on Central Park South, then entertained 150 people at the wedding party at Elaine's.

He also threw a black-tie bachelor party at Elaine's for his one hundred closest friends. I wangled a last-minute invitation. The affection in the restaurant was like a giant bear hug. Civil rights attorney Richard Emery praised Maple for knowing more about the U.S. Constitution than the best minds at the New York Civil Liberties Union, which Emery had headed. Maple's protégé at the NYPD, Ed Norris, who succeeded him as deputy commissioner of operations, said Maple had accomplished more than any politician in America to make cities safer.

Maple's employer in New Orleans said the Jackster had such a passion for helping people that he went so far as to challenge a black city councilman who had resisted funding for the crime reforms by saying, "Why is it that a fat ex-cop from New York cares more about blacks in New Orleans than you do?"

During one of his last healthy weeks, Maple decided to buy me a surprise present. First he led me on a stroll of his transit cop haunts around Times Square, pointing out scenes of past "scores." To Maple, that meant arrests. Then he pulled me into his favorite men's hat store on Broadway and bought me a Homburg like the one he was wearing. I was moved, but he brushed away my thanks. I wanted to tell him that I would think of him when I wore it but knew that such sentimentality would have provoked a wiseass remark. I wordlessly put it on. As we walked together south on Broadway in our homburgs, we passed an Asian shopkeeper who was struggling to pull down the metal gate to his store while arguing with a huge black man who was yelling nonsense at him. Never identifying himself as either a former cop or the Deputy Commissioner of the World, Maple placed himself between the two to protect the store owner, then began screaming until the menacing guy ran off.

Toward the end, I visited him at Sloan-Kettering, the renowned cancer center, which couldn't save him. Fluids had bloated his body and he couldn't get out of bed. He was lying there, propped up with pillows, but he remained feisty. I told him I had brought *him* a present to ease his pain. When nobody else was in the room, I gave him a marijuana joint. He waved it away. "C'mon, Lenny," he said. "I'm still a cop." Then he winked. "I had a pretty good run," he said. It was the last time I saw him.

Giuliani was among the first to pay his respects at Maple's wake. Unlike the rest of Bratton's crew, Maple had managed to remain on cordial terms with the mayor, even saying that he liked him. "C'mon, Johnnie," he would say to Miller, "I know you like him, too." Giuliani had also visited Maple at Sloan-Kettering. "It meant a lot to Jack," said Miller. "It made him feel he wasn't tarnished in the mayor's eyes because of his loyalty to Bratton."

Giuliani had his own reasons for such kindness. He used Maple's accomplishments to diminish Bratton's. The line out of City Hall had changed, crediting

Maple, rather than Bratton, with the city's dramatic crime decreases. Even Kerik got in on it, visiting him at the hospital. In *The Lost Son*, he called Maple "the architect of Compstat and much of the New York miracle," and "a true hero to me." Maple's wife said Jack barely knew Kerik.

His funeral at St. Patrick's Cathedral, in August 2001, just a month before 9/11, reunited Bratton, Timoney, Anemone, and Miller. If only for one sad day, the wild geese had returned. The mayor sat in the first row and gave a eulogy. If only for a day, he managed to put the past behind him. He had the NYPD give Maple a full inspector's funeral with police helicopters flying overhead and all the rest of the trimmings. In his eulogy, the mayor called Maple the city's preeminent crime fighter and even mentioned Bratton, Timoney, and Miller without grimacing. No doubt Maple would have seen through the praise and the posturing. "Come back in two weeks," he had told Miller. "As soon as I'm gone, they'll all be taking credit."

iv.

Tuesday, September 11, 2001. Every New Yorker has a story. This was mine: I was on a Metro North train into the city when, just after nine, a conductor made an ominous announcement. Without specifying, he said something had happened in the city and that passengers might not want to continue on to New York.

I continued on to Grand Central Terminal. From there my editors gave me the news: two jetliners had struck the Twin Towers. After the first, Giuliani, Kerik, and the top police brass rushed to the World Trade Center. So did cops and firefighters from all over the city.

The editors sent me to the news conference Giuliani was holding at the Police Academy on East 21st Street, which became the department's temporary command center because all communications had been lost at Police Plaza when the Towers collapsed. When I arrived, the academy was a madhouse. Amid hundreds of police and city officials, television crews, and reporters from around the world stood Giuliani. Kerik was at his side. I don't recall anything Giuliani said, but I wangled my way over to Kerik, who told me he and Giuliani were returning to the disaster site, newly dubbed Ground Zero.

"Can I go with you?" I asked.

"C'mon," he said, and arranged a place for me in his motorcade. We headed west to Seventh Avenue, making a stop outside St. Vincent's Hospital in Greenwich Village. Teams of doctors in green scrubs were lined up on the sidewalk alongside stretchers, waiting to treat the wounded. There were none. You either made it out of Ground Zero or you died. The police department would lose 23 officers; the fire department 343, including virtually all of its top command.

The motorcade headed south, down Seventh toward 7 World Trade Center, where Giuliani had established the Office of Emergency Management to coordinate the relief effort. But at Canal Street we stopped. There were fears that 7 World Trade was near collapse. Instead, we turned east on Canal and headed to Police Plaza, pulling into its underground garage. I didn't see where Kerik got out, but I followed others in the motorcade up the elevator into headquarters. I wandered into the Shack on the second floor, which was empty. Walking through the hallways, I realized the entire building was empty. Admittedly, the police department's losses were minuscule compared to those of the fire department, but there was a deathlike feeling in the building. As for 7 World Trade, it collapsed later that day.

I remained at Police Plaza through the evening and late into the night, the only reporter there. I used my cell phone to report, but I don't recall anything I learned. Nor do I remember how I returned to Grand Central. That's the state of shock that I was in. There were no cabs downtown. The Lexington Avenue subway wasn't running near Police Plaza. I remember walking west along Chambers Street, hoping to find a West Side line. I finally caught a subway, but as we traveled uptown, conductors held us at each station, where sirens were shrieking. None of us on the train spoke to one another, but it was obvious what everyone was thinking: There has been another attack. Mercifully, they were false alarms.

I was back at Police Plaza the next morning. The Lex was running only as far south as Houston Street, which meant walking a mile or two. Uniformed officers, city and state, stood on every corner. Somehow, they had been mobilized overnight. They were checking the identification of everyone heading downtown. I buried my press pass. I didn't want to risk being turned away by a yahoo officer from God knows where with his own agenda about the media. Instead, I talked my way through them as a civilian until I reached Police Plaza.

My first column after the attack focused on Giuliani, on how in those first days, when President George W. Bush was invisible, the mayor had stood alone, single-handedly, it seemed, holding the city together. His self-centeredness and self-righteousness, his unwillingness or inability to accept differing views were now his strengths. One of his staffers explained that not only had Giuliani appeared to be in charge on national television, he had been in charge behind the scenes. At all times he had appeared calm and focused, making certain that he even *looked* in charge, always fresh and clean-shaven, always in a suit and tie. In the week since the attack, he'd conducted meetings from two command centers at locations authorities refused to reveal for security reasons. Each meeting had included hundreds of city, state, and federal officials. Each meeting had a specific agenda. Participants sat around a long oval table, Giuliani in the middle, Kerik on his right, Deputy Mayor Joseph J. Lhota to *his* right, Fire Commissioner Thomas Von Essen to the mayor's left, Richie Sheirer, Safir's crony, whom Giuliani had made the head of the Office of Emergency Management to coordinate the city's response to the attack, to Von Essen's left. The head of the FBI's New York office attended some meetings. So did Governor George Pataki, although there was no question that Giuliani, not the governor, was in charge.

At the meetings Giuliani called on people after they raised their hands to speak. When officials complained of problems in their departments that the mayor considered trivial, he would answer, "I know this is important to you, but it is something you can solve among yourselves. Let's focus on the big picture."

At these meetings, they tackled major issues: how to bring in the heavy equipment to begin clearing the World Trade Center site, how to launch an economic package to help suffering businesses. At one meeting, the mayor gathered the city's business leaders to plan the reopening of the Stock Exchange and Broadway shows. At another, he summoned the clergy to plan a prayer service for the victims' families and invited psychiatrists and psychologists to arrange counseling for survivors and rescuers.

The week after the attack, I made it down to Ground Zero. I'd arranged passes for myself and Assistant Managing Editor Les Payne, who ran our New York operation. The site was off-limits to the public but the NYPD was providing police-escorted tours to news agencies and VIPs, including world figures like Vladimir Putin, Nelson Mandela, and Tony Blair. They all made sure to stand at Giuliani's side. French president Jacques Chirac dubbed him "Rudy the Rock."

Rupert Murdoch and his newspaper, the *New York Post*, also stood by Giuliani. The day after Murdoch visited Ground Zero, the *Post* endorsed Kerik in an editorial as police commissioner "for life." That's what it was like then amid the fear, the terror. You grabbed on to whatever you could, whatever seemed solid. Commissioner for Life.

Chief Fahey had arranged Les's and my police escort to Ground Zero. Les took the subway downtown, which was running then as far south as Canal and walked from there to Police Plaza. I met him outside the building in what had been declared a "frozen zone." But the lieutenant in charge refused to allow us to pass. "This is Les Payne, *Newsday*'s managing editor," I tried to explain, adding that Chief Fahey had arranged our escort.

"I know who Les Payne is," the lieutenant answered. "He's not going anywhere." What was going on? I suspected I knew. Years before, Les had written articles that some considered supportive of the Black Liberation Army, the radical group that had executed cops during the seventies. Some people had long memories. Amid 9/11, there was nothing to rein in their raw emotions. I called DCPI on my cell phone. Fahey wasn't there, but one of his officers came out and placated the lieutenant. While he seethed, Les and I set off down Broadway with our police escort.

Ground Zero was like the final scene in *Planet of the Apes*, where the Statue of Liberty has fallen, its face lying in the sand. But the destruction before me seemed far worse. The sixteen-acre World Trade Center site seemed like a moonscape, flattened to rubble. The only things standing were the riblike columns of what had been skyscrapers. Many of these shells listed like the Leaning Tower of Pisa. Smoke and steam rose from the ground. There was an acrid smell. Although the day was bright and clear, my eyes began tearing, my nose running. We had, I felt, taken a half step into hell.

When the funerals began—many at small, simple Catholic churches on Long Island, where *Newsday* circulated—I attended as many as I could. I had known John Perry, one of the twenty-three cops who died. He had been at Police Plaza the morning of the attack. It was his last day there before a transfer. Rushing into the Trade Center, he never came out.

At all the funerals I attended, Giuliani gave the eulogies. Bratton appeared at some. So did Ray Kelly. Former police commissioner Robert McGuire also turned up. Only Safir never showed.

In each eulogy, Giuliani addressed the victim's family—his widow and often small children—telling them that their father had died a hero, a distinction that could never be taken from them. It was as though Giuliani had been born for this moment of crisis. In the two years before the attack, his own life had unraveled. He had separated from his wife, Donna Hanover, and, in his bizarre fashion, announced his plans to divorce her at a news conference. At the same time, he had been diagnosed with prostate cancer. He considered running for the Senate against Hillary Clinton but at the last minute backed out, blaming his illness. His new girlfriend, a former nurse, Judy Nathan, helped him through six months of radiation treatment. (He had packed Lategano off to head the city's tourism bureau at a salary of $150,000.) In June 2001, he moved out of Gracie Mansion. Hanover had closed out his bank accounts and canceled his credit cards, so he turned up at the apartment of his friend Howard Koeppel, broke and carrying just two small bags. He lived there for the next six months.

Three months after 9/11, *Time* magazine made Giuliani Man of the Year, calling him "Mayor of the World." The story was written by Eric Pooley, now *Time*'s national editor. Five years before, Pooley had written *Time*'s cover story on Bratton that had so enraged the mayor. "I could have been the devil himself," recalled Pooley, "but coming from *Time* magazine with a chance to be Person of the Year hovering in the air. . . . Although that subject was never specifically mentioned, the mayor is not stupid."

Now in the post-9/11 world, Giuliani—whose policies Pooley had once portrayed as "inquisitions" and the "politics of aggression"—was a hero. "Giuliani became the voice of America. Every time he spoke, millions of people felt a little better. His words were full of grief and iron, inspiring New Yorkers to inspire the nation," Pooley wrote. He was "America's homeland-security boss," "a gutsy decision maker," "crisis manager," and "consoler in chief, strong enough to let his voice brim with pain, compassion and love." His performance, wrote Pooley, "ensures that he will be remembered as the greatest mayor in the city's history."

Yet "the old Rudy," as Pooley referred to him, still poked through. After 9/11, however, the type of bullying that in the past had upset so many people was now seen as toughness. Take his slight of Saudi Prince Alwaleed bin Talal, who on October 11 offered the city a $10 million check in honor of the 9/11 victims. At the same time, the prince said the United States should "re-examine its policies in the Middle East and adopt a more balanced stance towards . . . our Palestinian brethren [who] continue to be slaughtered at the hands of Israelis." Giuliani returned the check, saying, "I entirely reject that statement. There is no moral equivalent to this act. The people who did it lost any right to ask for justification." The prince helped dispel any doubts as to whether Giuliani had acted appropriately when he responded that the mayor had succumbed to "Jewish pressure."

Giuliani still showed his ruthlessness when it came to his definition of loyalty. His former emergency management head Jerome Hauer took it in the neck thanks to Giuliani's pettiness. Hauer made the mistake of looking ahead to the next occupant of City Hall. September 11 had been the day of the primary elections, and the two leading candidates had each positioned themselves with a former police commissioner. Bratton had attached himself to Mark Green, the Democratic frontrunner, and was rumored to be returning as commissioner. An unknown Republican, Michael Bloomberg, had secured the endorsement of Ray Kelly.

Hauer, who had served as Giuliani's first head of the Office of Emergency Management, was perhaps the mayor's only recognized professional in emergency management and counterterrorism. "I gave [Giuliani] complete loyalty for four years, twenty-four hours a day," Hauer said. "I was probably one of the people closest to him. He trusted me and believed in what I had to say." Two days after 9/11, Giuliani called Hauer, who had moved to Washington, and asked to meet with him. At the mayor's urging, Hauer signed back on at OEM as an unpaid volunteer under Sheirer. For the next eight days, he said he worked around the clock, often at the mayor's side at Ground Zero.

Then on September 22, Green announced a news conference on safety issues with Bratton and Hauer. Within fifteen seconds, Hauer said, Giuliani called him. "If you do this," the mayor told him, "you can't work with us anymore." Deputy Mayor Joe Lhota then notified reporters that Hauer had been dismissed because he was "self-appointive and disruptive." A friend of Hauer's in Washington called to tell him Lhota had telephoned the White House — "to inform them I was no longer welcome to work with the city," Hauer said.

The "old" Rudy surfaced a final time. He took advantage of the 9/11 crisis to try and abrogate the state constitution and city charter. Barred from seeking a third term, he sought a three-month extension of his mayoralty. Green went along. So did Bloomberg. Only the dark horse Fernando Ferrer balked at the idea, which implied that Giuliani was the only person in the city who could right

New York. Koch made the most salient point: If Giuliani cared so much about the city, Koch said, he could stay on for three months under the new mayor.

v.

Through all this, Kerik was at Giuliani's side. Silent. Dignified. As he drove up the West Side Highway with his detective detail the day after the attack, New Yorkers greeted him with applause. Turning to a passenger in his car, he said, "I'm a rock star." He, too, became part of *Time* magazine's Man of the Year coverage, touted as "a streetwise NYPD detective," who had "reduced violence by 95 percent in the city jails and kept crime on the decline in New York this year even as it spiked around the country." So bright was Kerik's aura that before the election Bloomberg maintained he didn't want to appoint the obviously qualified Ray Kelly as police commissioner. Instead, he said he had asked Kelly to convince Kerik to remain.

It was nonsense, of course. Kelly never asked Kerik any such thing. The terrorist attacks had provided a cover for Bloomberg to mislead the public, just as it would embolden Kerik to bend rules and break the law. But it would take the press, prosecutors, and the public six years to piece that together.

Nine months after becoming police commissioner, Kerik had signed a six-figure book deal with Judith Regan, without a questioning word from any corner of the city. Giuliani had accused Bratton of a conflict of interest when he had signed his $350,000 book deal with Random House. The *Times* had editorialized that Bratton's book deal raised "questions about his willingness to use his public office for private gain." But neither Giuliani nor the *Times* uttered a peep about the propriety of Kerik's deal with Judith's company, Regan Books, which was owned by Rupert Murdoch, meaning that Kerik was in essence on the payroll of one of the world's largest media conglomerates. Instead, Giuliani granted Kerik a waiver from the Conflict of Interest Board, no questions asked.

As for the *Times*, on November 11, around the day of the book's publication, it ran a story headlined "Sad Search by Kerik to Find His Mother; Family Secret Is Revealed in Autobiography." It began: "For years, Bernard B. Kerik, the New York City police commissioner, was haunted by the same dream. He said he would wake up drenched in sweat, feeling like a frightened child waiting for his mother to come home."

Kerik further blurred the line between public and private business by dispatching NYPD sergeant Lenny Lemer and a detective on three book-related research trips to Ohio. Kerik's mother had supposedly been murdered in Newark, Ohio, and the two officers traveled there supposedly to examine old police and newspaper files, visit her grave, and question witnesses. But it was Maple's pal at transit, Jimmy Nuciforo, now an NYPD detective assigned to the Drug Enforcement Administration's task force, who came up with much of the information about Kerik's mother by working the phones in his office. Nuciforo barely knew Kerik, and what he knew he didn't like.

"I called the funeral home where she was waked," said Nuciforo, "spoke to the owner whose family had run it for the past thirty years. He recalled the story. He knew it right off the top of his head. I also spoke to people in the police department there, contacted the medical examiner's office, the local Department of Health and some of Kerik's relatives."

Kerik maintained that none of the detective work was done on city time and reimbursed the city for the travel expenses of the officers who went to Ohio, $838.74. When stories appeared in the newspapers, however, Kerik was forced to pay a $2,500 fine to the Conflict of Interest Board for violating the city charter by using the three subordinates for a private project. In his settlement he stated that he had thought the work, if done off duty, would not be a violation. "I now understand that my assumptions were not correct. . . . I also understand that it was a conflict of interest for me as police commissioner to use subordinate officers . . . to help me with my private project."

Nuciforo was subsequently questioned by the Department of Investigation and the Conflict of Interest Board and later by the FBI. "They wanted to know about the whole incident, how it came about, what I did, how Bernie had approached me with it. (Nuciforo had actually been approached by Lemer.) They wanted to know all my investigative steps and where I was at the time. It was a nightmare."

Ironically, when Nuciforo bumped into Kerik three years later, Kerik didn't know who he was. In the summer of 2004, the NYPD assigned Nuciforo to the Republican National Convention, and seated in the section he was assigned to guard was Kerik. "I am in a suit and tie and he didn't recognize me. He said hello but thought I was someone else. I find out all this information about his mother and he didn't know who I was."

There was another reason Nuciforo didn't care for Kerik. It had to do with Jack Maple. "When Jack was on his deathbed Bernie came to Sloan-Kettering to visit him. He was no pal of Jack, but he had written an article in the *Daily News* that made them out to be close friends. I was appalled."

Nuciforo had been at Maple's bedside when Kerik appeared. "It was the only time he thanked me for what I had found out about his mother. Then he sent me a signed copy of his book."

But in the midst of the terror following 9/11, no one seemed to notice anything amiss with Kerik's book project. In July, two months before the World Trade Center attack, Kerik and Judith had made the rounds of Hollywood producers and celebrities, plugging his autobiography. There was talk Sylvester Stallone wanted to play him in a movie. Back in Manhattan, he began hanging out at Campagnola, an upscale East Side restaurant frequented by Bratton and attorney Joe Tacopina, who had defended Judith when her own divorce lawyer swore out a criminal complaint charging she had hired a private eye to steal her file from his office. She later awarded the private eye a post-9/11 book contract for *The Anti-Terror Checklist*, which she promoted as a "reassuring guidebook" about preventing "bombings, chemical terrorism, nuclear radiation."

Kerik also included 9/11 in *The Lost Son*. Judith had urged him to write another sixty pages about the attack, and her press release promised that the book would feature pages of "never-before-seen photographs covering the attack and the aftermath." Although Giuliani had forbidden city employees to use pictures of the site in commercial ventures, Kerik used sixteen Ground Zero photos shot by official NYPD photographers. Neither Giuliani nor Kerik explained how these photos ended up in Kerik's book or how publishing official NYPD photographs in his autobiography did not constitute another conflict of interest. After the newspapers wrote about this arrangement, Kerik paid $7,500 for the photos, making his check out to the Twin Towers Fund, a charity established by Giuliani.

Kerik also made time to take a call from Victoria Gotti, the daughter of Gambino crime family boss John Gotti, who had recently been hired to write for Murdoch's *Post* and starred in the reality television show *Growing Up*

Gotti—produced by Judith. Taking her call got Kerik a plug for his book in Victoria's September 30, 2001, column. Fahey acknowledged she had called Kerik in his office at Police Plaza but said she had "asked about a news story."

Just a week after the 9/11 attack, Kerik appeared on Murdoch-owned Fox Television to plug his soon-to-be published book on the show *Judith Regan Tonight*. No one questioned the propriety of the police commissioner's taking time from protecting the city to drum up sales for his life story while police officers and firefighters were working around the clock at Ground Zero.

When *The Lost Son* was published in November, just two months after 9/11, Kerik took off for a weeklong book tour. He appeared on the *Today* show, *Charlie Rose*, and *Oprah*, where Kerik burst into tears when discussing his mother. He also appeared on the *Howard Stern* show, where Stern cracked jokes about Kerik's motives for outing his mother as a hooker, shaming him into silence.

vi.

Under Judith's guidance, *The Lost Son* became a *New York Times* bestseller. Kerik, it appeared, was about to make some serious money by exposing his dead mother and capitalizing on 9/11. Perhaps this explains why he went to extraordinary lengths when Judith called him to say she suspected that, during a taping, Fox TV makeup artists had stolen her cell phone and a gold necklace Kerik had given her. That evening, detectives who normally investigate murders in Lower Manhattan showed up at the homes of the makeup artists in the middle of the night.

The police officer husband of Fox employee Debra Phillips Kunkel was surprised to see the lieutenant in charge of the Manhattan South homicide task force at their Manhattan home at 10:40 P.M. "You sent homicide people out to investigate a petty larceny?" said Kunkel, who was about to retire from the force.

"Well, you know, Judith did the book for the police commissioner," the lieutenant answered. Later, Debra Kunkel said, "Thank God my husband only has two more weeks, so he does not have to deal with stupid nonsense like this."

Fox employee Keira Iritano of Staten Island was so scared when an unmarked car pulled up outside her house at 11:30 P.M that she called 911 for her local precinct. "I asked who they were," she later explained. "I said I will not open the door because there could be some crazy person posing as a police officer. I did wind up opening the door prior to my locals arriving, only because I kept my dog right at my side. She growled the whole time [the detectives] were talking to me."

Antonio Huerta, another Fox employee, said a detective and a sergeant knocked at his door in Brooklyn shortly after midnight. They fingerprinted him in his kitchen, photographed him with a Polaroid, and said he would have to undergo a polygraph. "They said they would start making arrests if they had to," Huerta said.

Cynthia Faye, of Mountainside, New Jersey, saw two detectives at her door at 12:20 A.M. "They were in an unmarked car and did not show any credentials," she said. "My understanding of why the police had to come in the middle of the night was to retrieve her [Regan's] necklace before one of us sold it."

These detectives weren't merely on duty—they were on overtime. As for Judith's necklace, it turned up in her handbag. Her cell phone was found in a garbage can outside the Fox studio.

The Police Foundation also lavished money on Kerik. If the foundation had a weakness, it was indulging the whims of police commissioners. About the only time they had refused was when Safir asked them to pay for a full-page newspaper ad to attack the PBA, which had given him a vote of no-confidence. At Kerik's request, the foundation spent $3,000 for thirty small statues of Kerik's head as mementos for his friends when he left the department. Constructed of plaster of Paris, each bust weighed seven pounds and came on a wooden stand that displayed his name. When I headlined—pun intended—the busts in my story, Kerik whined, "You make me out to be like a Roman emperor." He then said he wanted them all destroyed, as did the embarrassed Police Foundation, which kept them hidden inside its Park Avenue offices. I, however, had gotten hold of a bust and announced in "The Confidential" that I would sell it to help defray the $3,000 the foundation had spent. Unfortunately, only one person was interested—a woman from Staten Island whose son was a police officer. She offered $4.

In his last weeks in office, Kerik continued breaking rules, flouting NYPD tradition. He short-circuited the department's procedures for awarding officers highly coveted medals. Normally these honors for performance and bravery, whose rules comprise half a dozen pages in the *Patrol Guide*, take at least a year from nomination to the solemn public ceremony. Instead, in a private ceremony five days before leaving office, Kerik presented the department's Medal of Valor to thirteen officers for their actions on September 11. They included members of his and Giuliani's security details, his former detective partner, and three of the department's top brass—Dunne, Chief of Department Joe Esposito, and Fahey, who had ordered the detectives to find Judith Regan's necklace. While each of them had acted heroically—Dunne had been hobbling around Ground Zero on crutches from a previous injury—they were no more heroic than the hundreds, if not thousands, of other officers who had rushed to the site.

Kerik also thanked the sergeant he had sent to Ohio for his book, awarding him the department's Combat Cross, its second highest medal, for "extraordinary heroism." And after Judith Regan donated nearly half a million dollars in proceeds from *The Lost Son* to the New York Police and Fire Widows, he thanked her with the sought-after civilian title and badge of an Honorary Police Commissioner.

Giuliani, in turn, made a public show of gratitude to his faithful police commissioner. On December 12, two weeks before leaving office, Giuliani renamed the two buildings, connected by a pedestrian bridge, that comprise Manhattan's storied city jail at 125 White Street. Built in 1838 and known colloquially as the Tombs, Giuliani renamed it the Bernard B. Kerik Complex.

vii.

Retired as police commissioner, Kerik now capitalized on his 9/11 fame. But money—always a problem for him—remained one. He went on the lecture circuit and on the board of Taser International, the Scottsdale, Arizona, maker of stun guns, which he joined in May 2002. Taser was expanding its sales to law enforcement agencies around the world and hired Kerik, its president said, because of his prominence as New York's City's police commissioner. With the 9/11 hero serving as its chief spokesman, pitching the stun guns to police forces and prisons around the country while defending its problematic safety record, Taser's sales quadrupled. By the end of 2004, more than six thousand police departments and prisons were using it. Its international sales grew from $6.9 million in 2001 to $68 million in 2004. When Kerik cashed in his stock in November 2004, he had made more than $6.2 million in pretax income.

That windfall financed a $1.2 million home for Hala and his children in tony Franklin Lakes, New Jersey, where Kerik flew the American flag. He also kept a secret home in Manhattan. Steve Witkoff, a commercial real estate developer and cop buff, allegedly provided Kerik with a rent-free luxury apartment on the Upper East Side and paid its annual rent of more than $100,000. Kerik allegedly accepted this gift without reporting it to the IRS.

In 1999, Kerik's only asset had been a New Jersey condominium, which been mired in decade-long foreclosure proceedings and lawsuits that accused him of nonpayment, prompting a judge to cite him for contempt. His appointment that year as first deputy in the Correction Department had brought him power but not enough money to satisfy his growing appetites. He turned then to Lawrence Ray, a shadowy figure with ties to the military and the mob, who had at one point provided security for former Russian premier Mikhail Gorbachev. With his shaved head, stocky build, and tailored suits, he mirrored Kerik in style and swagger. Ray liked to show people a picture he carried in his wallet of him, Kerik, Giuliani, and Gorbachev, during his visit to the United States that Ray had managed as advance man.

For a time, Ray would play a pivotal role in Kerik's life, becoming his financial godfather. At Kerik's 1998 wedding to Hala (which Donna Hanover but not Rudy attended), Ray served as best man and paid $7,000 toward the cost of the 230-person reception at the upscale Chanticleer Jersey catering house. When Kerik couldn't come up with the final $2,000 and the catering house threatened to sue, Ray also covered that.

E-mails from Kerik to Ray the following year sounded desperate as Kerik was spending more than he earned. Writing to Ray on May 19, 1999, as he closed on a $170,000 apartment in the Riverdale section of the Bronx, Kerik said, "If they start talking about points because of my credit history, I might have to get you involved . . ." He signed the e-mail, "Love B."

In another e-mail, five days later, he told Ray, "Can we spare $2500 to get me by until something else comes up?"

By July, with Hala pregnant, Kerik complained, in choice language, about a cash squeeze that prevented him from enjoying the luxuries he felt he deserved. "I can't go to the Caribbean or Florida on a three-day stint just because my dick gets hard or because I need a rest," he wrote. As for the apartment he was about to purchase, he wrote, "A bullshit $170,000. I had to beg, borrow and suck dick for the down-payment and I'm still shitting over the $5000 I need for closing if it happens."

Some of Ray's money came from a New Jersey construction company allegedly linked to the mob. He was a $100,000-a-year consultant to brothers Frank and Peter DiTommaso, the owners of Interstate Industrial, which was having troubles with city regulators. In 1996, Interstate had purchased a Staten Island debris transfer station from Gambino family capo Edward Garafola, the brother-in-law of the notorious underboss Salvatore "Sammy the Bull" Gravano, whose testimony had sent John Gotti to prison for life. Because of Garafola's links to the Gambinos, the city's Trade Waste Commission, formed by Giuliani to weed out mob-connected carters, investigated Interstate.

Ray helped Interstate use Kerik's office for a meeting with the head of the city's Trade Waste Commission, Raymond Casey, who happened to be a cousin of Giuliani. Around the same time, the DiTommasos hired Kerik's brother, Donald, as an $85,000-a-year supervisor of the transfer station's operations. Although Kerik denied a quid pro quo, Interstate then spent $225,000 to renovate Kerik's Riverdale apartment. The renovations included new plumbing and electrical wiring, hardwood floors, built-in cabinets, and a rotunda with a marble entryway. Four years later, Kerik sold the apartment for $460,000, nearly $300,000 more than he had paid for it, then bought his house in Franklin Lakes. Was it any wonder he called Ray his "best friend"?

Yet Kerik was to drop Ray in his hour of need. In 2000, prosecutors indicted him for securities fraud in connection with a mob stock scheme involving Garafola and eighteen others, including members of the Colombo and Bonnano crime families. Ray's indictment was bizarre because he had been secretly working as an undercover FBI informant against Garafola, who had threatened his life over the stock deal. It was Kerik who had introduced Ray to the FBI, which came to believe that Ray had been hiding information about his own role in the deal.

Now the roles of the best friends were reversed. Now it was Ray who begged for help from Kerik, who was about to become police commissioner. "I am sorry that I have to burden you with any of this at all," he e-mailed Kerik. "But I need you and my family needs you. I have done my best to keep you out of it all along. . . . [A]s a friend I was mindful of the sensitivity of your position. . . . Now I need you as a friend to do nothing more than be willing to state the truth as to the things you do know."

Ray pleaded for loyalty, reminding Kerik of the past two years. "When things were important to you, I was there for you. . . . I wish I did not even have to address this with you. . . . I have tried my best to avoid that. But I just don't know what else to do. I need your HELP."

Should Kerik's relationship with Ray and Ray's reputed mob ties surface, his job of police commissioner would be lost. He confided to a friend that as far back as 1993 when he had chauffeured the mayoral hopeful, Giuliani had promised that one day the job of commissioner would be his. In August 2000, as Giuliani prepared to appoint him to the position, Kerik worriedly asked that friend, "Suppose they find out about Larry Ray and the DiTommasos?"

Kerik wrote to Ray: "In the event that I am called to testify, I must tell you that my recollection of the events is not consistent with what you remember. And this would have a severely negative effect on your credibility. I would do anything for you but as I've said since the indictment, in my present position it is inappropriate for me to discuss the case with you any further." While Kerik's slight may have been expedient, it turned out to be shortsighted. Ray never forgave Kerik. A few years later their roles would again be reversed. Then Ray would take his revenge.

viii.

Ron Bellistri, a retired police officer who made a fortune in real estate and private security, replaced Larry Ray as Kerik's financial godfather. In 1985 Bellistri had formed Copstat Security with his former NYPD partner, Lieutenant Jim Wood, who had been Detective Kerik's boss. Just as Ray had paid for Kerik's wedding reception, Bellistri, celebrating Kerik's promotion to police commissioner, treated him to a party for two hundred at the Columbus Club on Fifth Avenue. In return, Kerik gave Bellistri the royal treatment whenever he visited One Police Plaza. Detectives waited inside the department garage, where Bellistri ranked among the favored visitors permitted to park their cars, then escorted him on the elevator reserved for the top police brass to Kerik's office on the fourteenth floor.

As Kerik prepared to leave the NYPD at the end of 2001, he made plans to go into partnership with Bellistri. Their firm would be called Kerik-Bellistri Associates International Investigations and Consulting. Kerik insisted that Picciano—"my number one man"—come aboard, and Bellistri agreed. He offered Kerik a salary of $350,000 and Picciano $150,000. By now Kerik was making enough money from other ventures that he convinced Bellistri that he should pay Pitch $250,000 and accepted only $100,000 in salary for himself. Although Bellistri's office was in the Bronx, he rented a suite for Kerik and Pitch in the Lincoln Building on East 42nd Street and signed a five-year lease for $6,000 a month. He bought antiques and forty-two-inch flat-screen televisions for both their offices. He purchased a high-tech telephone system, hallway security cameras, high-tech locks, special lighting, computers, and custom furniture, including a $2,000 leather chair for Kerik.

But Kerik-Bellistri Associates lasted only six months. Kerik's plan was to join Giuliani in his new security venture, Giuliani Partners. In the interim, he allowed Bellistri to waste his money. In those six months, he lost $500,000.

"Kerik and Picciano never brought in one client," Bellistri said, adding that they barely did any work. "I thought they were honorable guys. It took me a long time to figure it out. They didn't care who they hurt. They were using me as they prepared to go to Giuliani Partners."

For those six months, Kerik began his day by attending a 7:00 A.M. meeting with Giuliani, as though he were still mayor. Only afterward did Kerik appear at Bellistri's. "He insisted everyone call him Commissioner," said Bellistri. "Usually, he had the news media in there—lots of television crews. There were corrections officers coming and going, doing errands for him and Pitch." One was Eddie Aswad, Kerik's special assistant at One Police Plaza, now on leave from the Correction Department to work at Bellistri's for three months. Another was Kerik's Correction Department girlfriend, Jeanette Pineiro. One day when he entered his office, Bellistri found someone working at the company's investigative computer. "He turned to me and introduced himself as Richard Filipazzo and said, 'Thanks for the opportunity. I really appreciate it.' They had hired him without even asking me. They were paying him $60,000." As far as Bellistri could tell, he was doing work for Giuliani Partners, not for him.

Through Judith Regan, Kerik also hired a secretary. "I paid her $60,000 or

$70,000," said Bellistri. "But she was working only for Bernie. She was taking care of his personal needs, almost to the point of being disrespectful to me. Finally, I told him to fire her. He wouldn't. I set a meeting with him for 11:00 A.M. in his office. At just that time, he had a camera crew come in. They stayed until 1:00 P.M. Then Picciano walks by my office with his thumb in the air and points to Bernie's office and says, 'He's ready for you.' He's ready for me? It's my company. I said, 'Go tell Bernie I want to see him in here, in my office now.'"

Their parting was ugly, with Kerik and Pitch taking further advantage, Bellistri said. Bellistri had leased BMW 740 ILs for both Kerik and Pitch, for $2,800 a month. "When they went with Giuliani, I had my attorney formally dissolve our relationship. Bernie was supposed to put the lease in his name but he didn't do it. Instead, he used to get parking tickets. They would come back to me and I would send them to him for payment. He also took my laptop computer, which I had him return."

Bellistri said that after leaving the firm Pitch even charged $2,000 worth of restaurant tabs on the company's credit card. "He also kited a check from my checkbook and wrote it out for $2,500 for himself," though Bellistri did not take legal action.

Kerik brought another person with him to Kerik-Bellistri Associates—former Correction Department warden Ed Gavin, the closest thing New York City has to a present-day Serpico. I had met Gavin in 1991 when Larry Davis went on trial for killing a drug dealer, which would send Davis to prison for life. While in custody, Davis had threatened to kill Gavin, then a correction captain, saying he would obtain Gavin's home address. So Gavin reviewed the prison logbook of Davis's visitors. As Davis awaited trial, Gavin noted in a report, he was visited by Lorraine White, an IRS agent, who allegedly had given him the home addresses of judges, detectives, and prosecutors in his case. Gavin's report ended up in my hands. When I interviewed White, she acknowledged her visits to Davis but denied giving him the addresses. The day my interview of her appeared in *Newsday*, she resigned from the IRS. Two weeks later, on March 14, a jury convicted Davis of fatally shooting the drug dealer, Ramon Vizcaino, through the door of his apartment. As the verdict was announced, Davis's lawyer, Michael Warren, stood up in the courtroom and bellowed, "Are you happy, Lenny? You lowlife. You dog. You scoundrel."

In my twenty years of police reporting, Davis was the only person who threatened to kill me. He made the threat in a telephone call from prison to the press room of the Bronx County courthouse, where I was working. I hung up on him and never heard from him again. In 2008, he was fatally stabbed by another inmate.

Gavin, meanwhile, had risen through the ranks of the Correction Department, where he became known as the agency's go-to guy. Kerik was so impressed with a report Gavin had written about a machine that could detect narcotics and explosives that when Kerik became first deputy commissioner in 1995 he hired Gavin as his executive assistant. The job came with a warning. "If you ever cross me," Kerik told Gavin, "I'll ruin your fucking career."

Kerik also offered Gavin some advice that he himself might have heeded. "This is a very sensitive job," he said. "You can never embarrass the mayor."

Gavin lasted only six weeks. Proximity to Kerik was not important to him. He returned to his old job, where he could earn more money in overtime. Three years later, as the sick rate among correction officers was spiraling out of control (one thousand officers, or one-tenth of the force, were calling in sick each day, costing the city $500,000 a day in salaries and back up), Kerik sought out Gavin again. This time Kerik made Gavin the executive officer of the department's health management division. Gavin began visiting up to fifteen supposedly sick officers at their homes each day. Within six months, the problem was solved.

During 9/11, Gavin served as deputy director to the city's commissioner of emergency management, in charge of anthrax detection after anthrax-contaminated letters were sent to a number of New Yorkers, one of whom, a Filipino nurse, died. The following year, he exposed a top Correction Department official, Anthony Serra, for using Correction Department officers to renovate his home on city time. As a result, the entire leadership of the Correction Department was forced to retire.

Early in 2002, after he had left the police department, Kerik contacted Gavin and brought him to Bellistri Associates. Looking to capitalize on post-9/11 business opportunities, Kerik sought to use Gavin's anthrax expertise at Giuliani Partners. But after seeing what Kerik had done to Bellistri, Gavin declined Kerik's offer. "I liked Bernie. He was good to me," Gavin said. "But what he did to Bellistri was just wrong."

In joining Giuliani Partners, Kerik made even more money. Giuliani paid him $500,000 to head a subsidiary, Giuliani-Kerik Security. The firm would gain lucrative contracts, including a multimillion-dollar job advising the government of Trinidad on the rising number of kidnappings and murder, and a $4.3 million contract to reform the Mexico City police department.

Despite all this money pouring in, Giuliani, a private citizen now, continued to enjoy a perk funded by city taxpayers—NYPD bodyguards. Mayor-elect Bloomberg allowed him to keep a twelve-man detective detail, just as Giuliani had continued Safir's detail for sixteen months after he retired as police commissioner, ending it only when Giuliani's term expired. Supposedly, Safir's detail had been to provide "security." Instead, so far as I could tell, detectives spent their time doing personal errands for him and his family, like delivering laundry.

With Giuliani, the detail's stated purpose was to protect the former mayor from terrorists. Whether or not Bloomberg intended it, the detail gave Giuliani an air of official importance. With detectives at his side, he seemed to have an official position as he gallivanted around Europe, receiving awards for his role during 9/11, including being knighted by England's Queen Elizabeth at Buckingham Palace. Kerik defended the taxpayer-funded detail, saying Giuliani "deserves police protection because he is an ambassador for the city and the country." When I asked to see the detectives' overtime earnings, the department refused, citing "security concerns."

Kerik did not enjoy this perk himself, even while traveling to Mexico City for the Giuliani Partners contract. He was feuding with his successor, Ray Kelly, who, among other things, was investigating Pitch's purchase of the four high-tech doors. Kerik maintained he'd "rather be kidnapped than give Kelly the satisfaction of asking" for a detail.

Later, when Pitch visited Mexico City, I couldn't resist asking whether *he* had a detail. "Are you nuts?" Pitch answered.

ix.

In May 2003, two months after the United States invaded Iraq, Kerik turned up in Baghdad on a White House assignment to rebuild the Iraqi police force. He was coy on how this had happened. He said only, "My name came up in a cabinet meeting," and that the White House had summoned him to Washington for a meeting at the Pentagon. George Bush had met Kerik in the rubble of

Ground Zero when the president visited the city a few days after 9/11. They had talked again two months later when Bush commemorated Veterans Day in New York City. When Kerik broke the news to his boss, Giuliani answered, "Yeah, I know. They already told me."

Like the White House, the *Daily News* had high hopes for Kerik's mission. "Former NYPD Commissioner Bernard Kerik is heading to Iraq to help bring order to a ravaged nation plagued by looters and lawlessness," the *News* wrote. "His new office will help restore police, prisons, border security and other vital operations as coalition forces transfer control to an interim government." The *News* then cited Kerik's qualifications. "His résumé also includes work in Saudi Arabia, training security personnel and coordinating protection for the king and other heads of state." Kerik was quoted as saying, "I know the region, the culture, the people." His stay, he said, would be "in excess of six months . . . as long as it takes to get the job done."

Kerik, though, lasted less than three months in Iraq, even interrupting his presidential mission to travel home for a June vacation. He described his title to me at different times as "minister of the interior," head of "the Interior Division of the Ministry of the Interior for the Pentagon's reconstruction team," and "senior policy adviser to the Ministry of Interior," which had no minister. He gave me his cell phone number and occasionally picked up the phone when I called.

"So," I began, "how's Baghdad?" Temperature, 123 degrees, he answered. Water dripping down your body. Constant sweating. Inside the Republican Guard palace, he said, it was ninety and a fan blew dust. He added that he'd discovered a prison or detention cell in every ministry building, including the ministries of labor and agriculture, and the Baghdad police academy. He was horrified to learn about children buried in mass graves. Still, he sounded upbeat about his mission. He said he gave the opening speech at the first management and leadership class of the Baghdad police department's new senior staff. He greeted visitors like the actor Robert De Niro and retired FDNY captain John Vigiano, who had lost two sons on 9/11, one a firefighter, the other an Emergency Service Unit police officer.

According to *The Washington Post* and a memoir by the former commander of U.S. forces in Iraq, Lieutenant General Ricardo Sanchez, Kerik seemed a cross between a rock star and cowboy. "I'm here to bring more media attention to the good work on police because the situation is probably not as bad as people think it is," the *Post* quoted him as saying. But he apparently avoided real work, joining a paramilitary unit on all-night raids, paying for his own detail of South African bodyguards while packing a nine-millimeter semiautomatic as he rousted kidnappers and car thieves and raided a whorehouse. Instead of reorganizing Iraq's police department during the day, Kerik caught up on his sleep. He left Iraq not a moment too soon. The day after his departure, a bomb exploded at a police headquarters he had been scheduled to visit.

Resurfacing in New York three weeks later, he had a new mission—politics. He checked in with a phone call in September, telling me, "I will do everything I can to get President Bush reelected." Details of his behavior in Iraq hadn't reached stateside and his 9/11 mantle kindled talk of a political career in New Jersey. Some mentioned him as a candidate for governor or senator. "What about mayor of Passaic?" I asked him.

He didn't think that was as amusing as I did, so I said, "Okay, what about mayor of New York?" That was another wisecrack, but Kerik seemed to take it seriously. "Michael Bloomberg is doing a good job," he answered. "I have no intention of running against him."

He also defended his abbreviated stay in Iraq. "I completed the job," he said. "I reconstituted the Ministry of Interior," adding that its new head "was appointed two days before I left." When I asked about his successor, he said, "It's up to the Defense Department. They are processing someone right now. He's a civilian police type." So far as I could discover, there was no successor.

Despite his short stay, Kerik was full of ideas about Iraq—and full of himself. "Unless you've been there, you don't have a clue," he told me. "People at home know only one-tenth about how bad Saddam was. They should walk through the mass graves. There was torture of thousands and thousands of people. I've seen a video of Saddam watching his Doberman eating a military general alive. No one in this country understands."

You couldn't shut him up about the war and terrorism. "People are still hung up on weapons of mass destruction," he said echoing the Bush line. "There is a link between 9/11 and now, and the link is radical Islam. The suicide bomber that drove the bomb into the United Nations in Baghdad is no different from the suicide bombers who drove the planes into the World Trade Center. There is an element in this world that despises us, that despises our culture and our freedoms. We have a choice. We can fight it in Iraq and Afghanistan, in that region, or fight it at home, in New York, in California and Miami. I'd rather fight it there."

On October 3, Kerik briefed the president at the White House. I imagined him giving Bush the same spiel I had heard. Bush was apparently more impressed than I had been. As Kerik put it, "After a news briefing on the south lawn, I started to walk back to the Oval Office. Bush headed for his Marine 1 helicopter, then turned and called out to me, 'Bernie Kerik!'

"I turned around. 'Yes, sir,' I answered.

" 'You're a good man,' the president shouted to me."

Three weeks later, I heard Kerik try out his speechifying at the Harvard Club in New York City. It was quite the venue for a high school dropout who lacked the college requirement to become police commissioner. The Manhattan Institute, the right-wing think tank of conservative intellectuals, had invited him. As befitted an international soldier-statesman, military strategist, and possible political candidate, he arrived with his own think tank: Fahey, Tacopina, who had become his business attorney, and Giuliani spokeswoman Sunny Mindel, whom I termed "Sunny the Silent" for her refusal to provide any information about Giuliani or anything else.

For thirty minutes Kerik parroted Bush's Iraq war policy. "I don't care if they find [weapons of mass destruction] or not. Saddam tortured and killed one million people. Somebody had to go there." "It is better to fight terrorists in Iraq than in New York or Washington." "On September 10, 2001, would anyone say there was an imminent threat? At what point does it become an imminent threat?" "Saddam didn't do 9/11. But did Saddam fund and train Al Qaeda? The answer is yes. Then ask yourself, who hit the Towers?" To critics of the war, Kerik said, "Political criticism is our enemies' best friend." For this, the Manhattan Institute audience gave him a standing ovation.

Afterward, I couldn't resist asking him about his political plans, again bringing up mayor of New York. I got the same answer. "Mayor Bloomberg is doing a good job. I have no intention of running against him."

"What if his numbers are low?" I persisted. Before Kerik answered, Sunny walked up to him and whispered in his ear. Turning to me, Kerik said archly, "I don't deal in hypotheticals." He was now a pro.

Kerik spent much of the next year politicking for President Bush's reelection. At the Republican National Convention in August 2004, he delivered a testimonial to the president on national television. The next day, he told the Associated Press he had considered running for governor of New Jersey but learned he was barred because he hadn't lived in the state long enough. Asked about a run for mayor of New York City, he said he supported Bloomberg in 2005, but added, "I will keep my options open."

Then, that fall, President Bush announced he would elevate Kerik to a cabinet post. The president was nominating the Lost Son to be the director of Homeland Security, the multibillion-dollar agency formed in the wake of 9/11 and charged with protecting the country against another terrorist attack. Knowing what I did of him, I shuddered. A former top NYPD official who felt about Kerik as I did summed it up. "Good for Bernie," he said. "Bad for the country."

On Thursday, December 2, Kerik and Pitch drove down together to Washington. I called them as they were heading to the White House and heard the pride, excitement, and amazement in their voices. Standing at Bush's side the next day for an honor the president felt Kerik deserved, Kerik could see his wife and children in the audience, as well as Condoleezza Rice, Bush's nominee for secretary of state, and Karl Rove, Bush's key political adviser.

The president called Kerik "one of the most accomplished and effective leaders of law enforcement in America." "In every position, he has demonstrated a deep commitment to justice, a heart for the innocent and a record of great success. I'm grateful he's agreed to bring his lifetime of security experience and skill to one of the most important positions in the federal government."

Then Kerik spoke. "On September 11, 2001, I witnessed the very worst of humanity, and its very best," he said. "I saw hatred claim the lives of 2,400 innocent people, and I saw the bravest men and women I will ever know rescue more than 20,000 others."

The setting for these words seemed picture-perfect: the Roosevelt Room, filled with mementos of another ambitious police commissioner from New York. In that room stands a plaque holding the Nobel Peace Prize that Theodore Roosevelt won in 1906 for mediating an end to the Russo-Japanese War, the first time an American was so honored. Kerik, the world was soon to learn, did not belong there.

x.

The bombshells began dropping just a week later, on Friday night, December 10, when Kerik withdrew his nomination. He said he could not accept the president's offer because he had hired an illegal alien as a nanny for his children and paid her off the books. His excuse echoed the domestic servant problems that had famously sunk the nominations of two female appointees to the Clinton cabinet. Giuliani defended him. "It doesn't take away from Bernie's heroism," he said. "It doesn't take away from his decency."

Kerik informed President Bush in a telephone call that Friday night. In his withdrawal letter, he wrote that while serving in the cabinet post would have been "the honor of a lifetime, I am convinced that for personal reasons, moving forward would not be in the best interests of your administration, the Department of Homeland Security or the American people. . . . Under the present circumstances . . . I cannot permit matters personal to me to distract from the focus and progress of the Department of Homeland Security and its crucial endeavors."

How noble he sounded. I didn't believe a word. The following Saturday, I was asked about his explanation on *Good Morning America*. My answer was "Anyone who believes the nanny story believes in Santa Claus." Truth can be painful, and it stung me unexpectedly when an irate father e-mailed me that my remarks about Santa Claus had ruined Christmas for his small children, who had been watching the program. I e-mailed him back an apology.

As for Kerik, the nation would see him publicly humiliated, his secret financial entanglements with Larry Ray and the Di Tommasos and his affair with Judith revealed in all their tawdriness. Unknown to me, the day Bush announced Kerik's nomination both the *Times* and *Daily News* had begun investigating him. Reporters had apparently broached subjects that disturbed Bush officials. The *Times* published its first critical article on December 10, the morning Kerik withdrew, describing his potential conflict of interest because of the quick fortune he made working for Taser. With Kerik on its board, said the *Times*, Taser had "made an aggressive push to enter markets either regulated or controlled by the federal government, most notably the Department of Homeland Security." Although a White House spokesman said Kerik would leave Taser and sell his remaining stock if confirmed, the alarm had apparently been sounded. The White House quickly accepted his withdrawal.

The *Daily News* weighed in on December 12 with investigative reporter Russ Buettner revealing that Kerik had secretly accepted thousands of dollars in cash and gifts from Ray while Kerik was commissioner of Correction and the NYPD, without reporting them to the city as required by law. Buettner was the first to reveal that Ray had paid for Kerik's wedding and advanced him another $10,000, including $2,000 to buy a bejeweled Tiffany badge he admired and another $4,300 to pay for high-end furniture for his Riverdale apartment. Ray backed up his allegations by offering copies of the checks.

Next day, the *Times* revealed Kerik's link to Interstate and the Di Tommasos and the meeting in his office with the Trade Waste Commission. Again, Ray was at the heart of the story. Apparently, he was also talking to the *Times*. He appeared on national television, saying he felt it his duty as a loyal American to warn the nation about Kerik. While Kerik acknowledged to the *Times* that Frank Di Tommaso was his friend, he claimed ignorance of "wrongdoing or criminal activity." (Some months later, the *News* would report that when asked about the Di Tommasos' free renovations of his Riverdale apartment before a New Jersey state commission, Kerik had taken the Fifth Amendment nine times.)

Next came dirt about Judith Regan. Buettner reported that in the days after 9/11, Kerik had "conducted two extramarital affairs simultaneously, using a secret Battery Park City apartment for passionate liaisons." Liaisons plural because Kerik was secretly seeing both Judith and his longtime Correction Department girlfriend Jeanette Pineiro at different times in a donated apartment overlooking Ground Zero. About thirty apartments had been provided to the Red Cross and FEMA for weary rescuers after long shifts at the disaster site. Kerik took the most elegant of them, a penthouse with a harbor view. Pitch also got an apartment, with a terrace.

Sources "with intimate knowledge of both affairs painted a picture of passionate, and sometimes volatile, liaisons," wrote Buettner. "Dramatically," he added, "each woman learned of the existence of the other after Pineiro discovered a love note left by Regan in the apartment."

The two women later spoke on the phone. "She wanted to know if Judith was still seeing him," Buettner reported of Pineiro. "She told Regan about their affair and Regan told her she was shocked." Such specificity led me to wonder whether Buettner's source wasn't Judith herself. As I well knew, she was as angry at Kerik as Ray was.

Buettner wrote another article that I suspected Judith was behind, reporting that Kerik had kept $75,000 in book royalties that were supposed to go to charity. The money came from the sales of a book of photographs published by ReganBooks, entitled *In the Line of Duty*. Kerik had written an eleven-sentence foreword praising police and firefighters who "desperately fought and struggled and bled and died in a noble effort." Regan had published the book to raise money for the families of those who had died during 9/11, and it appeared on the *Times*'s Best Sellers list for four weeks. Kerik had *his* royalty checks sent to the Gryphon Strategic Group, an entity he had created in Delaware.

There was something else in that article that drew my attention. Judith, Buettner reported, had never known about Kerik's 79th Street apartment, the one he was living in rent-free, courtesy of the developer Steve Witkoff. For the first time, I began to understand why she had called me in 2002, fishing for information on Kerik. As intimate as they may have been, he had apparently kept plenty from her.

Prompted by these disclosures, the city's Department of Investigation announced a probe of Kerik's tenure as police commissioner. The DOI noted that Kerik had failed to file a background form detailing his finances when Giuliani appointed him in 2000. DOI commissioner Rose Gill Hearn ordered all city employees to cease contact with him.

Bronx district attorney Johnson announced he was investigating the remodeling of Kerik's Riverdale apartment. That could lead to a felony conviction for bribery. Bronx prosecutors began secretly wiretapping Kerik's phone. But the first victim of their investigation was a surprise: Kerik's well-liked spokesman at the Department of Correction and later at the police department, Tom Antenen. After Kerik's retirement, he had returned to Correction. He was picked up on a wiretap talking to Kerik about his girlfriend Pineiro, thus violating DOI's rule barring all contact with him. The Correction Department demoted him from his $131,000 job, slashing his salary to $55,000. He was the first of Kerik's collateral-damage victims.

The second was also a surprise. She was Jeanine Pirro, the former Westchester

County district attorney, then running for state attorney general. The wiretaps had picked her up talking to Kerik about allegedly planting a hidden recording device on her husband's boat to confirm her suspicions he was having an affair. Planting such a device is illegal in New York State and the FBI began investigating her. Though she was not charged, her campaign never recovered from the embarrassment.

She and Kerik had apparently known each other for more than a dozen years, as he said in a fund-raising letter he sent in the fall of 2006 in support of her candidacy. "I have know[n] and worked with Jeanine Pirro for more than twelve years and know first-hand her commitment to 'getting the job done,' whether that be pursuing white collar criminals, vicious thugs, child pornographers or scam artists. She's been in the trenches, knows the fight and has gotten results." Although Pirro's spokeswoman described their relationship as "strictly professional," others recalled that when Kerik was police commissioner, she had once become so angry at him, she had begun whaling on the hood of his car with him inside it.

The disclosures forced Kerik to sever his business ties to Giuliani. On December 22, less than two weeks after his nomination collapsed, Kerik announced that he was leaving Giuliani Partners, saying, as he had when he withdrew from consideration as Homeland Security director, that he had become a "distraction." He started his own security firm, the Kerik Group, based in lawyer Joe Tacopina's Manhattan office. In faraway places, he remained a hero of 9/11. He obtained a $7 million contract to train the army of Guyana. He turned up in Jordan as an adviser to King Abdullah.

I tracked him down by cell phone there, where he was working on—of all things—prison reform, while bemoaning his fate. "At least here in Jordan I have half a chance," he said. "Back home it's death by a thousand cuts."

"What about your friend Rudy?" I asked.

"It's like dying a slow death," he answered, "watching him have to answer for my mistakes."

Although down, he was still kicking. On his Web site he posted a picture of himself with Bush, along with the president's words: "Bernie Kerik is a dedicated, innovative reformer who insists on getting results." Much of the media still believed it. After the London subway bombing in July 2005, Kerik resurfaced as a terrorism expert on a half a dozen news shows. Here's how Lisa Pinto of CNN introduced him: "You've been all over. You were in Giuliani Partners. You weren't just [police] commissioner of New York. You visited a lot of different cities."

Tacopina became his full-time defender. "He's one of the strongest human beings I have ever met," he told me. "He spent four years in the Middle East, went to the war zone in Iraq when he had no obligation to do that. It is his nature to be mentally and internally tough. That's who he is."

Meanwhile, his buddy Pitch was also doing business overseas—and ducking creditors. Before leaving Giuliani Partners with Kerik, he borrowed $30,000 from Robert Tucker, a private-security big shot with scores of retired cops on his payroll. Kerik had vouched for Pitch. As Tucker put it: "I loaned the money to Pitch because I thought we were good friends, with a business relationship solidified by ties to the police commissioner's office."

Tucker made the loan to Gryphon Associates, of 23 Thompson Street, Kings Park, Long Island, the address of Picciano's home. I wondered whether Gryphon Associates was related to Kerik's Gryphon Strategic Group, recipient of his book royalties. Could the two have been in some scheme together?

Shortly after receiving Tucker's loan, Picciano wrote him a repayment check for $31,000, which included an extra $1,000 as a thank-you. But he asked Tucker not to cash it "for some time," until the Gryphon account had sufficient funds. Tucker held the check for a year, until October 26, 2005. When he deposited it, it bounced.

He then asked Kerik for help in getting back his money. "Do you think you're the only one?" Kerik replied.

A process server Tucker sent to Pitch's home on May 23, 2006, found it empty but discovered his wife living in her mother's house nearby. "She advised me that [Picciano] had left her and their five kids behind and went to Brazil," he said in a deposition. "They have not heard or seen him for five months at the time of my attempt. She stated that the address at 23 Thompson Street is in foreclosure and that 'a lot of people are looking for him.'"

I sent out an all-points bulletin in "The Confidential," and located Pitch in São Paulo, Brazil, where he was supposedly working for a New York–based security company. "Where I am and what I am doing is my business, not yours, and who I choose to speak to is also my business," he e-mailed me. "My family is well taken care of with my pension and other means."

Six months later, he announced his return to the United States in another e-mail to me but refused to divulge his whereabouts. "I am just a simple man with a few harmless vices," he wrote.

xi.

David Bookstaver was in a tizzy, pacing the corridors of the Bronx County Courthouse on Friday, June 30, 2006. As the court's press officer, he was worried the courtroom might not be large enough to seat all the reporters covering Kerik's criminal case. Eighteen months before, District Attorney Johnson had impaneled a grand jury to investigate whether Interstate had bribed Kerik by renovating his apartment and called Giuliani and the Di Tommasos as witnesses. That spring, I'd paid a visit to the Bronx and detected no sign of urgency on Johnson's part to take the case to trial. The reason was that he was uncertain whether he could prove the necessary quid pro quo between the renovations and Kerik's interceding for Interstate with the Trade Waste Commission to bring bribery charges. Such white-collar prosecutions are rare in state courts, especially in the Bronx. No doubt Johnson recalled the indictment of Labor Secretary Raymond Donovan by his predecessor, Mario Merola, two decades before. Merola's charges had been so complicated that, despite nine months of testimony, a jury acquitted Donovan after just a few hours of deliberations. On the other hand, Kerik's actions had created such an appearance of impropriety that Johnson could not let him off. A compromise was reached: Instead of going to trial and possibly to jail, Kerik agreed to plead guilty to two misdemeanors.

Supposedly, he had spent the past month in the Middle East and flown in on the eve of his court appearance, as though his criminal proceeding and evolution from hero cop to perp was but an interruption of his more important business ventures. Supposedly, too, he had asked an entourage of ex-police buddies to accompany him into the courtroom, signifying that he remained a person of influence. Whether he had scrapped the idea as poor taste or simply couldn't rustle anyone up, Kerik entered the courtroom with only Tacopina and Kenneth Breen, a young attorney I hadn't seen before. Impeccably dressed, Kerik wore a dark blue suit, red polka-dot tie, white handkerchief in his breast pocket, and an American flag pin in his lapel. Bookstaver's fears of a media crush were unfounded. Only a handful of reporters turned up. To much of the New York press corps, Kerik was history.

He was even fingerprinted and had his mug shot taken—"like every other perp," said the Commissioner of Investigation Rose Gill Hearn. Tacopina, though, pointed out that Kerik had "been afforded the opportunity to be processed in the district attorney's office and to walk to court."

The legal proceeding took but a few minutes. Inside the near-empty courtroom, Kerik pleaded guilty before Justice John P. Collins to accepting a gift and failing to report a loan. "I admit I took a gift from Interstate companies or a subsidiary," he said, "and thinking they were clean, I spoke to city officials about Interstate on two occasions and on another occasion permitted my office to be used for a meeting between Trade Waste authorities and representatives of Interstate." He also pleaded guilty to failing to report to the Conflict of Interest Board a loan of $28,000 from Nathan Berman, another real estate developer, who had hosted Kerik on a vacation at a seaside villa in Majorca. For these two offenses, Collins fined Kerik $221,000 but allowed him to keep his private investigator and pistol licenses. Acknowledging Kerik's service to the city on 9/11 and afterward, the judge said that the former police commissioner had nonetheless "violated the law for personal gain."

Giuliani issued a statement saying that Kerik "has acknowledged his violations but should be evaluated in light of this service to the United States of America and the city of New York." Such platitudes couldn't disguise Giuliani's problem: How could he have appointed Kerik police commissioner in 2000 when his relationship with Interstate was known to the Department of Investigation? As part of the vetting process, DOI lawyers would have briefed the mayor about Kerik. While she had aggressively investigated Kerik, Commissioner Gill Hearn refused to answer the key question: Just what had those DOI lawyers told Giuliani? Her predecessor, Edward Kuriansky, would die of cancer the following summer without publicly explaining what had occurred.

Outside the courthouse, Kerik remained unbowed as he spoke before a cluster of reporters and TV cameras. "You know it's funny, over the last year and a half I've watched and listened as people have picked apart my thirty-year career in fighting crime and fighting injustice and tried to destroy everything I've ever done." When a reporter asked whether he regretted his actions, Kerik cut him off. "Let's go," he said to Tacopina, and disappeared into a black chauffer-driven car.

That weekend, Kerik's name disappeared from its place of honor at the Tombs. Giuliani's tribute to his police commissioner vanished as city workers replaced the Bernard B. Kerik Complex signs with its old name, the Manhattan Detention Complex. Three weeks later, Kerik's guilty plea in the Bronx led to perjury indictments against the Di Tommaso brothers for lying to a Bronx grand jury. They had claimed they hadn't paid for Kerik's apartment renovations. They were placed in a no-win position after Kerik admitted the exact opposite in his guilty plea.

In subsequent interviews, Kerik continued to downplay his crimes as "mistakes," chalking them up to his "lack of sophistication." Giuliani echoed this, calling Kerik's misdemeanors "violations," a word that mitigated their seriousness. Six months later, Kerik told *Best* magazine that he had pleaded guilty because he "just fucking wanted [the case] to be over. I didn't take the pleas because I really thought I had done anything wrong. It was just, pay the fucking fine, give 'em their pound of flesh, whatever the fuck they want."

xii.

Kerik's lack of remorse apparently caught the attention of federal prosecutors. They quoted his words in *Best* magazine to let a judge know that "the defendant publicly claimed that there was no factual basis for his plea." That was a year later. Kerik was a defendant again, this time charged in a fifteen-count federal indictment on November 8, 2007. And this time he was in real trouble. The feds built on the Bronx case, sweeping through the dark corners of his life, accusing him of conspiracy, tax fraud, making false statements, and failing to report $500,000 in income from 1999 to 2004. This included $75,000 in book royalties and $230,000 in free rent for Witkoff's luxury Manhattan apartment.

The federal charges suggested that whenever Kerik could grab a buck or hit someone up for money, he did. The feds also accused him of lying on his application to become homeland security director by omitting a $250,000 loan from Eitan Wertheimer, an Israeli industrialist. It was a compromising omission since Wertheimer's companies did business with the U.S. military. According to the indictment, Berman, the developer who had loaned Kerik $28,000 toward the down payment on his Bronx apartment, had introduced him to an unnamed businessman who introduced Kerik to Wertheimer.

The U.S. attorney for the Southern District, Michael Garcia, appeared dis-

gusted with Kerik when he described Kerik's alleged crimes at a press conference. "During the time Kerik secretly accepted these payments, he lobbied city
officials on behalf of his benefactors—in effect selling his office, in violation of
his duty to the people of the city. Several of the payments were made on his behalf after he had taken an oath as the New York City police commissioner,
breaking the laws he had sworn to uphold."

Kerik, Garcia added, "went to great lengths to conceal the scheme. He did
so by filing four separate false financial disclosure reports with city officials,
which concealed the payments; by misleading city officials about his relationship with those who were paying him; and by obstructing the city's investigation
by causing multiple witnesses to lie to the investigators."

David Cardona, special agent in charge of the FBI's New York Criminal Division, then spoke of Kerik in language that Serpico would have appreciated.
"Moral relativism is not an appropriate yardstick for our public officials," he
said. "The only acceptable level of corruption in a trusted government office is
zero. A beat cop accepting a free cup of coffee or a meal 'on the arm' is properly
viewed by the public as wrongdoing. If the free cup of coffee is wrong, Kerik's
long list of alleged crimes is repugnant."

As a parting blow, Cardona cited Teddy Roosevelt's legacy. "He was the embodiment of rectitude, a man who held himself to a higher standard than he expected of others. A century apart, Teddy Roosevelt and Bernie Kerik held the
same job. There the similarity ends."

This time, reporters packed the White Plains courtroom for Kerik's arraign-
ment. Again, he was impeccably dressed, in a dark blue suit, red tie, a flag pin
in his lapel. This time, though, Tacopina was not at his side. In April, the feds
had forced him off the case, alleging that Kerik had lied to him about the cost of
the Di Tommasos' apartment renovations and that Tacopina had passed on
those lies to Bronx prosecutors in securing Kerik's plea deal. As District Judge
Stephen Robinson put it: Tacopina told the Bronx district attorney that Kerik
"had paid for all of the renovations to his Riverdale apartment himself." The
feds said they planned to call Tacopina as a witness against him. Instead, Breen
represented Kerik. Breen seemed devoted to him, quitting his former law firm,
which then sued Kerik for $202,384 in unpaid legal bills. The lawsuit was later
settled on undisclosed terms, Kerik said.

Kerik remained silent as the judge read the charges against him. But when asked his plea, he intoned, "Not guilty." He was released on $500,000 bail, secured by his New Jersey home, and ordered to surrender his passport and firearms. He was the first police commissioner since New York City established that position in 1901 to be indicted for crimes allegedly committed while in office.

I found myself both stunned and revolted by the charges. This was a man I genuinely liked, who had helped me in all sorts of ways, not the least of which was being available whenever I called him. Perhaps like other New Yorkers, I had been blinded to his actions on 9/11. I would never forget that on that terrifying day he had included me in his motorcade as we drove downtown to Police Plaza.

As I followed him down the courthouse stairs, I saw him pause and turn to address the crowd of reporters. "My life has been marked by challenges," he said. "Whether it was growing up, being a cop, Rikers Island, the New York City Police Department, or the worst challenge, until this time, my challenges during and after 9/11, this is a battle I'm going to fight." Part of me wished him good luck.

xiii.

I caught up with Kerik a couple of months later at a pretrial hearing. He was standing in the hallway outside the White Plains courtroom with Breen, whom prosecutors would later force from the case, alleging that Kerik had also lied to him. Their source for that was none other than Tacopina, whom Kerik was claiming had sold him out.

I wasn't certain how Kerik would feel about seeing me, as I'd written some hard pieces about the indictment. So before he could start complaining, I walked up to him, cupped his bald head in my hands and gave him a kiss on his forehead. Breen did a double take but my gesture settled things down. I asked Kerik about his family, as he did mine. His son, Joe, was about to join the Paterson Police Department. Joe subsequently joined the Newark PD. Paterson was a tough town, and Kerik hadn't wanted him to work there. In that he sounded like any parent.

Kerik seemed upbeat and combative. He was still granting interviews, reciting 9/11 mantras. Some months before, he had rejected a deal allowing him to plead guilty only to tax evasion but forcing him to serve up to six months in prison. Kerik refused to consider time behind bars.

On December 30, 2007, a month after his indictment, he wrote a year-end newsletter that he sent to a thousand of his closest friends: Again, he portrayed himself as a hero of 9/11 and an expert on terrorism, Iraq, and military strategy.

"With Al Qaeda claming responsibility for the assassination of Benazir Bhutto in Pakistan, Osama Bin Laden's renewed threats against Israel and Iran's announcement that their first atomic power plant will start operating in mid-2008, we can't put our guard down for even a second."

He started a legal defense fund, whose Web site described his Bronx indictment as a minor mishap. "In June 2006, Mr. Kerik settled an investigation by the Bronx District Attorney's Office. He accepted responsibility by pleading guilty to two New York City ethics violations (unclassified misdemeanors) and paid a substantial financial penalty. Shortly after he settled the Bronx case, the U.S. Attorney's Office began a new investigation. The Assistant U.S. Attorneys assigned to the investigation have charged Mr. Kerik, based in large part on conduct that was already addressed and resolved in the Bronx case." It concluded: "His heroic career and service to our country continues to be overshadowed by this investigation."

"So how are you handling this?" I asked him in the courtroom hallway.

"I stay mad," he answered. Since they'd taken his passport, he couldn't leave the country. That ended his contracts in Guyana and in Jordan. "They're killing me. I lost six million in contracts. Can you believe this shit? Give me a break. My wife is so mad at the government she wants to take down the American flag outside our house. She's from Syria. She said, 'This is what the government does to people in Syria.'"

I asked him about Pitch. He said he hadn't seen him in years and didn't know where he was.

"What about Antenen?" I asked.

"They screwed him," he answered. "That was so uncalled for what they did to him."

"And what of Giuliani?" I said. His presidential candidacy had collapsed. Kerik had been an issue, a liability—McCain was quoted saying that Kerik had done nothing in Iraq but posture. But Giuliani's failure as a presidential candidate had been larger than Kerik. Like Kerik, he had wrapped himself in 9/11. It had no longer been enough.

"I stay away from Giuliani," he said.

"Is he able to help you?"

"I don't want his help."

I asked him why he thought all this had happened to him.

"They're going after me to get Giuliani," he said.

"Who's 'they'?" I asked.

Apparently, he didn't have an answer. "They went after me to get Jeanine Pirro," he then said. "They wanted me to testify against her. I refused." (They never got her.)

Finally, I asked him about Judith. Like Kerik, she had been struck by an avalanche of bad publicity. HarperCollins had fired her after the uproar over her contracting to publish O. J. Simpson's so-called confession in the murder of his wife Nicole. Plenty of people she had crossed at HarperCollins were ready to strike back at her. They did, with the spurious but damning charge that in defending herself, she had used anti-Semitic language.

I'd seen her since then. She had been especially shaken by the anti-Semitism allegation. "How am I supposed to fight something like that?" she had said. But she did fight. She hired a lawyer, sued HarperCollins and its owner Rupert Murdoch, charging that the real reason for her dismissal was that a senior official in the company had urged her to lie to federal investigators about her affair with Kerik to protect Giuliani. HarperCollins, Murdoch, whoever, backed down. In the end, she won a settlement that amounted to $10 million. In announcing the settlement, Murdoch and HarperCollins said specifically that Judith was not anti-Semitic.

Yet fearless as she was of them, she remained fearful of Kerik. Over the years, I learned, she had told others what she had told me. Once, while she had dinner at a West Side restaurant, she said he had sat outside in his car and phoned her repeatedly. He had so frightened her that she had summoned a private detective to escort her home. She had even flown to California to get away from him. Los Angeles security consultant Rich Di Sabatino told me he tried to find a safe house for her after Kerik had sent a couple of his guys out to California after her.

I realized that I had known Kerik for nearly a decade. While he had charmed me, he had terrorized Judith. Though she never took legal action, to her he had revealed himself as a liar, a, fraud, a money-obsessed user who burned one friend after another. While I had never seen this side of him and he always denied having stalked her, she proved to be a Cassandra. How well did I know Bernie Kerik? she had asked me in that telephone conversation in my office years before. Not well at all, I supposed. Not well at all.

NINE

Never Appoint a Bitter Man Police Commissioner

i.

I had the exclusive. Someone high up in the NYPD had alerted me to the identity of the city's next police commissioner. That news had been buried under political double-talk. Mayor-elect Michael Bloomberg had been coy about his choice, despite the obvious signal when former police commissioner Ray Kelly endorsed him in the final weeks of the 2001 campaign.

Bloomberg, though, had hidden his intentions, maintaining he wanted to reappoint incumbent Bernie Kerik. Bloomberg had even stated that he and Kelly would double-team Kerik to convince him to stay. This unlikely coupling might have been conceivable had anybody believed Kelly when he professed no interest in returning to the job he had spent a lifetime struggling to attain.

The truth was that Kelly ached to return. All the Kerik talk had been just that, an election ploy because in those shell-shocked months following 9/11, New Yorkers believed Kerik was a hero. Bloomberg knew Kerik wouldn't stay, that he was departing with Giuliani. The mayor-elect had known who his police commissioner would be all along. So thanks to a well-placed source in the department, I was able to tell the world that Bloomberg was going to appoint Kelly.

I had known Kelly since his first term as commissioner, but it was only after Giuliani dismissed him that we became friendly. "The Confidential's" critical tone toward the new mayor had caught his attention. When President Clinton appointed Kelly under secretary of the treasury for law enforcement in 1996, I was among the invited guests at his swearing-in ceremony in Washington. When Kelly traveled to New York, we'd meet for lunch. During one holiday season, he called me in the Shack and invited me to join him, his wife, Veronica, and other family members at a pub on Hudson Street. At McAlary's wake, he introduced me to one of his sons as "the only reporter in New York with balls."

I'd also remained friendly with Kelly's factotum, Paul Browne. Like me, a graduate of Columbia's Graduate School of Journalism, he was a bear of a man with a reddish-brown beard who had been a former *Daily News* reporter and aide to New York senator Daniel Patrick Moynihan. He had joined Kelly during his first term as police commissioner, then accompanied him to Washington, and stayed when Clinton appointed Kelly commissioner of customs in 1998. Dedicated both to Kelly and to burnishing his image, Browne had even sent me a packet of testimonials from Kelly's retirement dinner, marking his passage from government official to a senior partnership with the Wall Street firm Bear Stearns.

My friendship with Kelly had helped me break the news of his return as police commissioner. While I couldn't reach him, and Bloomberg wasn't talking, someone who knew him well refused to comment but did not deny the story. That and my original tip were enough for me. The day my exclusive ran in *Newsday*, a police reporter from the *Baltimore Sun* called to ask how I could be so certain without official confirmation. I told him I trusted my sources. The next day the *Times* headlined the news "Under Bloomberg, Kelly Will Guide Police Again" and credited *Newsday* with breaking the story.

For me, Kelly's return could not have been sweeter. I respected his judgment, temperament, integrity, and ground-floor-up knowledge of the NYPD, where in a career of thirty-one years he had risen from trainee to commissioner. He himself was elated with his chance at redemption. Giuliani and Bratton had ignored his first term's accomplishments and derided his community-policing policy as "glorified social work." Although murders and crime overall had begun to fall on Kelly's watch, Giuliani and Bratton had taken credit for the city's dramatic turnaround. Kelly's return gave him a chance to set the record straight— and settle scores.

His return, as New York City's forty-first police commissioner, was also a historic event. Sworn in at Gracie Mansion inside a room so packed with well-wishers like me that one could literally not move a step, Kelly became the first man in the city's history to serve as police commissioner twice. There was a sense that justice had been done, that in returning to Police Plaza he was back where he belonged. His supporters ranged across the city's political spectrum. His first term under the city's first black mayor, David Dinkins, including his Sunday visits to black churches, had created a reservoir of goodwill among African Americans that would continue through his second term. Even Al Sharpton was a fan, saying during his failed 1997 mayoral run that he would be "comfortable with a white guy like Kelly" as police commissioner. As for conservatives, Kelly had maintained his relationship with the powerful Guy Molinari, who had tried to persuade Giuliani to keep Kelly as police commissioner back in 1993. In return, Kelly supported Molinari the next year in an unsuccessful run for Staten Island district attorney.

With feelings from 9/11 still raw, Kelly seemed the perfect choice to protect New York City. As police commissioner during the 1993 World Trade Center attack, he had stood shoulder to shoulder with the FBI's Jim Fox on national television, his silent, bull-like presence a source of reassurance to a stunned and frightened city. Nine years later, he still looked the part of the city's protector. Sixty years old, his hair, with a trace of gray, was cut short like the marine he once was. He still followed a military regimen, both running and lifting weights, and displayed his physique in custom-made suits. Who would have believed that after leaving the police department in 1999 he had undergone quadruple bypass surgery?

If the first World Trade Center attack in 1993 had infuriated him, the second had broken his heart. He and Veronica lived in Battery Park City, next to Ground Zero. "When we returned and looked from the roof down on the devastation, a part of our hearts were ripped away," he said. "I'll never be complacent, because I walk out of my building every day and I see the gap in the sky."

Kelly also seemed the perfect choice for Bloomberg, a self-made billionaire lacking experience in both government and with the police department. Unlike the Bratton-Giuliani dynamic, Kelly would pose no threat to the new mayor by hogging the spotlight. If Giuliani had been a control freak, Bloomberg delegated responsibility. He seemed content, if not grateful, to allow his police commissioner to become the department's public face. With Kelly, there would be no surprises or embarrassments. Unlike Safir, he did not purposely antagonize everyone he met. Unlike Kerik, he did not have his hand out. Rather, Kelly seemed ascetic. His sole interest was in running the NYPD. Or so I thought.

Under Bloomberg, Kelly would become the most powerful commissioner in the city administration. With Bloomberg's acquiescence, he would also become the most influential police commissioner in the city's history. Bloomberg placed so much confidence in Kelly that he would ignore the recommendations of the 9/11 Commission that the fire department should be the lead agency in responding to emergencies, as it is in every other major American city. Instead, in New York, Bloomberg assigned that premier role to the police department.

Speaking at his swearing-in, Kelly seemed to have forgiven the slights of the Giuliani years. This second-act police commissioner sounded tempered and conciliatory. He praised his three predecessors, Bratton, Safir, and Kerik, for their "outstanding service to the Police Department and the City of New York." They had, he said, "helped make New York a better, safer place and we are indebted to each of them."

Such generosity would prove as fleeting as the promises of a more open police department that candidate Bloomberg had promised. "Except for certain personnel documents, I am a believer in putting all the information out there," he had said in an interview at *Newsday* for "The Confidential" in September 2001. "The essence of a free society is the right to information."

The worldly Kelly, with his years in Washington, seemed the embodiment of this enlightened philosophy. "I think that obviously Ray Kelly is the right man for right now," Bloomberg said with no trace of hyperbole. Given what I perceived as our friendship, I felt Kelly was also the right man for me.

ii.

Within weeks of taking office, it was clear that Kelly's reach would exceed that of any previous police commissioner. He would set the NYPD upon a new course, marching it past traditional boundaries, both physical and legal. He would seek nothing less than to position the NYPD at the center of the country's fight against terrorism and reshape the department's culture as profoundly as Bratton had with Compstat.

Four months after 9/11, rescue crews were still digging for the remains of the dead. Smoke still poured from the pit that stretched across the west side of Lower Manhattan, where the Twin Towers had stood. FBI director Robert Mueller warned of suicide bombings on American soil. Secretary of Defense Donald Rumsfeld cautioned that terrorists might get their hands on weapons of mass destruction. Vice President Richard Cheney worried that attacks could come "tomorrow or next week or next year." In those uneasy months after 9/11, every day the city was not attacked seemed like a victory. The NYPD historian Tom Reppetto spoke for many New Yorkers when he said, "Kelly stood between New York and another terrorist attack. Under Kelly, the police department prepared itself not just for another attack but how they would handle it afterwards."

To Kelly, like millions of Americans, the federal government—in particular, the FBI—had failed to protect New York City. They had missed all warning signs, failed to see the connections, as one by one, the hijackers had entered the country and registered at flight schools. In the weeks after 9/11, the FBI had also refused to share information with Mayor Giuliani and the police department about another terrorist act—anthrax-contaminated letters sent to prominent New Yorkers. Kelly spoke for many in the city when he declared, "We feel we have to protect ourselves."

"The world has changed," he explained. "The days when you could just focus on crime and quality-of-life violations suppression are over." He added, "Unlike any other place in America, we have clearly been targeted here." Paul Browne put it this way: After 9/11, Kelly "took the position that the NYPD could no longer rely on the federal government alone, and that the department had to build an intelligence capacity worthy of the name."

Kelly's first two appointments reflected these priorities. Neither man had experience in policing New York City, but they came with "70 years of combined experience . . . sneaking spies into foreign countries, landing soldiers on foreign shores and navigating the bureaucratic back alleys in Washington," as the *Times* said. Recently retired marine lieutenant general Francis X. Libutti had commanded 80,000 marines in Asia, Hawaii, and California. The fifty-six-year-old Libutti became the department's first deputy commissioner of counterterrorism, reporting directly to Kelly. A Long Island native, his return to New York was heralded as "coming home."

Libutti's stated assignment was all-encompassing: Fashion a police response to any act of terrorism in New York City, which meant training the department's 36,000 officers to use protective suits, gas masks, and sophisticated sensors to detect chemical, radiological, and biological weapons. The general was also going to assess the vulnerability of such potential high-profile targets as the Empire State Building, Rockefeller Center, the United Nations, and the city's bridges and tunnels. In addition, he was to explore the use of backup police command centers, should Police Plaza again be put out of commission, and to select backup command teams so that if the highest levels of the department were killed, others could replace them. As if all those responsibilities weren't enough, Libutti was also supervising the detectives in the FBI-led Joint Terrorist Task Force (JTTF), formed in the 1980s to coordinate information between the FBI and the NYPD. Kelly quadrupled the number of detectives in the task force.

Kelly also hired a thirty-five-year veteran of the Central Intelligence Agency, David Cohen, who had spent his last years in the agency overseeing espionage operations around the world. Once a spook, always a spook, I suppose, even at press conferences. Cohen was so closemouthed that when Kelly introduced him to the media and I asked his age, Cohen refused to answer. (He was sixty.) As the department's first deputy commissioner for intelligence, he, too, would report directly to Kelly. Introducing him at City Hall, Kelly said, "The police department didn't have the global perspective it needed. In the wake of 9/11 we need a total professional."

Kelly would assign over seven hundred officers and civilians to Cohen's revamped Intelligence Division, whose previous mission had been to investigate organized crime and more recently was limited to protecting dignitaries. Under Cohen, Intel would recruit people fluent in Arabic, Urdu, and Pashto and able to read foreign newspapers and monitor jihadi Web sites. Under Cohen, Intel also cultivated informants to gather information on local mosques, believed to be hotbeds of home-grown terrorists. Kelly and Cohen also assigned a half-dozen NYPD detectives overseas, stationing them in such terrorism redoubts as Tel Aviv, Cairo, London, Paris, Madrid, and Amman. Their mission duplicated the FBI's, whose agents are assigned in those countries to U.S. embassies. Kelly stated, however, "We want to emphasize we're not looking to supplant anything that's going on in the federal government—this is to augment." Good intentions aside, the NYPD had no legal jurisdiction outside New York City. Nothing in the city charter allowed the NYPD to pay the detectives' overseas expenses— including housing, food, and travel. To pay those expenses, Kelly turned to the Police Foundation, the group of wealthy New Yorkers who for nearly thirty years had raised funds for the NYPD. After 9/11, the foundation solicited nearly $7 million a year from donors, nearly double that before the attacks. Kelly appeared before its board, explaining that the city placed limits on how much money could be given to city employees for longtime overseas assignments. These wealthy New Yorkers agreed to pay $75,000 a year for each overseas detective's expenses. That meant the supposed safety of New York City was financed not by its government but by private donors.

Kelly's antiterrorism measures seemed especially timely when reports of an attack on the Brooklyn Bridge surfaced in May 2002. The police department began operating checkpoints into the city's major bridges and tunnels. Kelly tightened security around the Brooklyn Bridge and expanded vehicle checkpoints at the city's bridges and tunnels. Six months later, an Ohio trucker, Iyman Faris, admitted plotting with Al Qaeda to destroy the Brooklyn Bridge. Kelly took credit for thwarting those plans, explaining at a news conference that a coded message Faris had sent—"The weather was too hot"—meant that Faris had backed off because of all the increased police security.

iii.

There was a price to pay for fighting terrorism. That fall the police department, with no announcement or explanation, stopped issuing permits for political protest marches in Manhattan. Not until the following February did the public learn of this cap on free speech. It came to light when a 100,000-member antiwar coalition, in solidarity with worldwide protests against the impending U.S. invasion of Iraq, sought to march past the United Nations. The police department refused to permit the march, citing post 9/11 security concerns. Instead, the department offered an alternative—a stationary rally that would allow 10,000 protestors into a block-long area on 47th Street, with the overflow massing north along First Avenue.

When the coalition sued for the freedom to march, federal judge Barbara Jones sided with the police department, ruling the city's need to protect the public in this "time of heightened security" overrode the rights of demonstrators. Mayor Dinkins's corporation counsel Victor Kovner blasted the decision as "a low point in New York's history." "Large marches are being held in cities throughout the nation and the world," Kovner said, "and it is incomprehensible that the finest police department in the world cannot accommodate a traditional peaceful protest." City councilman Bill Perkins agreed. "This is meant to send a message beyond New York City and it is going to have a chilling effect nationally. I think the Bush administration does not like political dissent and has influenced the Bloomberg administration to stop it." If those remarks sounded far-fetched, consider the February 6 editorial in the right-wing *New York Sun*, which ran a week before the demonstration. "Mayor Bloomberg and Police Commissioner Kelly are doing the people of New York and the people of Iraq a great service by delaying and obstructing the anti-war protest planned for Feb. 15. The longer they delay in granting the protestors a permit, the less time the organizers have to get their turnout organized and the smaller the crowd is likely to be. . . . [T]he smaller the crowd, the more likely that President Bush will proceed with his plans to liberate Iraq."

The day after Jones's decision, another federal judge issued a more sweeping ruling that gave the NYPD the power to spy on political protestors. Senior judge Charles Haight III eliminated virtually all restrictions on police investigations into lawful political activity. Similar investigations of domestic political activity had been sources of controversy in the past, most recently in the late 1960s and early '70s, with the emergence of such radical and violent groups as the Weathermen and Black Panthers. The NYPD had been caught in its own surveillance scandal. Some undercover detectives who had infiltrated political groups encouraged them to commit unlawful acts. The result was a consent decree known as the Handschu agreement, named after lawyer Barbara Handschu, which restricted the NYPD's political surveillance. Under the Handschu guidelines, in place since 1985, the department needed to show a "criminal predicate"—that is, suspicion of a crime—before conducting undercover surveillance or infiltrating a political group. In rescinding the guidelines, Haight said he had relied on the testimony of Deputy Commissioner Cohen, who had argued that suspicion of a crime was no longer relevant when it came to terrorists, who outwardly obeyed the law until they exploded a bomb or crashed a plane. "There is no disputing Deputy Commissioner Cohen's assertion," Haight wrote, "that [t]he world has undergone remarkable changes, not only in terms of new threats we face but also in the ways we communicate and the technology we now use and are used by those who seek to harm us."

Thousands of people appeared on February 15, 2003, to protest the impending war in Iraq. Pandemonium ensued, predictable when ten thousand people are penned into a blocklong area. Police horses charged the largely peaceful crowd. Officers arrested 274 protestors, including grandmothers and pregnant women. Intelligence Division detectives promised the jailed marchers a quick release if they answered the following questions: Why had they attended the demonstration? Who were their friends? Who had they attended the demonstration with? What schools did they attend? What organizations did they belong to? What other marches had they participated in? Had they traveled to the Middle East or Africa? What did they think about Israel and Palestine? What did they think about the September 11 attacks? Where had they been on 9/11?

Brendan Knowlton, an attorney, said police had crammed him into a holding cell at Police Plaza with 150 other marchers. "One by one, they took us to a smaller office," Knowlton said. "I was questioned alone by a detective. He asked me, 'Did you come alone? Are you a student? Are you a member of a student organization? Do you come to these often?' I said I was uncomfortable without a lawyer. The detective told me if I cooperated I could get out. There was no threat in particular but the implication was pretty clear. If we cooperated, it would expedite our handling."

Emilie Clark, who was seven months pregnant, said she spent seven hours in three police precincts deprived of food and water. "I was continually bombarded with questions about the upcoming rally by five detectives who questioned me, alone, in a cell at the First Precinct. I was warned of violence for my unborn child and told there were suicide bombers and rookie cops. 'You know how they are,'" they said about the rookies.

The detectives wrote down the responses on a document called a Demonstration Debriefing Form, which had a federal seal in the upper left-hand corner. The NYPD then entered the answers into a database. When the Civil Liberties Union wrote a letter to Kelly, and released a copy to the *Times*, raising concerns that the NYPD had violated the protestors' constitutional rights with those questions, Kelly—as sensitive to media criticism as he had been during his first term as commissioner—announced he had ended the demonstration debriefing forms as unnecessary. He also claimed that neither he nor Cohen had known about them. That was hard to believe. He and Cohen had been conversant with every detail concerning the march, even preparing legal arguments against it. How could they be ignorant of anything as organized as these debriefings? If Kelly and Cohen weren't behind it, then who was? Had a police chief dared on his own to implement these new procedures, even having special forms printed for the questioning? A runaway chief like this lives only in fairy tales.

Meanwhile, I wondered where Mayor Bloomberg was in all this. He seemed to disappear from view, as Giuliani had during the 30th Precinct scandal, making no statement on the matter, leaving it in the hands of Kelly. Unlike Giuliani, this would be a recurring practice.

At a news conference at Police Plaza the day after the *Times* broke the story, Kelly tried to finesse his role by pleading ignorance. But he never explained what his ignorance had consisted of. Had it been of in-putting the debriefing information into the data bank? Or had it been of the new and aggressive line of questioning? When I tried to pin him down, he cut me off.

Asked whether the questioning had been illegal because the detainees had been denied lawyers, Kelly, a nonpracticing lawyer, said, "In my judgment it was not illegal or unconstitutional." Answering the detectives' questions, he added, "was not compulsory in any way." He termed the questioning "debriefings," and said that nobody's rights had been violated because the debriefings were not an interrogation but "part of the arrest process."

Judge Haight cut through Kelly's hairsplitting and accused him and the police of abusing their powers. "A pilot who returns from a mission is debriefed," Haight stated. "A defector is debriefed by agents." Referring to the Iraq protestors, Haight said, "Those persons were in police custody." Haight further mocked Kelly's and Cohen's professed ignorance, likening it to the line in the classic movie *Casablanca*, where Claude Raines, playing a corrupt French official, bows to pressure from the Nazis and closes his favorite nightspot. "I'm shocked, *shocked* to find gambling going on," Raines announces. As he closes down the joint a croupier hands him his roulette winnings.

Haight's colorful lecture to the NYPD ended with his reinstating the Handschu restrictions on police surveillance that he had eliminated because of a fear of terrorism. Noting how the department had overreacted in handling the Iraq war protests, Haight now said he had lost faith in the NYPD's methods of investigating political activity. "Given the NYPD intelligence-gathering techniques," Haight said, "I no longer hold that confidence." Five years later, the city would end a federal lawsuit by paying fifty-two of those arrested a total of $2,007,000.

Nonetheless, Haight's initial easing of the guidelines had opened the door to trouble. To Cohen, surveillance of domestic political activity was essential to fighting terrorism. "Given the range of activities that may be engaged in by the members of a sleeper cell in the long period of preparation for an act of terror," he would write in a court affidavit, "the entire resources of the NYPD must be available to conduct investigations into political activity and intelligence-related issues." The noble mission of catching terrorists would turn into a bizarre and potentially illegal monitoring of legitimate political protest. Fighting terrorism had morphed into preventing disorder.

iv.

Barely a year after Kelly appointed him deputy commissioner of counterterrorism, Francis Libutti resigned. Curiously, the White House, not the NYPD, made the announcement. Libutti was joining the Department of Homeland Security and assuming the vague and incomprehensible title of undersecretary for information analysis and infrastructure protection. The police department said nothing about his departure until I asked about it the next afternoon. Something about Libutti had apparently gone awry.

Despite our past friendship, I had kept my distance from Kelly since his swearing-in. I had not wanted to fall into the trap I had with Kerik, valuing access above critical reporting. When I learned Kelly had provided a security detail for Guy Molinari as a private citizen, I wrote the story. Kelly discontinued the detail the same day. Then there was Giuliani's security detail, despite his earning millions of dollars as a private citizen. Knowing how Kelly felt about Guliani, I was certain that Bloomberg, not Kelly, had ordered it. Nonetheless, the detail's detectives belonged to the police department and were Kelly's responsibility. When I questioned him, he literally squirmed, forced to defend not only the indefensible but a policy that I believed he had opposed. I also wrote that story. Why was I so certain Kelly had opposed that favor for the former mayor? Well, a year later, when Bloomberg ended the detail, Kelly forced these detectives, some of them Staten Island residents, into a long daily commute—known in the department as "highway therapy"—by transferring them to the farthest reaches of Upper Manhattan and the Bronx. Giuliani interceded with Bloomberg, and Kelly was forced to rescind the transfers. The Staten Island detectives were reassigned closer to home—to the nearby office of Staten Island district attorney William L. Murphy, whom Molinari had run against unsuccessfully. I wrote that story as well.

With no explanation from the police department, I pursued the story of Libutti's departure. Why was he leaving? Why his sudden return to Washington and an ill-defined title? What had changed since his "coming home" to New York just fourteen months before? Given the fanfare over his arrival, these sounded like legitimate questions. Libutti declined to see me, so I started nosing around the department. No one seemed to have an answer. Some speculated his leaving stemmed from being a general and having to take orders from Kelly, a marine colonel. Someone said the reason was Libutti's wife: She had not been happy in New York. Because he been assigned so many things to do, I wondered if he had never been given a specific assignment of substance.

The following week I posed some of these questions in "The Confidential." The column ran under the headline "A Short-Lived Homecoming." Two days later, a letter to the editor appeared in *Newsday*. It was the beginning of the end of my relationship with the letter's writer—Police Commissioner Ray Kelly.

"Leonard Levitt, whose pettiness was matched only by his stunning ignorance of the facts, did a great disservice to Frank Libutti in attempting recently to ridicule and diminish his historic contribution to the New York City Police Department as its first deputy commissioner for counter-terrorism," it began. "In less than a year and a half, Libutti, a former three-star Marine Corps lieutenant general, transformed the NYPD into the premier terrorism prevention agency among municipalities nationally, if not internationally." After listing Libutti's success at the NYPD—including his construction and staffing of a "vast, state of the art counter-terrorism center that tracks potential threats to New York from within the five boroughs and around the world" and "his advocacy for the creation of a Northern command to defend New York and other cities from attack"—the letter listed Libutti's Marine Corps history, including his medals and added, "It is no wonder why Secretary of Homeland Security Tom Ridge recruited him away from us for a senior post in Washington.

"Yet, Levitt attempted to reduce General Libutti's role in the Police Department," the letter continued. "He is also under the misapprehension that Libutti does not talk to reporters. In fact, he has been interviewed by several of New York's major daily newspapers, magazine and television stations. At best, Levitt is profoundly ignorant; at worst, mendaciously vindictive. Why? Because Libutti had the audacity not to return the columnist's telephone call."

Well, that was quite a letter. It wasn't merely an attack on my reporting. It was an attack on me. I had diminished Libutti's role because he had "the audacity" not to return my phone call? People don't return reporters' phone calls all the time. That's the way journalism works. Especially at Police Plaza. Did Kelly actually believe I had "reduced" Libutti's role at the NYPD because he hadn't returned my telephone call?

Kelly and I had known each other for a decade. Was this what he thought of me? He had invited me to meet his family, to witness his promotions. I had happily complied. Now I could only suspect what his true motivations had been.

The most stinging phrase in his letter had been "mendaciously vindictive," which sounded as though he were accusing me of purposely lying. I may have disagreed with Kelly's providing a detective detail for Molinari. I may have come down too hard on him for providing one for Giuliani. But I'd never questioned Kelly's honesty or integrity. It sure sounded as though he were questioning mine.

I tried to comprehend the reasons for Kelly's over-the-top response. Perhaps I had failed to appreciate the pressures he felt himself under since assuming the responsibility of protecting the city. Perhaps he felt that the importance of his position placed him beyond criticism. Whatever his reasons, it was clear that the Ray Kelly who had returned as police commissioner in 2002 was not the same man who had left nearly a decade before.

The letter was just his first shot at me. Shortly afterward, my boss, Les Payne, called with the news that Kelly had traveled to *Newsday* to meet with him and *Newsday*'s editor in chief Tony Marro "to express his complaints about your reporting." Les remained silent when I asked for Kelly's specific complaints, saying only, "He wants your head on a platter."

God knows, I had faced reporting predicaments in the past. None, though, had featured the police commissioner of the City of New York's taking four hours away from fighting crime and terrorism to drive out to Exit 49 on the Long Island Expressway simply to bash me. It had been my experience that when officials became upset with a reporter, it usually meant the reporter was properly doing his job. When the district attorney's spokesman had threatened to run me out of the Bronx and cut off my sources inside the D.A.'s office, I had bested him by becoming a better reporter and developing new sources outside that office. Ironically, this led to his—not my—having to leave the Bronx. But that triumph had occurred fifteen years before, when *New York Newsday* had been running on all cylinders. By 2003, the paper's once-heralded New York City edition was a memory. *Newsday* had lost the spark that had made its national reputation. Our city coverage, as I had seen in the aftermath of 9/11, was now directed from Long Island. Within the year, Tony Marro would retire. By 2005, the entire New York operation would be dismantled.

Because the city edition was on shaky ground, I wasn't sure that *Newsday*'s editors would stand up to Kelly. To their credit, Les told me to continue writing "The Confidential" as before. On the other hand, the paper had little choice. Had it killed the column or suggested I ease up in my coverage, *Newsday* would have been perceived as caving in to police pressure. Instead, they made a subtle change, shifting "The Confidential" from Monday to Friday. Years before, then First Deputy Joe Dunne had told me that one of "The Confidential's" strengths was appearing on Mondays because readers at Police Plaza spent the rest of the week buzzing about it. Changing the column's day to Friday meant it could be forgotten over the weekend.

Perhaps I was being oversensitive, but I wondered whether the change stemmed from Kelly's visit. However, both Les and Tony were first-rate newsmen and I didn't bother trying to fathom their motives. I took Les at face value and continued writing "The Confidential" as I had. As for Kelly, I wondered why he had not come to me with his complaints. If he felt I had been unfair when I wrote about the detective details for Molinari and Giuliani, why didn't he tell me personally? Those columns had been on target. Kelly had stopped Molinari's detail the day I wrote about it. My columns on Giuliani's detail were probably part of the reason Bloomberg had put an end to it. The Libutti column had raised what I felt were legitimate questions about his quiet departure.

Why then had Kelly gone over my head and behind my back instead of speaking to me? Not even Giuliani or Safir, even after all my reporting about them, had tried such an end run. My so-called friendship with Kelly, I realized, had been imaginary. Like Mayor Lindsay's aide Jay Kriegel thirty years before, he had played me for a fool. His praising me as "the only reporter in New York with balls" had probably been meant only to egg me on to write critically about his enemy, Giuliani. Not that his praise had made any difference in that regard. I'd been writing critically of Giuliani long before. Angered that I had turned a critical eye on him, Kelly had driven out to *Newsday* to bully my bosses.

Back at One Police Plaza, a new reporting adventure began. "The Confidential" was no longer included in the daily clippings about police news that circulate through the building, although it was read surreptitiously—perhaps more than ever. Seeing me walking through the hallways, chiefs and inspectors I had known for years avoided me. Some actually rushed into their offices and slammed their doors when I walked by. The days of Jack Maple's inviting me into his office for a cup of espresso were long gone. An inspector I knew in Brooklyn told me his chief had warned him, "Being seen with Lenny Levitt is committing career suicide." Here were the commanders of the NYPD, supposedly the greatest, most powerful police department in the world, armed with guns, trained to kill, and they were terrified of a lone reporter, no less one from a dying newspaper. As intimidating as the NYPD could be, I realized they were more afraid of me than I was of them.

One afternoon, I visited the NYPD Chief of Internal Affairs Charles Campisi in his corner office on the twelfth floor. Ever since the days of Chief Guido some twenty years earlier, I had maintained a relationship with the head of Internal Affairs. That was an obvious contact to develop, given the NYPD's cycles of corruption. While Campisi lacked Guido's flair, he was a dedicated and honest man, though while always cordial, he never provided much information. He and I had a ritual. "Okay, what do I need to know?" he would say when I'd call, implying that I was plugged-in enough that I might know things he didn't. Instead of answering him, I would come back with the same question: "Okay, Chief, what do I need to know?" He would then answer, "I can't tell you anything," or "No comment," and hang up the phone.

When I left Campisi's office that afternoon, he walked me outside into the hallway, just as Rafael Pineiro, whom Kelly had recently promoted to chief of personnel, was standing outside his office at the hallway's other end.

Pineiro and I had been friends ever since Safir banished him to the Criminal Justice Bureau more than five years before. "Hey, Charlie," Pineiro called down jokingly to Campisi, "now I know where Lenny gets his information."

Within the hour, Chief Mike Collins—whom Kelly had brought back to replace Fahey at DCPI—telephoned me. He said Campisi complained to him I had come to his office without permission. Poor Campisi. With Pineiro as a witness, he felt he had to cover himself for having been seen with me.

Around the same time, Chief of Detectives William Allee retired. We, too, had been friendly. I had recently purchased a ticket to his retirement dinner. A week before the event, Collins called me again. This time he conveyed Allee's request that I not attend. "He's afraid," said Collins, "that you might make some people uncomfortable."

Soon, Collins himself was fleeing from me. Seeing him on the elevator, I tagged after him when he got off at the ninth floor and headed toward the cafeteria. Collins stands six feet five inches and weighs 250 pounds. Although he has bad knees, suffered in a fall years before while capturing a perp, he looks like a bruiser. As I fell into step with him, I realized he was walking as fast as he could on his bad knees to get away from me.

Yet as had occurred in the Bronx, my ostracism from official sources only made me a better reporter. This time, I didn't have to go outside the NYPD. Aggrieved officers, many of them of surprisingly high rank, began coming to me with tales I could not have imagined. As deep as I thought I had burrowed down inside the police department, yet another layer would be revealed to me.

v.

Everything had gone wrong. On May 22, 2003, police raided a warehouse in the Chelsea section of Manhattan to arrest a CD-counterfeiting ring. But the officers, from a team in Staten Island, didn't know the layout. They ignored their tactical plan, which had called for the specially trained Emergency Service Unit to lead the raid, and went in themselves. Stationed on the warehouse's third floor dressed as a mailman, undercover officer Bryan Conroy carried no NYPD identification, another oversight. Worse, his supervisors didn't realize they had posted him to a section of the warehouse isolated from the stairs and reachable only by elevator. So that when the unexpected happened—when a black man appeared from the maze of warehouse rooms—Conroy was on his own. The black man didn't belong to the counterfeiting ring. He was an art trader with a cubicle in the warehouse, a newly arrived immigrant from the West African country of Burkino Faso named Ousmane Zongo. Startled by Zongo's sudden appearance, Conroy called for backup, but the team, confused over his whereabouts, couldn't reach him. He and Zongo apparently mistook each for robbers and a terrifying chase began through the warehouse's maze-like rooms that ended with Conroy fatally shooting the unarmed Zongo.

Acknowledging "very troubling questions about the shooting," Kelly consoled Zongo's widow in his office at Police Plaza at a meeting arranged by Sharpton. Afterward, Sharpton told reporters Kelly had promised a full department investigation of the shooting.

Three years later, in Manhattan Supreme Court, Justice Robert Straus convicted Conroy of criminally negligent homicide. A jury had deadlocked in his first trial. Although Conroy faced up to four years in prison, Straus sentenced him to five years' probation and placed the blame for the killing primarily on the police department. "There was a time during the trial when I frankly felt there could be other people sitting at the [defendant's] table with Mr. Conroy," the justice said in an hour-long critique he delivered before passing sentence. "I think there is shared responsibility here." Conroy, Straus said, had been "insufficiently trained, insufficiently supervised, insufficiently led on the day in question, by people who had the responsibility to make sure he did nothing but protect and serve rather than end up taking a life." He was apparently referring to Conroy's superiors—his sergeant, lieutenant, and captain—each of whom had made tactical mistakes that proved fatal.

Yet despite the promise of a full investigation, Kelly did not reveal his findings to the public. As late as Conroy's trial in 2005, the department claimed ignorance of the supervisory lapses cited by Justice Straus. Kelly's spokesman, Paul Browne, blamed the impasse on a request by District Attorney Morgenthau that the NYPD wait until after the trial to investigate problems with the raid. Morgenthau's spokeswoman denied it. "No such request was ever made," she said.

The same month Conroy shot Zongo, Alberta Spruill, a fifty-seven-year-old Harlem woman, died in another flawed police raid. Spruill, a city employee for twenty-nine years, suffered a fatal heart attack after a dozen Emergency Service Unit officers threw a flash grenade into her apartment. They had acted on incorrect information from an informant that someone was using her apartment to store drugs and guns.

Amid the outcry over Spruill's death, Bloomberg took responsibility, telling mourners at her funeral, "As mayor, I failed to protect someone." Kelly also took action. He suspended the use of flash grenades and bounced Chief Thomas Purtell from his command of the Special Operations Division, which supervises ESU, although the chief had no direct involvement in the raid. "In light of what's happened in the last two weeks, we need a fresh look at supervision and training," Kelly said. Six months later, Kelly quietly transferred Purtell to the prestigious position of Bronx borough commander. Like the results of the Zongo investigation, whatever Kelly discovered from his fresh look, he kept to himself.

The following year, yet another unarmed black New Yorker died at the hands of police. At around 1:30 A.M. on a January night in 2004 in the Louis Armstrong Housing Projects in Brooklyn's Bedford-Stuyvesant section, nineteen-year-old Timothy Stansbury took a shortcut across his rooftop to an adjacent building. A senior at Thomas Jefferson High School, he worked part-time at McDonald's and had never been in trouble with the law. On the last night of his life, he was among twenty-five people who attended a Friday night birthday party for a teenage neighbor. Tragically, he tried to take a shortcut as two housing police offices were patrolling the roof.

Police officer Richard Neri and his partner had their guns drawn, as regulations permitted. As Stansbury pushed open the interior door to reach the roof, Neri's partner was pulling it open from the outside. In the darkness, surprised that Stansbury had suddenly emerged from the stairs, Neri fired a shot. In his twelve-year police career, he had never before fired his weapon while on duty nor been the subject of a disciplinary proceeding. His bullet struck Stansbury in the chest and killed him.

Braving jeers from an angry crowd, Mayor Bloomberg visited Stansbury's family, offering condolences. Kelly also weighed in, holding a news conference less than twelve hours after the shooting. Even before the department had completed its investigation, he announced, "There appears to be no justification for the shooting."

"It was an extraordinary statement," said Norman Siegel, the former head of the New York Civil Liberties Union. "In my years of monitoring police-community relations, I can't remember when a police commissioner made that kind of statement. When police commissioners do make statements, it is to defend their cops."

But even Siegel, who had spent most of his life attacking police abuses, had reservations. He felt that Kelly had violated Officer Neri's rights. No one else, though, seemed concerned. Rather, the media viewed Kelly's statement as saving the city from a riot. Every newspaper in town commented favorably on what they viewed as Kelly's candor. Under the headline "A Wrongful Death in Brooklyn," the *Times* editorialized that Kelly "quickly told the public that the shooting appeared to be unjustified. His announcement is consistent with how previous police missteps have been handled in Michael Bloomberg's administration—with an openness that was absent when Rudolph Giuliani was mayor."

Yet law enforcement officials throughout in the city were aghast. Kelly was a police professional, they argued, and a lawyer as well. His "no justification" phrase, they maintained, had been a calculated remark. It was a legal term, tantamount to finding Neri guilty. Using it could prejudice public opinion. "You can lay out the facts as you know them," said a former NYPD deputy commissioner. "You can visit the parents and attend the funeral. But you cannot comment if you know the case is going to the grand jury. A remark like that could influence the district attorney and even the grand jurors." Another former top NYPD official said, "While I understand what [Kelly] was saying and in a certain context he is correct, the starkness of the phrase doesn't take into consideration the possibility of an accidental shooting, which it probably was." That opinion was vindicated when a Brooklyn grand jury ruled the shooting accidental and declined to indict Neri.

The Stansbury family settled with the city for $2.1 million, and the shooting passed into history. As in the Zongo and Spruill cases, Kelly never publicly addressed the Stansbury case's most obvious concern—the practice of officers patrolling rooftops with guns drawn, even with no indication of violence. He never explained whether he had reviewed the practice and, if so, what he had concluded. Rather his "no justification" comment—like his promises of a full investigation in the Zongo case and his transferring a top commander in the Spruill case—had been meant merely as a gesture, to calm the city and avoid a racial explosion. And it had succeeded. Again, department reform was forgotten.

I realized that in all the years I had known him, I had overlooked perhaps Kelly's most skillful trait. No less than Bratton, or even Kerik, he was a master of public relations. He also possessed something both Bratton and Kerik lacked. Because he had served under David Dinkins, he retained the goodwill of most black New Yorkers.

On November 25, 2006, nearly three years after the Stansbury shooting, Kelly's public relations skills were tested again. Outside a Queens strip joint, five officers fired fifty shots, killing Sean Bell, an unarmed black man, and wounding his two friends. The three had just attended a bachelor party for Bell at the Club Kalua, a nightspot known for prostitution and drug dealing. That same night, a team of seven Manhattan-based officers, including three undercover detectives, had been investigating the club, looking for evidence of crimes in order to shut it down. While an undercover drank two beers inside the club, the other officers waited outside. When the Bell trio left, the undercover inside the club, Gescard Isnora, became alarmed. He mistakenly believed they were going to get a gun. He followed them as they entered their car. He testified that when he confronted them, Bell attempted to run him over. Isnora and two other undercover detectives reacted by firing nearly fifty shots. No gun was found on Bell or his friends. The similarity to the Diallo shooting of seven years before was stark. Again, there were fears of a riot. Again, Bloomberg and Kelly reacted immediately. Two days after Bell's death, Bloomberg convened a meeting of black religious leaders at City Hall and declared the shooting "inexplicable and unacceptable." "It sounds to me like excessive force was used," he added. Again, Kelly announced a series of bold-sounding reforms: Breathalyzer tests for cops who fire their weapons and hit someone; the Rand Corporation to examine the phenomenon of "contagious shooting"—presumably the reason the cops had fired fifty rounds. Again, Bloomberg and Kelly succeeded in forestalling a riot.

The Queens district attorney charged Isnora and the two other undercovers, Marc Cooper and Michael Oliver, with manslaughter and reckless endangerment. Like the Diallo cops, the detectives attempted to have their trials moved out of New York City but were unsuccessful. They then waived their jury rights and opted to be tried before a judge. Justice Arthur Cooperman—who had presided over the "stun gun" case two decades before—acquitted them.

Compared with the widespread outrages over past police tragedies like Louima's torture or Diallo's killing, the protests over the Bell case seemed tempered. The city's leadership had changed, the grievances during the Giuliani years had passed. Clearly, that took some of the sting out of the Bell debacle. The city's highest elected black official, Comptroller William Thompson, contrasted Bloomberg's approach to that of Giuliani's, saying, "Just the simple fact of meeting or discussion or expressing concern and outrage on the part of this administration was different."

After the acquittals, Kelly leveled internal NYPD charges against all seven officers at the scene. All faced the loss of their jobs. Sharpton called the internal charges "a step in the right direction." But by 2008, nearly three years after the shooting, there had been no public accounting of what had gone wrong. While Kelly's reform-sounding moves helped soothe the city, he again did not address the underlying police problems of oversight and training that had led to the shooting. Despite its stated purpose, the Rand Corporation's report said nothing about contagious shootings. Instead, it recommended issuing Taser stun guns to sergeants. How this was relevant to the Bell shooting, Kelly never explained.

Nor did mandated Breathalyzer tests for cops who shot someone have any bearing on the Bell case. How could they when department rules permitted the undercover who had fired the first shot to drink inside the club? Once again Kelly never disclosed whether those undercover rules needed changing. Again the crisis passed. Again reform was forgotten.

In fact, Kelly's mandated sobriety tests resulted in a major embarrassment. On July 13, 2008, an off-duty detective, Ivan Davison, was out with friends when at 2:00 A.M. he saw three men punching and kicking a man on the ground. Rushing to help, he identified himself as a police officer but was met by three shots from a Tec-9 automatic that luckily missed him. Firing back, Davison wounded the gunman, who was later arrested. Normally, the department would have hailed Davison as a hero. He had saved a stranger's life, properly defended himself, and helped arrest the thugs who had beaten another man—all responses the public seeks from its police officers. But because of Kelly's new policy, the department treated Davison like a criminal. When he tested slightly over the legal limit to drive, the department removed his gun and badge and suspended him without pay. The outcry was so loud, including a front page editorial in the *New York Post*, headlined "He Deserved a Hero's Medal, Not a Lashing," that Mayor Bloomberg called for Davison's full reinstatement, saying Davison had "acted correctly." Kelly had no choice but to reverse himself, restore Davison to full duty, and call him a hero.

As for the Club Kalua, two months after the officers' acquittals, it was finally closed. But not through any police action. The Health Department shut it down because of unsanitary pests: mice.

vi.

Despite his failed promises of reform and disclosure in these fatal incidents, Kelly would remain a favorite of New Yorkers. White New Yorkers praised him for sparing the city from racial turmoil even as he ignored necessary police reforms. Among black New Yorkers, the reservoir of goodwill he had built up by serving as police commissioner under Dinkins remained filled. Over 60 percent of New Yorkers approved of the way he did his job. He was so popular he even eclipsed the popular Bloomberg, and many touted him as Bloomberg's successor. One was former mayor Ed Koch.

It was obvious why Kelly was so popular. Most important, there had been no further terrorist attack. Whether or not this had anything to do with Kelly (as there had been no terrorist attacks anywhere else in the country), the memory of 9/11 still hovered over the city. Kelly seemed to personify the leadership that New York needed. In addition, the city had remained racially calm while he served as commissioner. True, he may have violated the rights of such officers as Richad Neri in the Stansbury shooting or Ivan Davison in the off-duty shooting and offered no reform in the wake of the Alberta Spruill, Ouswane Zongo, and Sean Bell cases. But no one seemed to notice these lapses. Finally, there was the declining crime rate. Despite diverting a thousand officers to fight terrorism and despite some five thousand fewer officers than had existed under Giuliani, crime continued to fall. Through the use of computer printouts, Kelly had taken crimes once denoted at Compstat by Maple's pin maps to a new level. When computers spat out a crime hot spot,

Kelly flooded the area with rookies under a program he called Operation Impact.

By 2007, homicides had fallen below 500, a level not seen since John F. Kennedy was president. A front-page article in the *Times* on November 29, 2007, heralded Kelly's achievement under the headline "City Homicides Still Dropping, to Under 500, Lowest Toll in Decades."

"Homicides began falling in the early 1990s, when Raymond W. Kelly first served as police commissioner," the story said, "and plummeted further under subsequent commissioners." Absent in the article were the gibes of the Giuliani years, mocking Kelly's earlier crime-fighting efforts under Dinkins. Absent, too, was the belittling term "social work," to describe his failed community-policing policy. Nowhere in the article's 1,064 words was there even a mention of Bratton, Maple, or Compstat. It had taken Kelly fourteen years, but he had seen his story told in the country's most important newspaper just the way he wanted it.

The crime picture looked so rosy that Kelly and Bloomberg began calling New York "The Safest Large City in America." They based their ranking on the FBI's 2004 Uniform Crime Report, although the Bureau said that index was misleading for the equal weight it gave to violent and the much more numerous nonviolent crimes. But this success had a darker side. Police sources were murmuring that crime was actually higher because some cops were suppressing complaints or downgrading them from felonies to less serious misdemeanors. Sources said that officers sometimes refused to accept civilians' reports of crime. It was part of an unwritten policy, they whispered, to lower the official crime rate. A former Brooklyn commander was said to discourage robbery complaints by insisting that only detectives at the precinct take the cases, not the officers responding to the crime. A former police official said he personally had to call the desk sergeant at a Brooklyn precinct to report a $5,000 theft because detectives refused to take the victim's complaint. A retired squad commander said that cops who low-balled the figures hid their paper trail by reusing complaint form numbers for crimes they had ignored. A Manhattan squad commander said, "Many victims are talked out of filing complaints [because] they have told their story to three or four precinct-level cops and to bosses who question them with an eye to sculpting the victim's story to fit the criteria for a downgrade from a felony to a misdemeanor." A lieutenant in the Bronx ordered an officer to reduce the estimated value of merchandise stolen from a Genovese Drug Store from \$1,815 to \$500, which downgraded the crime from a felony to a misdemeanor. The officer refused and both he and the precinct's PBA delegate, who backed him, were transferred.

Allegations like these had been around since the Bratton years, an unfortunate by-product of Compstat. The computer tracking of crimes had made it possible to measure accountability through statistics. Crime totals could make or break a commander's career as well as a police commissioner's. No one was more sensitive to this than Kelly. As he wrote in the *News* after a slight monthly increase in murders, "It is curious that commentators waited until now to express alarm about a modest midyear uptick in murders but remained silent in 1999 or 2000 when homicides increased for two successive years."

During the past decade, the department had demoted or transferred half a dozen commanders caught doctoring crime figures. Now inside sources maintained the cheating was increasingly widespread. After *Newsday*'s Rocco Parascadola and I reported their concerns and provided some examples, PBA president Patrick Lynch and sergeants' union head Ed Mullins held a news conference and declared the problem to be systemic. "It is a truth that is widely known by members of the department," said Lynch. Paul Browne dismissed our reporting as "inventions" and declared it was "baffling that a police union would assert that its own members are failing to suppress crime as effectively as we know they are." He was able to convince the city's other newspapers that the charges had no merit and stemmed from a dispute between the department and the PBA over the Bronx delegate's forced transfer over the Genovese drugstore case. No one bothered to ask why, if that was the case, the sergeant's union had seconded the allegations.

The sole agency mandated to investigate these charges of lowballing crime was the toothless Mayor's Commission to Investigate Police Corruption. Bloomberg had recently appointed a new chairman, a former federal prosecutor, Mark Pomerantz. As chief of the criminal division of the U.S. Attorney's Office in New York, he had helped convict officer Frank Livoti of the choke-hold death of Anthony Baez in the Bronx in 1994. Pomerantz announced he would investigate charges that the department had deliberately and systemically downgraded crimes. But Kelly refused to cooperate. Pomerantz and his deputies were stonewalled. "Our entire tenure," said a city commissioner who worked with him, "was characterized by jurisdictional disputes about what constitutes corruption. The police department does not feel that such issues as falsifying crime statistics and lying about them constitute corruption. And when they disagree, it can take them months to get back and say no. Then we set up a meeting a year down the road and nothing happens."

This city commissioner added that Kelly had resisted questions more vigorously than any previous police commissioner. "It was not a question of Kelly's personal integrity," the city commissioner said of him. "He lets you ask all sorts of questions. But he feels he can't be bothered by what he considers insignificant. He feels the department can take care of itself and doesn't need outside help."

Testifying before the City Council two years after he began his investigation, Pomerantz explained Kelly's refusal to cooperate by saying Kelly had decided that the alleged crime-doctoring was an "administrative," not a "criminal" matter. When Mayor Bloomberg remained silent, Pomerantz resigned. "This was a mayoral commission," Pomerantz later explained. "When he refused to intervene, there was no point in remaining."

To succeed Pomerantz, Bloomberg appointed Michael Armstrong. Thirty-five years before, Armstrong had been the aggressive counsel to the Knapp Commission on Police Corruption. He had served briefly as Queens district attorney. But over four decades, his point of view had changed. As a defense attorney, he represented government officials and white-collar criminals, most notably Queens Borough President Donald Manes, who committed suicide amid a corruption probe. Describing Armstrong's change since the Knapp Commission, a colleague said of him, "He is now an older man."

Taking over the corruption commission, Armstrong said he did not believe it was necessary to investigate the police department as long as Kelly remained commissioner. "The best formula for a corruption-free department," he told *The New York Sun*, "is to have a tough, knowledgeable, hands-on police commissioner and we have one now." Official oversight of the NYPD had ended.

vii.

Despite Bloomberg's campaign promise of more transparency, the police department under Kelly became more sparing of information than under Giuliani. Often, Kelly used security concerns to justify the secrecy, sometimes not convincingly. He refused to reveal such minor details as his public schedule—Bloomberg, FBI Director Mueller, and even President Bush released theirs—because, Kelly said, disclosure "could endanger lives or hurt ongoing investigations." More importantly, he refused to release the weekly schedule of officers facing charges in the department's trial room, ensuring that the public would know little, if anything, about cases of corruption.

But Kelly couldn't suppress all bad news. In the fall of 2006 retired detective Thomas Rachko was sentenced in Brooklyn federal court to seven years in prison for stealing $800,000 from drug dealers. He had been assigned to the Northern Manhattan Institute, a narcotics unit targeting drug dealers in Harlem and Washington Heights. That was the same territory of the Dirty Thirty scandal of a decade before. Retired lieutenant John McGuire, who had supervised Rachko and forty other Upper Manhattan narcotics detectives, was sentenced to fourteen months for stealing $110,000 in drug cash over three years. And Rachko's partner, Detective Julio Vasquez, was sentenced to six years for robbing drug dealers of $740,000 over an eight-year period.

A hidden camera had videotaped these corrupt officers in 2003, stealing $169,000 from a drug-money courier. The videotape had not been made by the NYPD but by a federal task force investigating unrelated money laundering and tailing the courier. The feds watched as Rachko, who had retired the year before, and Vasquez—both wearing NYPD jackets—arrested the courier and stole the money.

Their scheme echoed the drug shakedowns rampant in the corruption scandals of the recent past. It should have sounded the alarm bell for Kelly and IAB that there were plenty of other dishonest cops out there. Indeed, the arrest of drug-dealing NYPD cop Michael Dowd by Long Island police in 1992 had led to the Mollen Commission and the uncovering of the 30th Precinct scandal. Rachko, McGuire, and Vasquez, like Dowd, had run wild for years. Worse, the corruption had included the supervisory ranks. McGuire was a lieutenant. Yet here there was no public outcry, no calls for a wider investigation. Why not? Well, with terror threats frightening people and with local crime at all-time lows, neither the public nor the media focused on police corruption. Unlike the Knapp Commission of the early 1970s, the current problems did not suggest a cover-up at the top. If anything, the current top brass resembled the chiefs of the Ben Ward era, so scared of upsetting the police commissioner with bad press, they ignored corruption warning signals, as the Mollen Commission testimony had revealed. Kelly, too, was sensitive to bad press. Maybe even more than Ward did. And the top brass was at least as fearful of upsetting Kelly as they had been of Ward. The last thing Kelly wanted was an independent body poking around One Police Plaza in search of corruption.

So in 2007, for posterity's sake, I decided to start my own tally. I found myself making entries right away. Suffolk County police arrested Glen Smokler, a veteran 30th Precinct cop, along with twenty-eight others who were part of a multimillion-dollar marijuana ring that had smuggled drugs from Canada to Long Island. The Long Island police seized $3 million in cash, a hundred pounds of marijuana, Uzis, and shotguns. The Suffolk district attorney said Smokler, who drove a BMW and had recently moved to a plush apartment in Coram, served as both a narcotics distributor and an enforcer.

Nassau County police arrested Hubertus Vannes, a cop in the 110th Precinct in Queens, for allegedly dealing drugs and selling guns he had stolen from his precinct house. "This case represents the most egregious betrayal imaginable," said the Nassau County district attorney, who showed reporters three pistols that were traced back to Vannes. He pleaded guilty to selling handguns and was sentenced to five years in prison.

Narcotics cop James Calderon, a thirteen-year veteran, was arrested for allegedly running a cocaine and heroin ring with his girlfriend and two Bronx drug lords that stretched as far south as Virginia. Prosecutors learned of the drug ring when Calderon tried to get cops in the 44th Precinct to release to him a stolen minivan that had been impounded. Police later found a kilo of heroin stashed in a secret compartment inside the car.

Former cop Joe Torrado was sentenced to ten years for smuggling cocaine and marijuana from Mexico as part of a drug-trafficking ring. Torrado was arrested after federal agents seized 135 kilos of cocaine, hidden behind the false wall of a truck in the Bronx. The ring was headed by Torrado's brother. In all of 2007, nearly two dozen officers were arrested for drug-related crimes.

In January 2008, Sergeant Roosevelt Green allegedly took a sweat suit and sneakers from a Long Island drug lord in exchange for helping him evade federal drug enforcement agents, according to a federal complaint. Green, an eleven-year NYPD veteran, was arrested after he reputedly used a police department computer inside an unmarked car to run license plates checks on several cars the dealer thought had been tailing him. Green was indicted and as of this writing he is awaiting trial.

On the day of Green's arrest, federal agents charged Luis Batista with protecting a friend's cocaine ring. He pleaded not guilty and is awaiting trial. The feds also charged Henry Condo, an Internal Affairs sergeant, with checking police records and warning Batista that IAB was on to him. A day earlier, the feds had busted a prostitution ring enforced by Detective Wayne Taylor. Taylor was alleged to have been pimping a thirteen-year-old runaway. Prosecutors alleged that Taylor and his madam girlfriend forced the thirteen-year-old to party throughout the city and have sex with twenty men. He pleaded not guilty to the charges.

Queens police officers Dennis Kim and Jerry Svornoros were arrested for reportedly protecting a brothel in exchange for sex and bribes of $125,000. The pimps paying off the two cops provided tips about competing brothels that led to raids that advanced the cops' careers. Kim pleaded guilty and Svornoros cooperated in the case against Kim. A Manhattan South narcotics sergeant was charged with stealing from the cash register of a nightclub. A team of narcotics cops was under investigation for falsely charging four patrons of a Queens club with selling two bags of cocaine after a secret surveillance tape revealed the cops never bought drugs from them. Brooklyn South narcotics sergeant Michael Arenella and police officer Jerry Bowens were arrested for allegedly stealing cash and drugs from an undercover officer posing as an informant after the two were suspected of skimming from drugs they had seized on other occasions. Bowens was later charged with killing his girlfriend, Catherine Donofrio. In what appeared to be a growing scandal in the unit, police officers Sean Johnstone and Julio Alvarez were arrested after being heard on a surveillance tape bragging that they had confiscated twenty-eight bags of cocaine from a Coney Island dealer. Only seventeen bags were invoiced. This mess was too big for even Kelly to dismiss. He replaced the citywide narcotics commander, transferred the Brooklyn South narcotics unit inspector, together with two captains, and recruited another chief to fix the entire division. Brooklyn prosecutors said they might have to invalidate five hundred narcotics convictions and release countless convicted dealers back to the streets. The officers are awaiting trial.

While I was keeping my corruption count, the *New York Post* had also caught on that something in the department was amiss. The once-slavish, surrogate voice of the NYPD had turned into a trumpet of critical and embarrassing stories on police corruption. I attributed the *Post*'s change to another Kelly crackdown on public disclosure—this one directed at reporters and their police sources. In the winter of 2006, Kelly became uneasy with the details appearing in the newspapers about the kidnapping, rape, and murder of graduate student Imette St. Guillen, who was last seen leaving a Soho bar in Manhattan and whose body was discovered off the Belt Parkway in Brooklyn. The leaked information was not compromising to the case. Nonetheless, Kelly took an unprecedented step. He ordered detectives and other police officials to turn over their private cell phone records to determine whether they had spoken with reporters. Besides this "dumping" of cell phones, a tool used against criminals, the Internal Affairs Bureau questioned scores of detectives and several of their bosses, including two chiefs.

The *Post*, which had the most experienced police reporters in town, was especially upset because its reporting had provided detectives with a break in the case—a witness linking St. Guillen to the suspect, a bouncer at the Soho bar where she had last been seen. "The effect [of Kelly's crackdown] was more severe than anything during the Giuliani years," said the *Post*'s bureau chief Murray Weiss. "There hadn't been anything so chilling in the police department since Giuliani wiped out the entire Public Information Office under Bill Bratton."

While Giuliani's wholesale transfers at DCPI were public—John Miller had even held a news conference—Kelly's crackdown on the NYPD's Detective Bureau occurred behind the scenes. Not one newspaper, not even the *Post*, reported it. The story appeared only in "The Confidential." But Kelly's actions liberated the newspaper from its uncritical support of him. Its police reporters began coming up with embarrassing disclosures. It broke the scandal in the Brooklyn South narcotics unit. It uncovered a steroids scandal involving twenty-seven officers whose names turned up in a Brooklyn pharmacy that sold $8 million worth of these drugs. One of the alleged customers was a deputy chief.

Then, in October 2007, the *Post* showcased on page one a secret Internal Affairs report, showing that corruption in the ranks was worse than anyone suspected. Corruption arrests had jumped 25 percent from 2005 to 2006, including 114 cops charged in 2006 with such acts as soliciting sex in exchange for overlooking crimes, stealing credit cards from the homes of the dead, and hiring a hit man.

Still, there was no public outcry. The mayor said nothing. There were no editorials asking what was going on at Police Plaza. The entire city seemed afraid to ask hard questions of Ray Kelly.

viii.

"Never appoint a bitter man as police commissioner," a top department official said to me. Despite his accomplishments and successes, Kelly remained bitter toward those he felt had wronged him. His bitterness ran so deep I sometimes suspected he shaped his actions, even measures against terrorism, through the prism of his resentments.

When Bratton—who in 2002 became chief of the Los Angeles Police Department—came through town, Kelly refused to take his calls. Upon learning Bratton would play a central role in an international terrorism conference that the NYPD was cosponsoring with the Manhattan Institute, Kelly withdrew at the last minute. He then threw together a rival conference and held it at Police Plaza on the same day.

When Safir attempted to see Kelly, a Kelly aide told him he would have to write a letter to get an appointment. Apparently at Kelly's direction, Deputy Commissioner for Intelligence David Cohen also shunned Safir. "David," Safir lamented in a letter I was given a copy of, "I have called you four times and you have not returned my calls. There was *never* a time when I was P.C. that I did not return the calls you made to me, nor did I ever fail to help you. Friends do not treat friends this way."

Kelly also harbored a grudge against the FBI, although what this stemmed from remained unclear to me. After the first World Trade Center bombing in 1993, the Bureau had been his partner, at least on national television. After the 9/11 attack, they became the bumbling agency that had failed to protect New York City.

Top law enforcement officials are hardly the stolid, stoic figures as Hollywood presents them. Rather, they are more like high-strung thoroughbreds. The slightest criticism can spook them.

In addition, each law enforcement agency has its own culture. Since the days of its founder, J. Edgar Hoover, the Bureau has disdained local police departments, including the NYPD, which it considered both corrupt and unable to keep its collective mouth shut. The NYPD, in turn, mocked the FBI as hicks, lacking the street smarts necessary to blend into New York City life.

But Kelly's anger at the FBI seemed less institutional than personal. A well-placed source told me that after FBI director Louis Freeh fell out with President Clinton, Kelly angled, unsuccessfully, for Freeh's job. Apparently, even the threat of terrorism was not enough for Kelly to overcome past grievances and welcome the FBI as partners.

In July 2003, I learned of a secret meeting between Kelly and current FBI director Robert Mueller. FBI sources told me it was prompted in part by a *New York Post* article in which Kelly had criticized the Bureau for withholding terrorism information. Referring to the Joint Terrorism Task Force, comprised of FBI agents and NYPD detectives, Kelly told the *Post*, "It's not quite joint." While to the public this may have seemed like a quibble, Kelly's remark violated an unwritten code of law enforcement ethics: Never publicly criticize another law enforcement agency. Equally upsetting to the Bureau, the *Post* article quoted an anonymous source, stating that the FBI "couldn't pick out a Yemeni from a Palestinian." When I asked whether Mueller and Kelly had discussed that crack, a Bureau official answered, "The director was aware of the article," adding that the FBI assumed the anonymous source "was someone high in the NYPD." He stopped short of stating the obvious: The Bureau believed the source was Kelly.

What had been especially irritating, to the FBI, I learned, were Kelly's public comments taking credit for disrupting the terrorist attack to destroy the Brooklyn Bridge. It had been the FBI's tip that led the NYPD to ramp up security, thwarting the scheme. It had also been the FBI who arrested the Ohio plotter, Iyman Faris.

Kelly's sending NYPD detectives on out-of-state antiterrorism operations caused further friction. The detectives were not from the Joint Terrorism Task Force, the body of NYPD detectives and FBI agents established to coordinate the agencies' joint activities. Rather, in the fall of 2003, Cohen dispatched detectives from his Intelligence Division to New Jersey and Pennsylvania. Although lacking legal jurisdiction outside New York City, the NYPD kept local authorities and the FBI in the dark about their missions, which ended in embarrassment and recriminations. In New Jersey, the Intel detectives conducted an antiterrorism telephone sting to determine whether scuba shops along the

Jersey shore would notify law enforcement after receiving suspicious queries from strangers; they asked to pay for scuba lessons in cash without filling out required paperwork. But the scuba shop owners acted properly and notified New Jersey's Office of Counter-Terrorism (OCT) about the calls, who spent days trying to determine whether terrorists had been making them. When they learned the callers were NYPD detectives, they were furious. In an "advisory" to the FBI, Director Sidney J. Casperson wrote: "On Wed., Oct. 15, 2003, it was brought to the attention of the Office of Counter-Terrorism [OCT] that calls . . . regarding suspicious inquiries at four dive shops were part of a test the NYPD's Intelligence Division was conducting. OCT was not aware that the tests were being conducted and has since informed the NYPD Intelligence Division to cease and desist all such activity in the state of New Jersey."

The Pennsylvania mission involved explosives that were reported stolen from a local business in Carlisle in the western part of the state. Two NYPD detectives appeared at the crime scene, which was controlled by the FBI, the Bureau of Alcohol, Tobacco, and Firearms, and Pennsylvania's North Middleton Township Police Department, and began conducting interviews. The feds and the locals asked them to leave and return to New York.

"We mainly instructed them that the investigation was being handled by us and the FBI and that if we need their help we will give them a call," explained Jeff Rudolph, the North Middletown Township police chief. "After what happened on September 11, we all have great sympathy for New Yorkers. If I had any idea that anything was headed their way, I'd be the first to call them through proper channels."

Three months later, in January 2004, Mueller had apparently had enough and sent a subordinate to "rein in" Kelly, as a source put it. Pasquale D'Amuro, one of the agency's top international terrorism experts, became the new head of the New York office and immediately began sparring with Kelly. A continuing flashpoint of friction concerned the NYPD's overseas detectives. When in March 2004 terrorists bombed a commuter train in Madrid, Spain, the NYPD and the Bureau squared off. Cohen dispatched two Intel detectives from London to Madrid to interview the Spanish National Police (SNP), ignoring the FBI agent assigned to the U.S. Embassy. An FBI official later maintained that the SNP had refused to meet with the detectives and called the embassy's legal attaché to say the SNP had no time for them. "The SNP was aware that two NYPD detectives were on the way or were already there, and wanted nothing to do with them," the official said. The NYPD had a different version. Contrary to what FBI sources had told me, Intel officials said the detectives had met with the SNP and that it was the FBI that had been shut out. "We came in just before the Moroccans," said an Intel official, "which was where the investigation was heading."

That summer, Kelly sparked another flap with the Bureau. After the JTTF arrested radical Muslim cleric Abu Hamsa al Masri in London, Kelly publicly praised an NYPD detective with the JTTF who had helped arrest him. At a news conference with U.S. Attorney General John Ashcroft, Kelly identified the detective as George Corey. Deputy Chief James Waters, who commanded the NYPD side of the JTTF, added, "Nobody is better than the New York City cops at this kind of thing."

The police department then e-mailed reporters the text of Kelly's remarks with a picture of Corey and details about him, including his age, college background, and the fact that he lived on Long Island. The FBI appeared stunned— not just by Kelly's grab for credit in al Masri's capture but by Kelly's public identification of Corey. "In twenty-four years of the JTTF," said the Bureau's New York spokesman, Joe Valiquette, "I can't recall a JTTF investigator having his photo published in the midst of a prosecution."

Such information made it easy, with today's technology, to locate Corey's unlisted phone number and his home on Long Island. Teams of reporters and photographers camped out there, terrifying his wife, who contacted officials at Police Plaza. Corey, who had been sent to London with his FBI counterpart to testify at al Masri's pretrial hearing, was whisked home.

D'Amuro then took the extraordinary step of chastising Kelly in a scathing internal memo, which the FBI released to the media. Kelly's identification of Corey, the memo said, had led to "security concerns," prompting his premature return from London. Kelly's remarks, D'Amuro added, had also upset Scotland Yard, prompting a call of complaint from the commander of Britain's Anti-Terrorist Branch. "The newspaper articles . . . credited the NYPD with breaking the case," D'Amuro's memo continued. "There were quotes attributed to an NYPD official, on the record, that 'Nobody is better than the New York City cops at this kind of thing.'" The memo concluded: "This is NOT the way we do business."

Kelly appeared undaunted. The day after the London subway bombing the following summer, he held another news conference. This time, he identified the NYPD detective based in London and said he had been working with London cops and provided key information to Kelly within twenty-four hours of the blasts. Later, an Intel official told me what the detective had actually done. He had been a few subway stops away and gone immediately to the site, then, like any reporter or private citizen, phoned in what he saw. What key information he provided, Kelly never said.

The FBI was not the only agency Kelly feuded with in fighting terrorism. He also battled the Port Authority Police Department (PAPD), which had jurisdiction over the World Trade Center site. Formed eighty years ago, the Port Authority's jurisdiction includes both New York and New Jersey. Its 1,500 police officers patrol the bridges and tunnels connecting the city to New Jersey, to Kennedy and LaGuardia Airports, and to the World Trade Center. On 9/11, the Port Authority police lost thirty-seven officers, including its superintendent, nearly double the loss of the NYPD.

Initially, Kelly had no problem with the PAPD because, in 2002, he had successfully lobbied New Jersey's then governor James McGreevey to appoint Kelly's friend, retired NYPD inspector Charles De Rienzo, as its superintendent. De Rienzo, though, was forced out after two years because top PAPD officers felt his loyalty was to Kelly, not to the PAPD. In 2006, Kelly objected to what he termed the PAPD's lax security measures at the Ground Zero construction site. The PAPD guarded the site's four entrances, at Church, West, Vesey, and Liberty Streets, placing officers in parked patrol cars just inside the gates to each entrance. In an urban version of a Mexican standoff, Kelly placed NYPD officers in patrol cars just outside the gates. Though only a few feet apart, the officers from the two agencies did not communicate. Instead, they warily eyeballed each other from their patrol cars. After a few months of this wasted manpower, Kelly withdrew his officers.

Ironically, the man Kelly increasingly reminded me of was the man he most despised—Rudy Giuliani. Like Giuliani, Kelly had to be in charge. Like Giuliani he brooked no rivals. As mayor, Giuliani, too, had tried to take control of PAPD duties at Kennedy and LaGuardia Airports. He had been no more successful than Kelly had been at the entrances to Ground Zero. During the 9/11 Commission's public hearings in New York in 2004, I was struck by another similarity. Seeking answers for the lack of coordination between the police and fire departments, the 9/11 commissioners aggressively questioned past and present top city officials. But when Kelly and Giuliani testified, the 9/11 commissioners turned deferential. Was it the fear of the World Trade Center attacks and the fact that these were the two men charged with protecting the city? Or was it that their mere presence commanded respect? Whatever the reason, the 9/11 commissioners appeared in awe of both of them.

ix.

After nearly two years year of battling with Kelly, D'Amuro retired from the FBI—and joined Giuliani Partners. I marveled at how, at the highest levels of law enforcement, some coincidences are arranged.

With D'Amuro gone, the Bureau's line toward Kelly changed. The new FBI guy in town, Mark Mershon, explained the FBI's capitulation to me: "I got word of my appointment on a Monday. . . . My first business call was to Ray Kelly. He took my call. He knew who I was. I said, 'Ray, I really need to address something with you about the real or exaggerated differences at our level. I have profound respect for your command presence and your ownership of the safety of the good people of New York. I hope we will stand shoulder to shoulder, reassuring those same people that we will do the right thing.'"

As evidence of this new unity, Mershon pointed to an October 2005 press conference at which the NYPD and the FBI joined Mayor Bloomberg to warn New Yorkers of a terrorist plot involving rigged baby strollers on subways, an alert that turned out to be false. Immediately after the news conference, Mershon's office phone rang. "It was the director's [FBI Director Mueller] secretary Wanda," Mereshon said. "Before I could say a word he [Mueller] said, 'Mark, thank you, thank, thank you. I am so glad we have you up there. Thank you for the manner in which you handled yourself.'"

Later, as Mershon drove home, Mueller called him again. "He said, 'Mark, I hope you don't mind. I just called Ray Kelly to thank him for working together.'" Mershon said that he and Mueller had even come to accept Kelly's stationing detectives overseas. "Ray Kelly views this as the signature accomplishment of his administration," Mershon said. "Those detectives are doing something we are not. They sit in the bullpen with the foreign police agencies eight or ten hours a day. Their primary mission is to get right to the scene, and to light up a cell phone and call back to the NYPD in the event that simultaneous attacks are planned for New York City. I would love to be able to say the FBI can do that. But we are not staffed to do that. That is not our mission."

The key question, I asked Mershon, was this: Which agency is in charge of fighting terrorism, the FBI or the NYPD? Mershon didn't answer directly. Fighting terrorism, he said, requires "maturity and judgment from the top. It will not be done in an atmosphere of subordinating another agency. They are full partners and decision makers. . . . You have to share completely and make it crystal clear that anyone who violates this is not part of the team."

It wasn't clear to me that Kelly had joined that team. In marking the fifth anniversary of 9/11, it sure didn't look like it. First he bailed out of the international terrorism conference over Bratton's participation, then Deputy Commissioner Cohen infuriated the Secret Service, the federal agency that protects the president. To mark the fifth anniversary of the attack, President Bush had planned to visit Ladder Company 10 and Engine Company 10 on Liberty Street, the firehouse closest to Ground Zero, which had lost five firefighters in the burning towers. When Cohen learned the Secret Service was inspecting the firehouse in advance of the president's visit, he rushed over, then declared the site vulnerable to a terrorist attack. This was news to the security experts at the Secret Service, who had no problem with the firehouse's safety. An Intelligence Division detective told me the Secret Service's special agent in charge of the presidential detail had been so furious at Cohen that he stalked out, saying that, because of Cohen's interference, Bush would not visit the firehouse. The next day Cohen was rumored to have been summoned to Kelly's office and told to go immediately to City Hall. Bloomberg had received a call from the White House. He ordered Cohen to apologize to the Secret Service for his meddling.

I could never confirm this incident actually occurred, beyond what my Intel source had told me. Cohen, Kelly, and Bloomberg did not return my phone calls. In checking past news clippings, I saw that Bush *had* visited the Liberty Street firehouse—but on the sly. Press accounts described it as an "unscheduled" stop the evening before the 9/11 anniversary.

There was no doubt, though, about Cohen's actions at Kennedy Airport when the Iranian delegation accompanying its president, Mahmoud Ahmadinejad, arrived in New York to address the United Nations the following

September. Once again, the Kelly-Cohen combination proved that the NYPD was not part of any team. When the plane landed, officials from four agencies—the Secret Service, Port Authority, State Department's Diplomatic Security Service (DSS), and the NYPD's Intelligence Division—were ready with motorcade cars. The plan was that Port Authority police would escort the motorcade to the airport exit, where the NYPD and the Secret Service would take over for the ride into Manhattan. The four agencies held a run-through at the airport command post. Everyone was in synch.

But when the plane landed, Cohen's newly appointed Intelligence Division deputy chief Thomas Galati blocked the Iranians from leaving the airport. He insisted on a weapons check. The Secret Service, Port Authority, and Diplomatic Security Service all objected, maintaining this violated diplomatic protocol and would lead to retaliation against our diplomats. Galati backed off. But he then held up the Iranian delegation for forty minutes while the other agencies fumed. Only after a top Port Authority official contacted the NYPD's chief of department Joe Esposito were the Iranians permitted to leave for Manhattan.

Still, Cohen had his supporters. The loudest were at the *Daily News*. Columnist Michael Daly sounded gleeful, describing "a forty-minute standoff where the NYPD vehicle at the head of the motorcade stayed put and the Iranians milled around on the tarmac. The scene was complete with a rough-hewn cop, Deputy Chief Thomas Galati," wrote Daly. "Galati is with the Intelligence Division, headed by David Cohen, formerly of the CIA." The *News*'s editorial that day echoed Daly's tone. "The NYPD stood tall against the heavily armed entourage of Iranian President Mahmoud Ahmadinejad," it began. "[T]he cops put the Iranians in their place until the feds insisted New York had to abide by diplomatic niceties." The NYPD, it said, tried "to check how many guns the Iranians were packing. Galati and his boss, Deputy Commissioner David Cohen, did their best to find out. For which we salute them heartily."

I suspected I knew why the *Daily News* was so enamored of Cohen. A couple of years before, I discovered, Cohen had used Intel detectives to conduct what appeared to be a private investigation for the *Daily News*'s billionaire owner, Mortimer Zuckerman. Late in 2004, Zuckerman's chauffeur noticed he was being tailed. At the same time, Zuckerman maintained he was receiving threatening phone calls. Although his spokeswoman said Zuckerman felt the threats were "business related," he told the police that as a supporter of Israel, he could be targeted by terrorists. So instead of notifying his local precinct or detective squad, he called Cohen.

Cohen dispatched a team of Intel detectives to tail the Zuckerman tail, with instructions to commit nothing to paper. The detectives picked up the tail and followed it toward New Jersey. Aware that they could not legally enter another state unless on official police business, the detectives called their supervisor, who ordered them to break off the pursuit. Cohen was said to be furious, accusing the supervisor of timidity.

Zuckerman's pursuers, it turned out, were private eyes—former NYPD detectives to boot, including one who had actually worked in Intel. According to Zuckerman's spokeswoman, the police department "satisfied him that he was not in any danger and that there was nothing for him to worry about." But who were the private eyes working for? Some Intel detectives believed that a rival businessman had hired them. Others at Intel suspected they were working for Zuckerman's estranged wife, who was suing for divorce. Whatever the truth, neither Cohen nor Zuckerman was talking.

x.

The worst of Cohen's Intelligence Division exploits stemmed from the 2004 Republican National Convention (RNC) held at Madison Square Garden in midtown Manhattan. As they had at the anti–Iraq war demonstration the year before, cops made mass arrests of 1,806 protestors, holding scores of people for three days in a West Side bus depot that had been converted into a temporary jail. Critics charged the police purposely slowed the legal process to keep the protestors away from the convention. Not one of them was convicted of a serious crime—only of misdemeanors or violations. Protestors filed claims for false arrest, but Kelly refused to cooperate with the investigation by the city's Civilian Complaint Review Board. Although his refusal violated the city charter, Mayor Bloomberg again said and did nothing.

Not until three years later did the public begin to learn how the police had prepared for the convention. Cohen had sent detectives across the country and the globe to spy on Americans and others who didn't like President George W. Bush and the Republicans and wanted to make their voices heard. A police unit

called the "R.N.C. Intelligence Squad," conducted surveillance in Massachusetts, Florida, Illinois, Texas, New Mexico, California, Oregon, Canada, and
Europe, according to the *Times*'s Jim Dwyer, who broke the story in March
2007. In fairness to Cohen and Intel, the R.N.C. squad identified groups that
had discussed creating havoc and even urged violence. However, the squad also
spied on peaceful citizens who had a right to express their dislike of George
Bush or anyone else. Hundreds of police reports from this surveillance, said the
Times, described "the views and plans of people who had no apparent intention
of breaking the law," including three elected officials, street theater companies,
church groups, antiwar organizations, environmentalists, and death penalty op-
ponents.

One such group was the Boston-based Black Tea Society, whose Web site
read like an updated version of the strident but nonviolent leftists of the 1960s:
"This November if you want to vote for a rich white male, pro-war, pro-cop, pro-
god, pro–death penalty, pro–Israeli Occupation of Palestine, pro–U.S. occupation of Iraq, pro–national ID card, pro–Patriot Act, pro-NAFTA, anti–Gay
Marriage, pro–video surveillance, pro–prison industrial complex, pro–no children
left behind, anti–universal health care candidate, then this is the election for you."

Early in 2004, Intel detectives drove to Boston to secretly monitor workshops
the society was holding at a local church. Like the New Jersey scuba-diving sting,
the NYPD did not inform local authorities or the FBI. Because the Black Tea Society was also planning to demonstrate at the Democratic National Convention
in Boston, the Massachusetts State Police were also staking out the church. Seeing men arriving in a car with New York license plates, the staties grew suspicious
and tailed the car after the meeting ended, stopping it on the Massachusetts Pike
for speeding and nearly arresting the detectives when they refused to identify
themselves.

The New York Civil Liberties Union sued in federal court for the department's internal records of its RNC spying. Cohen resisted, turning for support
to an unexpected source—former *New York Times* reporter Judith Miller. Her
reporting before the Iraq war had described nonexistent Iraqi weapons of mass
destruction, and she had spent a few months in jail for refusing to testify about
conversations she had with a high-level White House aide, Lewis "Scooter"
Libby, who was subsequently convicted of perjury. Writing in *The Wall Street
Journal* on May 3, 2007, Miller said she had reviewed "600-plus pages of still-

secret [NYPD] intelligence documents"—apparently the documents the NYPD refused to release to the Civil Liberties Union.

"Stung by the [*Times's*] criticism," Miller began, Kelly, Cohen, and Browne "outlined in interviews the nature of the police's concerns, its conduct and the goals of its intelligence surveillance." She then quoted Cohen as saying that the "co-mingled threat of terrorism, anarchist violence and unlawful civil disobedience" had led to the NYPD's surveillance and mass arrests at the convention. Explaining his concerns, Cohen said that since September 11, 2001, the city had "experienced or prevented eleven separate terrorist plots." Cohen told her that "the 18-month period between selecting New York and the convention itself was the most intense threat period of the post-September 11 era to date." Apparently reflecting Cohen's views, she added, "Six terrorist attacks by al Qaeda-related or inspired groups in far-flung Casablanca, Jakarta, Istanbul, Moscow and Madrid killed nearly 300 people and wounded more than 3,000." To justify the spying and mass arrests at the convention, Cohen was linking overseas attacks by Al Qaeda–related groups to legitimate political protestors at the RNC.

In a letter city lawyers filed in court the next day, Kelly, Cohen, and Browne denied providing Miller with the police reports and said they "did not direct anyone else in the NYPD to do so and that to the best of their knowledge no one in the NYPD had provided them to her." That seemed difficult to believe. Still, Miller was familiar with the NYPD's counterterrorism program. She'd written about its preparations for a possible chemical-biological terrorism incident. Assuming Kelly-Cohen-Browne et al. were telling the truth, we might conclude that probably one of the former CIA people Cohen had brought into the department had shown her the documents.

Cohen continued to resist disclosure of the documents after the Civil Liberties Union filed suit. The following month, he filed a "declaration," claiming that making public any "raw data" from the Intelligence Division could lead to the naming of undercover detectives or confidential informants, whose identities, he said, were "the most protected personnel information in the NYPD." This raw data, he maintained, included the "case number, date of report, date of opening of investigation, person reporting, unit reporting, date, time and location of activities being reported on, description of activities, including code name or organization[s], name and description of individual[s], meeting attended, topics discussed, conversations engaged in or overheard, things observed." Reading his declaration,

I wondered whether the pressure of fighting terrorism had gotten to Cohen. He sounded like the CIA's notorious counterspy chief James Jesus Angleton, who was convinced that his colleagues were Communist agents.

Federal magistrate James Francis IV rejected Cohen's arguments and ordered the NYPD to release the reports, redacting whatever the department considered sensitive. The police department appealed. On August 27, 2007, Cohen filed another declaration, explaining why even redacted police files should not be released. "I prepared the Aug. 27 Declaration," he wrote, "to demonstrate how the specific strands of information ordered disclosed by the court [i] could reveal the identities of sources of information, including undercover and confidential informants; [ii] disclose methods of operation; and [iii] be used as a means to undermine NYPD law enforcement operations." Cohen felt his explanations were so sensitive that whole sections of the document filed in federal court were also redacted so that neither the public nor the press could see them.

Still, Cohen had his supporters, most notably, again, the *Daily News*. In an editorial on June 18, 2007, the *News* wrote: "[Judge] Francis must heed the warning of David Cohen, the department's deputy commissioner for intelligence, who stated in court papers: 'The damage to the NYPD intelligence program, a program that has become an essential element in the public security and safety of New York City in this post-11 September 2001 era, from the release of such material would be severe and irreversible.'"

That fall, the Anti-Defamation League awarded Cohen its first Giovanni Palatucci Courageous Leadership award. Palatucci, the chief of police of Fiume, Italy, had saved the lives of over 3,500 Jews destined for Nazi death camps by forging documents and visas. In a news release, the ADL said it had established the award "to recognize Italian and American police officers who have demonstrated extraordinary leadership in the fight against extremism, bigotry and terrorism." The ADL's head, Abraham Foxman, said Cohen had been selected because he "works against forces of hatred and extremism to make New York City safe for people of all backgrounds to live, work and worship."

On January 22, 2008, Magistrate Francis again rejected Cohen's arguments—specifically that the information in his latest declaration was so sensitive Cohen wanted to file the entire declaration under seal. That meant only the judge would see it. Francis called Cohen's attempt at secrecy "antithetical to our adversary system of justice."

"It is the rare case where the very arguments presented to the court in order to influence its decision may justifiably be shielded by opposing counsel and from the public," he wrote. "This is not that case."

The judge's decision did not slow Cohen and Kelly. On the contrary, in the fall of 2008, there occurred an extraordinary exchange of letters between Kelly and the U.S. Attorney General Michael Mukasey over the NYPD's domestic surveillance of terrorism suspects. Kelly began the exchange when he wrote to Mukasey and accused the U.S. Justice Department of hindering investigations of "high priority subjects of international terrorism in the New York area." He added that the federal government was "doing less than it is lawfully entitled to do to protect New York City."

Specifically, Kelly accused senior Justice Department officials of denying the NYPD's requests for wiretap warrants. In 1972, the Supreme Court had ruled that, despite national security concerns, the government must obtain a judicial warrant before conducting domestic electronic surveillance of American citizens. Six years later, Congress enacted the Foreign Intelligence Surveillance Act (FISA), which allowed the government to spy on American citizens without probable cause that they are involved in criminal activity. To conduct this surveillance, the government had to obtain authorization from the special, FISA-created Foreign Intelligence Surveillance Court (FISC). All applications from local law enforcement agencies such as the NYPD were routed through the FBI and the Justice Department, and needed the approval of the attorney general.

It was this arrangement—under which the Justice Department and the FBI control NYPD authorization for FISA surveillance—that led to the Kelly-Mukasey exchange. Three days after receiving Kelly's response, Mukasey answered that Kelly was "incorrect and the alarming conclusions you draw are unfounded." He then accused Kelly of ignoring probable cause standards. "In effect, what you ask is that we disregard FISA's legal requirements, which are rooted in the Constitution," Mukasey wrote. "This view, which appears to be a driving forced behind [the] NYPD's complaints about the FISA process in New York, is contrary to the law."

In Intel's six years under Cohen, what had been the result? Most significantly, there had been no terrorist attack on New York City. Whether this was due to Cohen's vigilance or merely to good luck, who could say? The department supposedly kept a list of fourteen terrorist plots it said the NYPD had disrupted. All but one had been thwarted with the assistance of federal agencies—from Faris on the Brooklyn Bridge to Iranian agents photographing city bridges and structures to a subway cyanide plot, leading to the arrest of a jihadist in Saudi Arabia. Kelly would add that many of Intel's successes went unheralded, resulting in the early curtailment of plans by countless unknown plotters. Perhaps, this, too, was true. Again, who could say?

The NYPD did make one terrorism case on its own, leading to the conviction and thirty-year imprisonment of a Pakistani immigrant, Shahawar Matin Siraj, for conspiring to blow up the Herald Square subway station. On the surface, this alone might seem to justify Cohen's mission. But the impressionable, twenty-year-old Siraj was hardly the terrorist one imagined. At his sentencing hearing in Brooklyn federal court, with his parents cowering in the rear of the courtroom, he appeared to be slow of mind. Furious at the atrocities at Abu Ghraib prison in Iraq, he had discussed his subway-bombing plan with his Egyptian "spiritual sanctioner," Osama Eldawoody, saying he wanted to "burn these motherfuckers." Eldawoody, a man twice his age, who egged him on, turned out to be a police informant on the NYPD payroll to the tune of close to $100,000.

A top former NYPD official put it this way, "Yes, he [Siraj] had it in his heart to do these things. And a potential murderer is behind bars where he belongs. But what did we accomplish? How much are we culpable? Who knows?"

As I write this I remain undecided, as I do about Kelly's grand antiterrorism scheme. Has he created this worldwide antiterrorism web with virtually no federal input to protect the city? Or is it to serve his own ego so that he and he alone can dictate every move?

Equally disturbing is whether anyone is monitoring the NYPD, a municipal agency that in its antiterroism measures has become a mini CIA. What safeguards are there to ensure that the NYPD doesn't break the law? What mechanisms are in place to ensure that the NYPD does not become a rogue organization?

As I write this, I do not know.

xi.

At the end of 2004, *Newsday* underwent another round of cuts and virtually ended its New York City edition. We agreed that I would continue writing "The

Confidential" for another year, but on a contract basis, not as a full-time employee. Learning of this arrangement, the police department immediately revoked my building pass to Police Plaza.

When I entered the building in February 2005, a group of officers surrounded me. For the first time in my life I thought I was about to be arrested. They never raised their voices. Nor did they lay a hand on me. Instead, they demanded I give up my building pass. I took it out of my wallet and handed it over.

I was then provided with an escort, a "minder," as I termed him. He was Sergeant Kevin Hayes of the Public Information Office, who materialized with the officers who had surrounded me. Kevin informed me I would be restricted to my office in the Shack on the second floor. To leave it, he said, even to go to the Public Information Office on the thirteenth floor, required a preapproved appointment and a police escort. But Kevin was generous. Because we'd known each other for years, he allowed me to go unescorted to the cafeteria on the ninth floor to buy a Coke.

This nonsense lasted a couple of weeks. By then, I suppose, Paul Browne, or whoever had thought up the idea, realized it wasn't getting him anywhere. Although I never got my pass back, I was again allowed to roam the building, unescorted.

Then, at the end of 2005, my contract with *Newsday* expired and I began writing "The Confidential" online. Whether or not I could cover the police department on my own, with no newspaper affiliation or news organization behind me, remained problematic. Although the department granted me a press card as an "Independent," when I tried to enter Police Plaza in January 2006, I was again banned from the building.

First, I was stopped at the outside security station. "Mr. Levitt, I recognize you," the young cop manning its metal detector said apologetically. "My orders are that you are not allowed in the building."

"Is this a joke?" I asked.

"No, those are my orders."

"Can you tell me why?"

"I don't know why. I was only told you are not allowed inside the building."

This time I fought back. Not physically, of course. I called Christopher Dunn, the associate director of the New York Civil Liberties Union, and told him I was under the apparently mistaken impression that Police Plaza was a public building, open to anyone who had police business. I don't know whom Chris contacted, but the following week I was again permitted to enter the building.

Now I was both a pariah and a celebrity. The officers manning the metal detector outside of Police Plaza and inside the building's first-floor security pod were alerted to my arrival. Again, I was given a minder, this time an Officer Rodriquez, who said he had instructions to accompany me to the fourth-floor trial room where officers face departmental charges, and to remain with me. Officer Rodriquez was also polite. When the trial adjourned for the day, however, he would not permit me to stop down in the Shack, where I had worked for the past decade. Instead, following his instructions, he escorted me down the elevator and out of the building.

I returned the following week and guess what? No more minder. Instead, after a frantic telephone call from the metal detector's security officer—"It's Lenny Levitt. He's back. What do we do with him?"—I was given a pass that permitted me to travel, unescorted, on the elevator to the Public Information Office. But when I asked again to stop down in the Shack, the two desk sergeants said they would have to check with Paul Browne. Minutes later, one returned from Browne's office: permission denied.

A month later, I discovered why my presence at Police Plaza had set off alarms and why my every step was monitored. A cop I didn't know tipped me off. Without speaking, he pointed to the circular security pod on the first floor. I walked over and peered inside. There on its inner wall were posted eight mug shots of people described as "security" threats. Each had either threatened someone or committed a form of mayhem. A woman had come into the building drunk and created a disturbance. A retired officer had regularly tried to sneak inside. Two others were said to have threatened the life of Commissioner Kelly. Beneath their pictures, at the bottom of the pod, a ninth photo had been posted. It was of me.

There was a final drama to be played out. In January 2007 the department refused to renew my press pass. Their reasons, as described to me in a letter, were that I was not a full-time employee of a news-gathering organization. Again, I contacted Chris Dunn. In February 2007, he accompanied me to a formal hearing at DCPI. Chris requested all documents relating to the department's handling of my press passes for the last ten years; the names of everyone participating in the decision to deny my most recent application; and all police documents concerning me, including files maintained by DCPI, the police commissioner's office, of any other NYPD unit.

In March, the department announced it would not provide any documents and denied my appeal. Its written explanation said only that I "did not provide any new evidence or documentation to establish your eligibility." It was signed by my friend, recently promoted to assistant chief, Michael Collins.

xii.

But it wasn't over. In fact, "The Confidential" online was just beginning. The Internet had invigorated it, attracting all sorts of new readers—and sources. People too afraid to contact me in the past were now able to e-mail me anonymously. I began hearing from scores of NYPD officers and officials from other law enforcement agencies. Many were detectives from the Intelligence Division and the Counterterrorism Bureau. Others were of surprisingly high rank. It has been my experience in covering the NYPD that there are no whistle-blowers. That is not how the police department works. Except for Serpico, no police source provides information to a reporter without a self-serving motive. Usually it involves a slight or a grudge against a fellow officer or superior. But self-serving motives do not invalidate the information they provide. Without officers like these, information would be restricted to only what the police commissioner and the top brass want released.

None of the officers who contacted me did so to expose police corruption, at least not at first. But their stories were real, and their insights and information about an increasingly closed police department were invaluable. Under Kelly, these disgruntled officers provided the most reliable—indeed the only—check on the department that the public had.

Those stories I could confirm, I wrote. And the more I wrote, the more e-mails I received. Some officers who contacted me were willing to reveal their names but warned me their careers would be over if they were discovered. Some officers agreed to meet with me. Because they were risking their careers, I began traveling to clandestine locations all over the city. I met a detective on a street corner outside a church in Lower Manhattan. We walked round and

round the block as he told me of an overseas detective pulled off a plane because he was drunk, of another who had been reassigned to Police Plaza because he'd angered his hosts in the country to which he'd been sent. An officer
from the Counterterrorism Bureau feared he was being followed in Manhattan
so I suggested we meet in my classroom at Brooklyn College, where I taught a
course in journalism.

I realized I was succeeding when I received information about the elite
group of detectives who guard the police commissioner. To detectives, the commissioner's detail is considered the most prestigious in the department, a lock
on overtime money, grade promotions, and a window into the department's
most confidential goings-on. Grateful for its benefits, these detectives are prepared to take a bullet for the boss. For that small, closed circle to reach out to an
outsider like me meant something was amiss.

No one had been more loyal to Ray Kelly than the detail's head, Sergeant
Manny Lopez. As a detective said, "Manny never took. He only gave." Lopez
had headed the detail during Kelly's first tour as commissioner, when Kelly was
informal enough that he cooked dinner for the detail in his office. But as I had
personally discovered, Kelly had become a different man upon his return. As one
of the detail's detectives put it, "The detectives thought they were joining the old
Ray Kelly. But the old Ray Kelly never showed up. He was nowhere to be found."

Despite Lopez's years of loyalty, Kelly had turned on him over the Stansbury
shooting. What had Lopez done to disillusion the commissioner? Instead of
awakening the boss at 1:30 A.M., immediately after the shooting, Lopez let Kelly
sleep until dawn. Kelly expressed his displeasure by restoring to the detail another sergeant, dismissed just months before, as Lopez's equal. Lopez took the
hint and filed for retirement. Kelly then ordered him investigated for overtime
abuses. None was found.

Next, Kelly went after Lieutenant John Lyke, whom Lopez had recruited as
the detail's supervisor. Kelly began berating Lyke for petty issues—walking too
close to him, then too far ahead. Lyke, too, filed for retirement. Kelly ordered
him investigated for overtime abuses. Again, none was found. By 2007, when I
wrote my story about the detail, sixteen detectives had quit. Only one of the
original detectives remained.

I also continued writing about David Cohen and the Intelligence Division,
where morale was so low its 2007 Christmas party had to be canceled because

only fourteen people had signed up. E-mails arrived, saying the party had been rescheduled for January. That was amusing—a Christmas party a month after the holiday.

After I wrote that story, more e-mails arrived. To ensure a full house at the January Christmas party, Cohen had ordered his chiefs to pressure staffers to pony up $75 a head. The chiefs and inspectors ordered lower-ranking officers to keep lists of who was coming and to warn detectives that it was "in everyone's best interest to attend." Supervising this roll call was Deputy Chief Galati, the same Galati who had detained the Iranian president. Galati had also begun an investigation into why staffers had boycotted the first party.

Word then came to me about the cavalier tastes of a new hire—Deputy Commissioner for Counterterrorism Dr. Richard Falkenrath, a former academic and deputy homeland security adviser. The department had assigned him not one but two luxury cars—a 2007 Chrysler Touring Car and a 2007 Ford SUV Expedition. Each had leather upholstery, a GPS navigational system, and the full lights and siren package. Both were leased by the NYPD at an annual cost to taxpayers of $20,000. Falkenrath was soon spotted roaring around town in his Expedition, lights and sirens blazing. Some years before, Cohen, too, had been spotted roaring up the West Side Highway. In his case, the spotter had been Mayor Bloomberg. Both Kelly and Cohen maintained Cohen had been on official business, although they refused to provide details.

In Falkenrath's case, the spotter worked for a television station. He ran the license plate number, which came back to a leasing company in North Haven, Connecticut, which leases dozens of cars to the NYPD. At least forty—Ford Explorers, Nissan Altimas, Toyota Camrys, Dodge Durangos, Chevy Suburbans, even a Cadillac DeVille as well as Falkenrath's Chrysler 300 and the Ford Expedition—were assigned to the Counterterrorism Bureau, parked in an open-air lot at its vehicle pool in Brooklyn. The leasing company alerted the police department to the station spotter's call. The Counterterrorism Bureau's top brass decided to dump the Expedition and provide Falkenrath with a less flashy Dodge Charger. One of his two drivers—he had a driver for each car as well—drove the Expedition out to the Brooklyn vehicle pool and left it there. So I drove out to the lot to see it. Although the lot was supposed to be secured, I had no trouble entering. I parked my car, and there, just a few away, among the Explorers, Camrys, Altimas, Durangos, and Suburbans, sat the Expedition. I had just finished checking out its GPS system and leather upholstery when an officer approached and told me the lot was closed to the public. I nodded my understanding and drove off. Then I went home and wrote the story.

Falkenrath also liked to go on junkets. Three months after he joined the NYPD, he went off on a $13,000 weeklong jaunt to London and Singapore. My source showed me e-mails between Falkenrath and his friend Kumar Ramakrishna in Singapore, who had invited Falkenrath to give the "Distinguished Dinner Lecture" for the Asia-Pacific Program for Senior National Security Officers. Falkenrath requested a round-trip business-class ticket on a nonstop Singapore Airlines flight, a room in a topflight downtown Singapore hotel, and a car and driver. He left for Singapore on a Friday and stayed three days in a suite at the Hyatt at $348 a night. After his speech, he flew to England on another nonstop, business-class Singapore Airlines flight. After two nights in London, he flew back to New York on American Airlines, also business class.

The department could offer no justification for his trip. It could show no benefit for the NYPD. A copy of the Singapore program revealed that the NYPD already had a representative at the conference—Lieutenant Scott Stein, one of its overseas detectives.

After my stories ran, I learned Kelly had ordered an investigation. Not into Falkenrath's royal treatment but how I had learned about it. Thanks to the Internet, an insider who wanted the public to know about Falkenrath's perks contacted a reporter without a newspaper who penetrated the top-secret Counter-terrorism Bureau.

More information arrived. Detectives warned me the department was monitoring my phone calls and e-mails. I was skeptical. Unless a crime is suspected, spying on a private citizen is against the law. I wasn't committing a crime. I was merely reporting. Okay, so Kelly mistreated detectives in his detail. Okay, so Cohen had gone overboard on the Christmas party. And, yes, the department had indulged Falkenrath with luxury cars and trips. As much as those stories may have embarrassed the department, I felt Kelly was too disciplined to risk breaking the law.

"Don't be naïve," said my source at the Counterterrorism Bureau. "Didn't they ban you from the building and post your picture as a security threat? They'll claim you obtained confidential information that could potentially be terrorist-related."

Now the stories I wrote became more than merely embarrassing. Some concerned corruption issues that the department hid. Some involved criminality. I learned of an Intel detective who used the pretext of conducting a terrorism investigation to spy on his girlfriend. He had convinced two Queens prosecutors to subpoena her phone records. After obtaining them, one of the prosecutors noticed something strange. The detective's phone number was among them. Said a law enforcement official: "We got enough to know this was not a counterterrorism investigation and notified up the line."

"Up the line" meant the Internal Affairs Bureau. The Queens prosecutors believed IAB's investigation would lead to the detective's dismissal or, at the least, to his being placed on modified duty without his badge or gun. Instead, the detective's job status remained the same. He was merely transferred. He retained his badge and gun. Was Cohen protecting him? Was Kelly protecting Cohen and the image of the Intelligence Division?

Then a detective e-mailed me about an Intelligence Division deputy inspector. "I want to expose [Cohen's] top-dog Deputy Inspector Vincent Marra, who has basically destroyed the Intelligence Division's ability to function from right under Cohen's nose," he wrote. "The information I can provide you with should lead to a multifaceted investigation on him and others not only in the police department but possibly the fire department. [It] is 9/11-related and should get some people rather irate."

The detective wasn't exaggerating. He made the same allegations in letters to Chief Campisi of Internal Affairs and other law enforcement agencies. "The corruption and abuse of authority has gone on long enough," his letter began, "and it is time that someone outside of the Intelligence Division and for that matter outside of the NYPD needs to address the situation."

When I asked the detective to meet with me, he refused. "I do not believe we need to meet," he stated. "We can communicate via e-mail. I am willing to answer any and all questions." In the end we did meet, at a spot in Greenwich Village. As we sat down, a uniformed police officer happened to pass. Without a word, the detective jumped up and ran off. I chased after him. "I can't afford to take any chances," he explained when I caught up to him.

Then he started telling me about Deputy Inspector Vincent Marra. In 2002, Marra had had cosmetic surgery to remove a benign tumor from his chest. To avoid possible scarring, he elected to have it removed via his back, but his medical insurer refused to cover the cost. He then devised a plan to collect $50 per detective and $100 per supervisor. Those refusing to contribute were warned their future assignments and promotions could be affected. He collected approximately $25,000.

He then approached a female subordinate, an old girlfriend now dating a fireman, Bill Eisengrein. Eisengrein was a founder of the Bravest Fund, a charitable organization that benefited victims of 9/11. Marra promised the female detective a promotion if she could persuade Eisengrein to give him $10,000 from the Bravest Fund to pay for the surgery. Eisengrein agreed to pay Marra — but only $1,000. Marra then informed the subordinate he could not get her promoted "due to D.C. Cohen not knowing who she was."

The detective and I spent an hour together as he laid all this out for me. He still refused to give me his name. Nonetheless, I was able to confirm everything he said. Nonprofit charities have to register with the state attorney general's office. Their records are open to the public. According to the Bravest Fund's mission statement, it had been established to raise money "for the ultimate benefit to the victims of Sept. 11, 2001 World Trade Center disaster, as well as for firefighters, police officers, emergency service workers and their families who are victims of tragedies in general." Eisengrein was listed as the fund's treasurer and one of its three directors. In 2002, the file showed, he had given Marra $1,000.

After I wrote the story, Marra retired. Like the detective who had subpoenaed his girlfriend's phone records, no charges were filed against him. Once again, Kelly had protected Cohen and the image of the Intelligence Division.

"You owe me a steak dinner," the detective e-mailed me again.

"Name the place," I wrote back.

I never heard from him again.

Then another detective passed on more unsettling news. He told me a friend of his had seen an Intelligence Division folder with my name on it and the words "Top Secret." When I again expressed skepticism, he said, "Do you know that a surveillance team in Queens has been assigned to follow you? You teach at Brooklyn College, don't you? Now how would I know that?"

I was stunned. For the first time, I found myself wondering whether this could be true. Admittedly, any number of people in the police department could have found out about my teaching at Brooklyn College. The information was probably available online. But why would this detective know about it? Why would anybody in the police department be looking for it? What had been my crime to justify an Intelligence Division file on me? I was a police reporter. Nothing more, nothing less. And I had another reason for concern. I had met one of my intelligence sources at Brooklyn College. He had been the source for my stories on Deputy Commissioner for Counterterrorism Richard Falkenrath. We had met once in Manhattan but, concerned that he might have been followed, he was afraid to meet me in Manhattan again. I suggested we meet late one afternoon after I finished teaching in my classroom.

Had the police department followed him? Had they followed me?

I looked over my shoulder.

I couldn't see anyone.

Afterword

After his plans to run for president, vice president, and governor went nowhere, Michael Bloomberg dropped a bombshell in the fall of 2008. He decided he wanted to remain at City Hall and serve a third term as mayor. The obstacle was that city voters had twice endorsed a two-term limit on election to the office. So Bloomberg tried to change the law. A billionaire can only suffer so much disappointment.

Although, as mayor, he had supported term limits, Bloomberg used his money and power, and the excuse of the country's financial meltdown, to bend the City Council to his will. He argued that only he could steer the city through the tough economic times ahead. Only he—who during his first two terms had claimed to be above partisan politics, placing New York's interests above his own—could save the city.

Not even Rudy Giuliani had attempted such a grab for power. Even at the height of his popularity following 9/11 he had dared ask only for an extra three months in office. At the first hint of criticism, Rudy abandoned the idea.

Bloomberg, however, pressured enough City Council members to repeal the two-term law. His reelection in 2009 now seems assured.

So ended the mayoral dreams of Police Commissioner Ray Kelly, whose recognition and approval rating among New Yorkers had topped all other mayoral candidates. While many prominent New Yorkers—most notably former mayor Ed Koch—supported Kelly, one person had appeared noticeably cool as Kelly rose in the polls in 2006 and 2007. That person was Bloomberg.

The week the City Council cleared the path for him to run for a third term, former police commissioner Bill Bratton was in town, speaking at the John Jay College of Criminal Justice. Since 2002 Bratton has served as the police chief of Los Angeles, instituting the same reforms there as he had in New York. During his short presidential run, Rudy Giuliani had twice traveled to L.A. to visit him, apparently to secure Bratton's promise not to criticize him publicly. Bratton's silence, however, proved to be no help to the former mayor. After spending $50 million, Giuliani received the support of only one Republican delegate.

Bernie Kerik had been an issue. The charges against him remained pending. Rival John McCain said Kerik had done nothing but posture during his three-month military tour in Iraq. Ultimately, Giuliani endorsed McCain and gave the keynote address at the Republican National Convention.

Hoping for a new mayor in New York, Bratton had talked for the last year about returning as police commissioner. Though the NYPD pays about half as much as his $300,000 salary in L.A., he said he would accept the near 50 percent pay cut. Bratton had also lobbied two Democrats preparing to run in 2009. Bloomberg's virtually guaranteed third term appeared to dash his hopes, and shortly before the presidential election, Bratton endorsed Barack Obama, saying he did so to counter recent criticism of Obama by Giuliani. That sounded as though Bratton might be seeking a job in Washington.

And what of Kelly? With Bloomberg the likely mayoral winner in 2009, what will the future hold for him? Will he remain police commissioner for another four years under Bloomberg in what may now be a marriage of convenience? Should he remain, he will serve longer than any commissioner in the department's history, surpassing the eleven-year tenure of Lewis J. Valentine under Mayor Fiorello LaGuardia.

In his speech at John Jay, Bratton could not resist an implied criticism of Kelly, declaring that inclusiveness and transparency, both notably absent under the commissioner and Bloomberg, are vital to running a police department. Kelly's extended tenure would seem to bode ill for that, as well as for an outside police monitor and public accountability. Yet with today's technology, Kelly may be forced to live with more exposure than even he can smother. In this high-speed digital age, when practically everyone carries a cell phone with a camera and can share his pictures with the world via the Internet, transparency seems to be breaking out everywhere. No longer can the police spin their version of events when pictures tell another story.

In March 2003, police claimed they had arrested anti–Iraq war demonstrators for being unruly and refusing to disperse. Video footage, however, showed this was a lie. The protestors couldn't disperse because police barricades had pinned them down just as police mounted units began to advance. Video cameras also showed that many people arrested at the Republican National Convention in 2004 had not broken any law, leading the Manhattan district attorney to drop virtually every case.

A year later, a teenager's MP3 player caught a veteran detective in an apparent lie that could end his career, if not send him to prison. Bronx detective Christopher Perino repeatedly denied under oath that he had interrogated a seventeen-year-old shooting suspect at the 44th Precinct, urging him to sign a confession before his relatives arrived. Perino never imagined the kid was secretly recording his conversation, including his warning, "And our conversation right now does not exist, you following me?" Two years later, when the recording was revealed in court, Perino was charged with perjury. Even though a surveillance camera had captured the kid shooting his victim in the face, Perino's lie allowed him to get seven years off his sentence.

In July 2008, video shot by someone in always-crowded Times Square contradicted rookie cop Patrick Pogan's sworn complaint that a bicyclist had deliberately driven into him and resisted arrest. Instead, the video, seen by a quarter of a million people after being posted on YouTube, showed the rookie charging the cyclist without warning and violently flinging him off his bike to the ground. "It looks . . . totally over the top and inappropriate," said Bloomberg. "In terms of the officer, it certainly looked like— Inappropriate is a nice way to phrase it." The Manhattan district attorney dropped the charges against the cyclist and began an investigation of rookie Pogan. He resigned from the NYPD.

The day after this footage aired on YouTube, another video surfaced. This one showed an officer three weeks earlier striking a man on the Lower East Side ten times with the modern version of a police nightstick—a collapsible metal baton. It looked like the cop had used far too heavy a hand in subduing someone he thought was committing the minor crime of carrying liquor into the park. The NYPD ended up investigating the officer for excessive force.

Then the *Daily News* broke the story of a damning police video that has yet to be released. In the summer of 2008, a security camera at a Manhattan housing project allegedly caught an officer beating a man whose mother lived in the project, even though he was already on the ground and handcuffed. Worse, the officer, David London, reportedly paused to answer his cell phone, then continued to hit the man. Criminal charges against the civilian were dropped. The Manhattan district attorney indicted London for assault and fraud.

The ever-present camera has its limitations. Even though civilian video and audio reveal problems inside the police department, they cannot compensate for a lack of official oversight and transparency, whether under Kelly and Bloomberg or anyone else. With cowed public officials, only a flagrant act of corruption or brutality will galvanize public opinion to accomplish necessary reforms.

And while the camera can help keep the police honest, sometimes it has unexpected consequences. It may well have contributed to the pressures on an elite Emergency Service Unit lieutenant. The lieutenant made a mistake, a monumental one, which was captured on videotape and played over and over on television and the Internet.

On September 24, 2008, Lieutenant Michael Pigott ordered his officer to Taser Iman Morales, a naked, emotionally disturbed man, perched on a second-floor ledge of his Brooklyn building. Morales was menacing with an eight-foot-long fluorescent lightbulb the cop who was trying to rescue him. After Pigott ordered the officer to fire, Morales fell headfirst to the pavement and died, his awful end filmed by witnesses.

The police department charged that Pigott's order violated guidelines. The department stripped him of his badge and gun and placed him on desk duty in another unit, away from his colleagues and support system while the district attorney and the department investigated. The anguished lieutenant took full blame for Morales's death, absolving the officer who fired the Taser of any responsibility. He also publicly apologized to the dead man's family, a rare step for a cop under investigation. But nothing he did eased his pain. Eight days later, Pigott committed suicide with a gunshot to his head inside ESU's locker room. He had secretly returned to his former unit at 4:00 A.M., broken the lock on a fellow officer's locker, taken his gun, and fired a bullet into his head. A suicide note said he feared being arrested and didn't want his family seeing him in handcuffs or behind bars. He left his note alongside pictures of his three children.

Pigott's union leader, Thomas R. Sullivan, put it like this. "It is worth remembering that our police officers are not supermen but rather flesh and blood human beings who deal with life and death situations on a daily basis that most of us cannot even imagine."

Bibliography

Barrett, Wayne. *Rudy! An Investigative Biography of Rudolph Giuliani.* New York: Perseus Books, 2002.

Barrett, Wayne, and Dan Collins. *Grand Illusion: The Untold Story of Rudy Giuliani and 9/11.* New York: HarperCollins, 2006.

Bratton, William, with Peter Knobler. *Turnaround.* New York: Random House, 1998.

Conant, Jennet. "The Ghost and Mr. Giuliani." *Vanity Fair,* September 1997.

Conlon, Edward. *Blue Blood.* New York: Riverhead Books, 2004.

Farber, M. A. "Unreasonable Doubt." *Vanity Fair,* October 1995.

Gelb, Barbara. *Varnished Brass: The Decade After Serpico.* New York: G. P. Putnam's Sons, 1983.

Girgenti, Richard H. *A Report to the Governor on the Disturbances in Crown Heights.* Albany, N.Y.: New York State Division of Criminal Justice Services, July 1993.

Giuliani, Rudolph, with Ken Kurson. *Leadership.* New York: Hyperion, 2002.

Junod, Tom, "The Last Cop in Camelot." *Esquire,* June 2000.

Kerik, Bernard B. *The Lost Son: A Life in Pursuit of Justice.* New York: ReganBooks, 2001.

Kocieniewski, David. *The Brass Wall: The Betrayal of Undercover Detective #4126.* New York: Henry Holt, 2003.

Lardner, James, and Thomas A. Reppetto. *NYPD: A City and Its Police.* New York: Henry Holt, 2000.

McAlary, Mike. "The Last Cop Story." *Esquire*, December 1997.

———. *Sore Loser.* New York: William Morrow, 1998.

Maple, Jack, with Chris Mitchell. *The Crime Fighter.* New York: Doubleday, 1999.

New York Commission to Investigate Allegations . . . Milton Mollen, Chairman. *Commission Report.* New York, N.Y., July 7, 1994.

Reppetto, Thomas A. *The Blue Parade.* New York: Free Press, 1978.

Safir, Howard, with Ellis Whitman. *Security: Policing Your Homeland, Your City.* New York: St. Martin's Press, 2003.

Steffens, Lincoln. *The Autobiography of Lincoln Steffens.* Berkeley, Calif.: Heyday Books, 2005.

Index